MAGISTRACY AND THE HISTORIOGRAPHY OF THE ROMAN REPUBLIC

The study of Roman republican magistracy has traditionally been the preserve of historians posing constitutional and prosopographical questions. As a result, one fundamental aspect of our most detailed contemporary and near-contemporary sources about magistracy has remained largely neglected: their literariness. This book takes a new approach to the representation of magistrates and shows how the rhetorical and formal features of prose texts – principally Livy's history but also works by Cicero and Sallust – shape our understanding of magistracy. Applying to the texts an expanded concept of exemplarity, Haimson Lushkov shows how a rich body of anecdotes concerning the behavior and speech of magistrates reflects on the values and tensions that defined the republic. A variety of contexts – familial, military, and electoral, among others – flesh out the experience of being, becoming, and encountering a Roman magistrate, and the political and ethical problems highlighted and negotiated in such circumstances.

AYELET HAIMSON LUSHKOV is Assistant Professor of Classics at the University of Texas at Austin. She studies the Latin literature of ancient Rome, focusing on historical accounts of the Roman republic. She is co-editor of *Reception and the Classics* (2012), and author of a number of articles on aspects of Livy's language and historical practice. Her work has also appeared in the *Huffington Post* and the *Guardian*.

MAGISTRACY AND THE HISTORIOGRAPHY OF THE ROMAN REPUBLIC

Politics in Prose

AYELET HAIMSON LUSHKOV

CAMBRIDGE
UNIVERSITY PRESS

CAMBRIDGE
UNIVERSITY PRESS

University Printing House, Cambridge CB2 8BS, United Kingdom

Cambridge University Press is part of the University of Cambridge.

It furthers the University's mission by disseminating knowledge in the pursuit of education, learning and research at the highest international levels of excellence.

www.cambridge.org
Information on this title: www.cambridge.org/9781107040908

First published 2015

A catalogue record for this publication is available from the British Library

ISBN 978-1-107-04090-8 Hardback

For Pramit
and
for my grandparents

Contents

Acknowledgments

Various people and institutions have lent their time, resources, and support to this project. I thank all of them. Chris Kraus offered efficient, calm, and unwavering support throughout and read the manuscript more times than either she or I care to count. Jane Chaplin, Matthew Roller, and Bob Kaster have read the manuscript in whole or part and offered their usual trenchant criticism, as did an anonymous reader for Cambridge University Press. Tony Corbeill and Carlos Noreña discussed earlier versions with me and encouraged me to make more assertive claims. I have not always taken the good advice offered, and I reserve sole responsibility for the consequences.

Portions of this material have been presented to audiences at Johns Hopkins, University College London (with assistance from the George P. Macatee III Centennial Lectureship Fund), and Amherst College, as well as at various meetings of the American Philological Association (now Society for Classical Studies); I am grateful to all those audiences for their comments. Closer to home, my department has heard multiple versions of this material and offered comments both incisive and collegial. I owe particular thanks to Andrew Riggsby, Stephen White, and Lesley Dean-Jones for their various acts of kindness.

I finished the bulk of the writing during a sabbatical leave from the University of Texas at Austin in 2012–13. During this time I enjoyed the splendid hospitality of the Leslie Center for the Humanities at Dartmouth College; I am grateful to the Center's former and present directors, Adrian Randolph and Colleen Glenney Boggs, and to Isabel Weatherdon, for being so unstinting with their help, and for giving me the biggest office I am ever likely to have.

Michael Sharp at Cambridge University Press, together with Elizabeth Hanlon, Jonathan Ratcliffe, and Jan Chapman have been supportive and attentive throughout. Charles Westfall Oughton fact-checked the book; he and Margaret Clark compiled the indices. I am grateful to the

Office of the Vice-Provost at UT Austin for their financial support, and to Chuck and Margaret for their hard work and good cheer. Whatever errors or infelicities remain are entirely my own.

This book has its origin in a Yale doctoral dissertation, of which little survives in its present form. What cannot be eroded, however, is my debt of gratitude to my supervisors, Chris Kraus and Celia Schultz, for all the very many things they have taught me. I see their influence in everything I do and can only hope to pass on even a fraction of that generosity to my own students.

My parents – indeed my whole family – have been supporting my classical interests since I was a small child, and I hope this book is some compensation for all the hours they spent driving me to and from Latin lessons. The book is dedicated to my grandparents, Avner and Zachia Zuk, as an entirely insufficient token of how much I love them. But it belongs above all to my husband, Pramit Chaudhuri, who needs no words to know the debt I owe him.

Abbreviations

Abbreviations of journals follow the conventions of *L'Année philologique*; those of ancient authors' names and works, the *Oxford Classical Dictionary*. Other abbreviations are as follows:

Beck and Walter	Beck, H. and U. Walter 2001. *Die frühen römischen Historiker*. Darmstadt.
CIL	*Corpus Inscriptionum Latinarum*. Berlin.
FRHist	Cornell, T. J. (ed.) 2014. *Fragments of the Roman Historians*. Oxford.
HRR	Peter, H. (ed.) 1906. *Historicorum Romanorum Reliquiae*. Leipzig.
ILS	Dessau, H. (ed.) 1892. *Inscriptiones Latinae Selectae*. Wiedemann.
MRR	Broughton, T. R. S. 1951–2. *The Magistrates of the Roman Republic*. New York.
OCD	Hornblower, S. and A. Spawforth (eds.) 1996. *The Oxford Classical Dictionary*, 3rd edition. Oxford.
OLD	Glare, P. (ed.) 1968–82. *Oxford Latin Dictionary*. Oxford.
ORF	Malcovati, H. (ed.) 1967. *Oratorum Romanorum Fragmenta*. Turin.
RE	von Pauly, A. F., G. Wissowa, and W. Kroll (eds.) 1893–1980. *Real-Encyclopädie der classischen Altertumswissenschaft*. Stuttgart.
RS	Crawford, M. (ed.) 1996. *Roman Statutes. BICS Suppl.* 64. London.
TLL	*Thesaurus Linguae Latinae*. Berlin.

Introduction: exemplarity, magistracy, and narrative

Livy's account of the otherwise uneventful year 199 BC ends, according to annalistic custom, with the election of the following year's magistrates. Rather than the typically laconic announcement of the new consular college, however, Livy in this case elaborates on the unusual nature of the campaign:

> neque ipse consul memorabile quicquam gessit, comitiorum causa Romam reuocatus; quae ipsa per M. Fuluium et M'. Curium tribunos plebis impediebantur, quod T. Quinctium Flamininum consulatum ex quaestura petere non patiebantur: iam aedilitatem praeturamque fastidiri nec per honorum gradus, documentum sui dantes, nobiles homines tendere ad consulatum, sed transcendendo media summa imis continuare. res ex campestri certamine in senatum peruenit. patres censuerunt qui honorem quem sibi capere per leges liceret peteret, in eo populo creandi quem uelit potestatem fieri aequum esse. in auctoritate patrum fuere tribuni. creati consules Sex. Aelius Paetus et T. Quinctius Flamininus. (Livy 32.7.8–12)
>
> However, the consul achieved nothing worth remembering, because he was summoned back to Rome to hold the elections. These were held up by M. Fulvius and M'. Curius, tribunes of the plebs, because they would not allow T. Quinctius Flamininus to seek the consulship after the quaestorship: they said that noblemen now spurned the aedileship and the praetorship and did not strive for the consulship through the steps of office, thus giving proof of themselves; instead, through skipping the middle offices, they joined the lowest to the highest. The matter was debated in the Campus Martius and then reached the senate. The senators determined that, so long as a person sought an office which the laws allowed him to hold, it was fair that the people should have the power to elect whomever they wish. The tribunes accepted the authority of the senate, and Sex. Aelius Paetus and T. Quinctius Flamininus were elected consuls.

This account, notable merely because the elected consul went on to much greater glory, is one of any number of anecdotes in Livy and other authors in which a political problem specific to the republican system arises, is negotiated, and finally solved.[1] The anecdote is, primarily, about magistracy, albeit in the rather broad sense that a magistrate, and the conditions for his tenure of magistracy, are the subject of the debate. The crux in this particular case is Flamininus' accelerated progress up the *cursus honorum*, and the episode offers us a rhetorically crafted reconstruction of two reasonable but conflicting positions: Flamininus wishes to stand for office prematurely; the tribunes wish to protect conventional practice. However, although the episode ends with a functional resolution – the tribunes accept the authority of the senate and the elections proceed – there is no actual reconciliation or synthesis of the two positions: the moral validity of the tribunes' objection remains, as does the validity of the senate's reliance on law and the people's wishes.[2] Further, although the language of the passage is carefully crafted as a symmetrical exchange – the tribunes' metaphorical *documentum* is answered by the senate's concrete *leges* – in reality this symmetry is purely formal. The basis of the two different positions exists in entirely different realms, one ethical, the other legal. While the resolution achieves the consensus necessary for the functioning of the electoral process, the lack of synthesis between the two leaves the reader to consider the validity of each position, free from the pressure either of active engagement or of an imminent tear in the fabric of the state. The anecdote thus encourages the reader to reflect simultaneously on a welter of political concerns, from the qualifications of Flamininus to the authority of senate and people; from the power of the tribunes to the force of law; from the conventions of the *cursus honorum* to the innovations of political ambition; and finally from ethical principle to the need for pragmatism.

These anecdotes do not exist in isolation and can be read against a number of comparable episodes which fall into two main groups. The first consists of parallel iterations of the same episode across a range of authors. Plutarch, for example, preserves a slightly different version in the *Life of Flamininus*, probably drawn not from Livy himself but from a common source.[3] The second, perhaps more important, group consists of

[1] On Flamininus' early career, see also the account in Plut. *Flam.* 1–2. Badian 1971: 109–10 and Carawan 1988: 211–12 and Pfeilschifter 2005: 31–52 reconstruct Flamininus' career before this election. On the episode: Briscoe 1973: 180–1, Pfeilschifter 2005: 52–65. Translations of quoted passages are my own.

[2] *Per leges* is here anachronistic (compare Plut. *Flam.* 2.1 παρὰ τοὺς νόμους): the *lex Villia annalis*, which regulated the minimum ages for progression up the *cursus honorum*, would not be passed until 180 BC. On the *lex Villia*: Astin 1958, Brennan 2000: 170–1. Flamininus was not yet thirty in 199 BC (Polyb. 18.12.5; Plut. *Flam.* 2.2). so *per leges* emphasizes the inapplicability of the future *lex Villia.*

[3] For the traditions of Flamininus' career, see the discussions in R. E. Smith 1944 and Carawan 1988: 209–12.

episodes that treat similar themes. The general topic of progress through the *cursus honorum*, for instance, features in a number of episodes in Livy and elsewhere, as in Scipio Africanus' premature candidacy for the aedileship some seven books and thirteen years earlier (25.2.6–8), with which Flamininus' candidacy shares certain features and interests.[4] Read within either grouping, Livy's Flamininus episode is a set piece, a single iteration of a larger narrative topos, which is itself part of the annalistic theme of political activity in Rome.[5] Our episode is also an *exemplum* of a sort, typifying a whole set of political behaviors – of candidates, tribunes, and senators – as well as, at a further level of analysis, the various historiographical ways of writing about those behaviors. It is thus possible to view these debates, and others like them, through a number of different lenses, each emphasizing different issues or reinforcing common concerns. At times these debates are connected intra- and intertextually, at other times they share only discursive or thematic similarities. What they all have in common, however, is a distinctively dialectical view of Roman politics, one that originates in the narrative formulations of the event. These formulations highlight the internal and external polysemy of perspectives that govern political behavior and the conflicts of values that underscore the workings of the Roman republic.[6]

The argument of this book is twofold, proceeding through a series of close readings of political anecdotes or *exempla*, largely drawn from Livy but supplemented by other authors. First, it takes advantage of the god's-eye view of events characteristic of narrative to study the historiography of Roman political behavior, and more specifically of magistracy as a textual phenomenon. It argues that these anecdotes construct a distinctive image of political culture and political ideas, which juxtaposes and scrutinizes competing values and exemplifies the methods involved in resolving the consequent tensions within the community. This discursive construction of magistracy leads into the second part of the argument: that magistracy offers a uniquely rich instance of the exemplary habits that suffuse Livy's work, because the historical protocols, procedures, and institutions which governed it lent themselves especially well to the exemplary preoccupations of the *Ab Urbe Condita* (*AUC*).

[4] Briscoe 1973: 181. See my more detailed treatment in Chapter 4: 151–9 below.

[5] Kraus 1994b lays out the case for the importance of topoi as an organizational tool within Livy's text.

[6] In the Anglophone philosophical tradition, Berlin 1958: 29–39 and Williams 1981 remain seminal on moral dilemmas and the idea that there is no perfect calculus by which to solve conflicting obligations.

This affinity not only made magistracy a powerful tool for understanding the economy and sociology of exemplarity within Livy's work but also opened the narrated republic itself to constant redefinitions of its character and features. In articulating an approach to politics and political thought that is inherently dialectical, the *exempla* show the republic, at least in its textual manifestation, to be an imperfect compromise, which often struggles to reconcile rival principles, authorities, and opinions, and in doing so exposes these elements for consideration and invites reflection on their merits. The intersection of narrative, exemplarity, and magistracy thus ultimately yields a unified theory of literature and politics, interrogating not only public office, but also the rhetorical mannerism that shaped its textual presentation.

The semiotics of magistracy

Fundamental to the project of this book is the idea that magistracy is a useful heuristic paradigm for both the literary and the political systems that make up Livy's text, and by extension that magistrates are "good to think with" for the substance and the formal features of the narratives they participate in. A reasonable opening question, therefore, is why that should be case, and subsequently, what it is about magistracy that sets it apart from other types of phenomena or *exempla.* As a preliminary answer, this book will suggest that magistracy naturally possesses a triple valence when it comes to exemplary discourse. It participates in the construction of other *exempla* (of *severitas*, *pietas*, *fortitudo*, *uirtus*, and so forth); it offers a vehicle for the creation and negotiation of exemplarity through the political procedures of election, contional oratory, and other types of magisterial behavior; and finally, it is not only an object of study in itself but also a way into thinking about republican ideology, at least as understood by Livy and other, principally late republican and early imperial, authors. The consuls, for instance, have recently been styled "the very personification of the republic itself,"[7] a paradigmatic status which made the consulship, and by extension the other elected offices too, a convenient shorthand for thinking about political culture, political problems, and political exemplarity. Although there is little need now to belabor the complexity of the Roman constitutional system, or the scope of competencies the magistrates exercised within it, the special place the magistrates held within the state is worth

[7] Beck, Duplá, Jehne, and Pina Polo 2011: 9.

stressing on three related levels: institutional, cultural/historiographical, and semiotic.[8]

From an institutional point of view, which observes the system of government at Rome, the magistrates performed a bewildering range of tasks and roles. As a group, they maintained the city, sat as judges, led armies, performed various religious functions, advocated for certain interest groups, managed their own as well as a portion of the state's finances, implemented and sometimes determined Roman foreign policy, and had a hand in any number of more mundane administrative tasks.[9] As such, they are consistently referred to as one of the three pillars of the Roman state, representing, to pick two famous formulations, the element of *potestas* (Cic. *Rep.* 2.57, complementing the senate's *auctoritas* and the people's *libertas*), or the monarchical element (Polyb. 6.11–12, complementing the senate's aristocracy and the people's democracy).[10]

From a literary and cultural point of view, the magistrates hold a central role as both subject and organizing principle of Roman history. The elite bias of much of Roman historiography necessarily entailed a focus on great individuals, whether admired or notorious, who tended to perform their most memorable, or infamous, actions during their times either in office or when endowed by the senate with magisterial powers.[11] Cato the Elder, as often, is the exception that proves the rule: his insistence on withholding the nomenclature of consuls and generals from the *Origines* demonstrates clearly that theirs were the normal names on people's lips, and consequently on the pages of history.[12] Thus, when Livy or other writers describe the

8 Lintott 1999 remains a good overview of the system. Shorter treatments can be found in *OCD* s.v "Magistracy, Roman," 911; *Der Neue Pauly* s.v. "magistratus" 7.679–83; Berger 1953: 571–2, s.v. "*magistratus*." There are also useful charts in Brennan 2004: 63–5 (with added information about other constitutional bodies), and North 2006: 264. More specialized treatments: Develin 1979, Hopkins and Burton 1983, Eckstein 1987, Sandberg 2001, and Sivonen 2006.

9 On the individual magistracies: Consuls: Henderson 1957, Lippold 1963, Badian 1990, and now Pina Polo 2011, and Beck, Duplá, Jehne, and Pina Polo 2011. Praetors: Daube 1951, Stewart 1998, Brennan 2000. Censors: Schmähling 1938, Suolahti 1963, Astin 1982, Nicolet 2000. Aediles: Taylor 1939 (on Cicero's aedileship). Quaestors: Harris 1976. *Tribuni plebis*: Niccolini 1934, Bleicken 1955, Badian 1996. *Magister Populi*: Valditara 1989.

10 For Polybius' views of the Roman polity, see Walbank and Brink 1954, Walbank 1957–79, vol. 1: 673–97, 1964, 1998; see also Hahm 1995. Champion 2004: 67–99 reads Polybius' discussion of the Roman polity in the context of the cultural struggles between Greeks and Romans. For Cicero's *de Republica* see Zetzel's 1995 commentary, and most recently Asmis 2005. The connections between the *de Republica* and the *de Legibus* are the subject of a 2001 collection of essays edited by J. G. F. Powell and J. A. North.

11 On consuls and consulars as the most prominent actors in Roman politics and Roman historiography, see the collection of essays in Beck, Duplá, Jehne, and Pina Polo 2011, especially part III, with articles by Hölkeskamp, Roller (esp. pp. 183–4), Jehne, and Fronda.

12 Nepos, *Cato* 3.4, Pliny, *HN* 8.11 = *HRR* F 88 = *FRHist* F 115. Astin 1978: 213 suggests that Cato could hardly have omitted all the names of *imperatores*, although he acknowledges that such names

political life of the republic, they necessarily also describe the political life of the magistrates, and vice versa. The magistrates further provided one of the fundamental organizational principles of Roman history, whose basic unit was the consular year, identified and labeled by the relevant consuls' names. Magistrates played an especially important role, moreover, in the constitutional changes which structure the familiar narrative of Roman history. Indeed, constitutional development in Rome is tantamount to a change in the identity of the ruler (kings or consuls), the number of the rulers (decemvirs, military tribunes, or consuls), the hierarchy of office (the gradual codification of the *cursus honorum*), and, finally, the control and definition of access to the magistracies (patricians, plebeians, and the struggle of the orders). Thus, republican magistracy possessed a double valence in Roman political thought: not only were the magistrates the actual, historical players who enabled political action by the Roman people, they were also the unit according to which Roman time was divided and Roman history narrativized. The magistrates were therefore ubiquitous and vital, both in the city itself and in the various forms of its representation and commemoration, and as such were frequently at the center of debate, whether as active participants or passive subjects, or, as in Flamininus' case, both.

Finally, on the semiotic level, the magistrates were, in many ways, a shorthand for speaking about an entire ideological system. Scipio Aemilianus famously pronounced that *ex innocentia nascitur dignitas, ex dignitate honor, ex honore imperium, ex imperio libertas* (*ORF* 32 "standing is born from moral purity, office from one's standing, command from office, and freedom from command"). Though perhaps a naïve view of the relationship between ethics and political deserts, the emphasis on *honor* and *imperium* clearly connects the moral qualities (*innocentia*) of the office-holder with social and political outcomes, namely public standing and public office. But especially relevant here are the two steps following from public office – *honor* and *imperium* – and their connection to *libertas*. Aemilianus makes Roman freedom contingent not on the benign *honor* but on the more aggressive *imperium*. That choice in turn shapes how *honor* is to be understood: not as a social good similar to *dignitas* but rather a political good – magistracy – from which individual authority (*imperium*) and the characteristic independence of the republican state (*libertas*) flow.[13]

may have appeared in non-military contexts. One might also compare Caesar's treatment of his officers in the *Bellum Gallicum*, which uses them to showcase Caesar himself in the best light and prioritizes the centurions over Caesar's legates: Welch 1998.

13 Wirszubski 1968: 38 sees in this formulation a "sectional and exclusive *libertas* belonging to a Scipio and his likes." Whether or not Aemilianus' concept of *libertas* is class-derived, which to some

The same connection between magistracy and freedom is pronounced too in the historiographical tradition. When Livy begins narrating the history of the republic in the second book of the *AUC*, he defines his topic not only as the *res gestae* of the newly free people, but also, more specifically, as annual magistracies (2.1 *annuos magistratus*). He refers here to the literary convention of the consular year, but his coupling of magistracy with the rule of the law (2.1 *imperia legum*) at the dawn of the republic immediately situates magistracy at the heart of the new ideology. Likewise Cicero, formulating a law code for his idealized republic in the *de Legibus*, writes that a magistrate is a speaking law, and law a silent magistrate (*Leg.* 3.2 *uereque dici potest, magistratum esse legem loquentem, legem autem mutum magistratum*), thus further cementing the connection between magistracy and the foundations of republican liberty.[14] The Decemvirs, on the other hand, the body responsible for the laws of the Twelve Tables, and especially its president Appius Claudius, quickly became an archetype of tyrannical conduct.[15] Whether positive or negative, in other words, tinkering with the idea of magistracy was a useful and productive way of thinking about what the republic was and what the republic meant, and the image of magistracy became, as the figure of the emperor would later become, exemplary not only of itself and of the aristocratic battle for honors, but also of the state and its ideology.

It is possible, of course – indeed desirable – to adopt a similar approach to the study of either of the remaining elements of the Roman state, that is, senate and people. The scope of this book leaves little room for those two important bodies, but I do not mean to suggest that they were any less representative of republican ideology. On the contrary, senate, people,

extent it must have been, his articulation of *libertas* in terms of magistracy holds true. Arena 2012: 142–3 follows Wirszubski's view of Aemilianus' *libertas* as limited and connects Aemilianus' view to the exponents of democracy in, e.g., Cicero's *de Republica*.

14 On Cicero's transformation of the Greek "doctrine that the laws are over the magistrates," see Dyck 2004a: 432–3. In particular, as Dyck points out, the idea that law is a silent magistrate derives from Xenophon's *Cyropaedia* 8.1.22, where it is applied to a king rather than a magistrate. Note, however, that Dyck translates *legem loquentem* as "living law," which somewhat downplays Cicero's attention to speech and speech acts. For the idea of animate law (*nomos empsychos*) embodied in kingship developed by the pseudo-Pythagorean tradition see Noreña 2011: 53. For the more pedestrian measure of reading the laws out loud, see my discussion on pp. 164–7 below. Arena 2012: 48 argues that laws and citizen rights were "the institutional means through which the status of political liberty was established and maintained, rather than the incarnation of liberty itself." Given the complexity of the Roman political thought-world, there seems little need, however, to see the two opinions as mutually exclusive.

15 For the formation of the annalistic tradition on the decemvirate: Ungern-Sternberg 1986. Livy cements the connection with a reiteration of the Lucretia motif (cf. n. 22 below). On Claudian arrogance: Vasaly 1987.

and magistrates each offer the reader a distinctive entry into the conflicting discourses which formed Roman political theory, and one might with equal profit look at anecdotes on assembly or contional speech, senatorial procedure, and the clashes between the two.[16] The distinctive contribution of magistracy, however, is necessarily focused on their essential quality: the ability to act on behalf of the Roman people, the most concrete manifestation of which was the *imperium* given to the curule magistrates and the more limited *potestas* of the tribunes. *Imperium*, however, represents only one type of individual authority more broadly conceived, and it is in the relational or situational aspects of authority – the negotiation between law and pragmatics, between constitutional and familial obligations, between success and failure, and between universalizing *exemplum* and the contingencies of the moment – that this book finds its animating questions.[17]

This conception of magistracy has been neatly captured by Hans Beck. In response to a question posed by Plutarch – "Why was it that when [the Romans] gave a public banquet for men who had celebrated a triumph, they formally invited the consuls and then sent word to them requesting that they not come to the dinner?" (*Quaest. Rom.* 80) – Beck observes the following:

> Moreover, while the consuls claimed the right of highest honor, the story makes it clear that there were other distinctions, such as a triumphator's rights and privileges, which under certain cirumstances challenged the superior power of the consul, whether present or not . . . Plutarch reveals that if such a conflict between authorities arose, the Romans were not shy about practical solutions that enabled them to navigate around the provisions of their constitution without actually abandoning it.[18]

Beck's formulation applies precisely to the Flamininus example above: two valid demands meet in an attempt to negotiate some defining element of magistracy – the *cursus honorum*, and the *decorum* expected of up-and-coming magistrates in adhering to its steps. The Livian episode's conclusion

16 For an example of the plebs' perspective, see my discussion of Val. Max. 5.4.5 in Chapter 1. For plebeian views of contional speech: Morstein-Marx 2004: 207–30. For plebeian culture more generally, Horsfall 2004, and for the world of the citizen, Nicolet 1989. For a senate-centered approach to historiography, see Pittenger 2008.

17 On relational approaches and "scripts": Kaster 2005: 8–9, and *passim* (see index s.v. "scripts"). Goldhill 2012: 262–3 suggests replacing "text" with "script" as a more useful critical term. He sees scripts as "a written or oral template which has the strange ability of maintaining itself through innumerable re-incarnations – and which only comes to voice in and through performance" (262), and which retains its integrity even when the script is performed (i.e. read, acted, or interpreted) partially or with rhetorical distortions.

18 Beck 2011: 78. Cf. Val. Max. 2.8.6, at the close of a section devoted to *ius triumphandi*.

further illustrates Roman pragmatism, even at the expense of vocal and principled opposition, in an effort to reconcile the competing demands of ambition and ideology. Likewise, the tension Beck describes between the *triumphator* and the consuls is more than a problem of mere decorum; it also exposes a contention over honor and supremacy. In the presence of the consuls, as both Plutarch and Valerius Maximus state, no one else can hold the highest honors, and their absence from the feast therefore protects them from diminishment, albeit temporary, just as it protects the *triumphator* from having his limelight stolen. The deliberate avoidance of direct negotiation, however, also poses further revealing questions about the unique status of both consul and *triumphator*, and about what each of them represents in relation to the other. In a real sense, a *triumphator* was a magisterial *exemplum*: a consul or praetor exercising his *imperium* to the fullest, with beneficial results to himself and the Roman people. *Triumphatores* were thus a privileged sub-category of the bigger set of magistrates, and the requested absence of the consuls constructs them, too, as equal to the *triumphator* in potential.

What is especially salutary about Beck's framing of the episode is his focus on the "pragmatic solutions" the Romans came up with for such problems, an approach that opens up, rather than reduces, the scope of inquiry into the Roman constitutional sensibility. The contribution this book has to make, while fully in agreement with such broad horizons, takes Beck's insight in a different direction: it argues that the literary depictions of this problem-solving process rely on a heuristic framework which is exemplary in its logic, that is, one that looks to imitation, replicability, precedent, and decorum as its guiding principles. More specifically, this book looks to the literary techniques through which politics is depicted and argues that those formal and rhetorical mannerisms give important structure to the representation of magistracy in historiographical texts.[19]

The operation of exemplarity

In thinking about the ways in which historiography participated in political discourse, exemplarity presents itself as an especially useful heuristic device which provides the moral and literary infrastructure for much of Roman commemorative production. Indeed, historiography, and especially Livy, made ample use of the Roman penchant for exemplary discourse, which

[19] For a similar approach to the problem of history writing as a literary text, see Elliot 2013: 198–232 on Ennius' *Annales*.

explicitly connected the rhetorical form of the anecdote with the cultural values the anecdote explored.[20] Exemplarity, and the habits of thought it engendered, governed and shaped the movement between universals and particulars, a capacity it shares with other units of narrative composition such as topoi, allusivity, and intertextuality. It also fueled an inclination, for both author and reader, to evaluate events and characters along certain lines and towards certain commemorative goals. Exemplarity is thus one of the main hermeneutic frameworks of this book. Studies of exemplarity to date, however, have typically focused on attention-grabbing deeds and their inculcation of moral values, or alternatively on establishing the ways in which internal audiences teach the audience how to read *exempla*. This book differs by examining, for the most part, a different type of anecdote, which in turn suggests a different account of its didactic function. It also views exemplarity from two related aspects: one internal, wherein exemplarity governs the way in which certain episodes are delivered to the reader, relying on recognizable and acknowledged *exempla*; and one external, which views exemplarity as a heuristic device which governs not only the content of *exempla*, but also their modes of production. What this second function amounts to, as this book will argue, is a type of meta-exemplarity, wherein *exempla* invite the reader to think not only about their moral content, but also about the way in which that content was produced, and the consequences of that evaluation in the broader context of both literary and political writing. In a nutshell, this book will argue that magistracy offers a convenient figure or even mannerism through which to articulate a number of issues, pertaining both to the literary economy of Roman historiography (though especially of Livy's *AUC*) and to any articulation of the republic and its ethical dimensions. To explain how this type of exemplary discourse works, and what benefits can be drawn from it, we might profitably return to the Flamininus episode to ask what it is exemplary of, and how it functions as an *exemplum*.

[20] The role of the anecdote in the writing of history has received a great deal of attention from New Historicist critics. See, e.g., Gallagher and Greenblatt 2001: 49–74. For the use of anecdotes for details of Roman history, see Saller 1980, esp. 82: "In contrast, anecdotes can be valuable evidence for the attitudes and ideologies of peoples." On exemplarity in Livy: Jaeger 1997, Feldherr 1998, Chaplin 2000, and Langlands 2011; on possible connections between Livy and Ennius: Elliot 2009b and 2013: 213–18. On exemplarity in Roman culture: Hölkeskamp 2003 and Roller 2004. Morgan 2007: 122–59 discusses *exempla* as part of an ethical discourse in the early empire. Roller 2009a discusses exemplarity as a mode of historical knowledge, as does the growing bibliography on exemplarity as *memoria* in n. 21 below. For exemplarity as a theoretical approach to literature: Goldhill 1994. For a reception-centered view of classical exemplarity: Hampton 1990 on the uses of exemplarity in Renaissance literature, and Vlassopoulos 2009: xiv on the use of historical narrative as "patterns in order to elucidate the present and future of modern communities."

In order to answer those questions it is helpful first to clarify the operation of exemplarity as it pertains to the standard cases, as well as pointing out the two models of exemplarity currently available. In the most recent systematic study of exemplarity as a cultural phenomenon, Matthew Roller, whom I use here as a representative of a broader current of interest in exemplarity and historiography as components of cultural memory, has suggested that the exemplary discourse consisted of four components: action, audience, commemoration, and imitation.[21] Roller's paradigms are Horatius Cocles and Cloelia, two figures whose stories conform to the usual image of the exemplary hero as a lonely figure performing a great deed against all odds. These deeds leave behind a concrete and visible sign, specifically a statue, but also physical scars, and, of course, literary texts too. A more complicated standard reference point is the story of Lucretia. Her action (suicide) is performed in order to manifest a value (*pudicitia*, "chastity"), and she performs it in front of witnesses – her brother, father, and Brutus (as well as Livy's readers) – who transmit the story to the Roman people at large. Those audiences, too, act as the commemorative agent, as does the republic itself, founded in an act of vengeance on Lucretia's rapist and his regal family. Lucretia even refers to her own act as a tellingly ambivalent *exemplum*: Livy 1.58.10 *nec ulla deinde impudica Lucretiae exemplo uiuet* ("so that no unchaste woman should henceforth live, citing Lucretia's example"); she wishes to avoid becoming an *exemplum* of *impudicitia*, even as her suicide becomes exemplary of female agency and indeed of wronged *pudicitia* itself. However, as Jane Chaplin points out, Lucretia is neither cited as an *exemplum* nor taken as a model of conduct, although Livy himself deploys her narrative repeatedly as a template for exploring changing political values.[22] What further prevents imitation is the commemorative medium itself. The very foundation of the republic is designed to prevent

[21] Roller 2004: 4–6. Roller himself acknowledges that not all elements appear in all *exempla* (7). The bibliography on *memoria* is considerable, and quickly growing. Timpe 1996 (reprinted as 2011: 150–74) and Farrell 1997 give a good introduction to the phenomenology of memory in Rome, the former with an eye on historiography in particular. For discussion of specific historians: Walter 2004: 212–356 surveys most of the fragmentary annalists, Grethlein 2006 discusses the dialectics between history and memory in the proems of Sallust; for the same tension in Livy, Miles 1995: 8–74. On *exempla* as *lieux de memoire* and their function within the Roman "memory culture," Walter 2004 is both seminal and comprehensive, but see also Hölkeskamp 1996 (reprinted as 2004: 169–98), Coudry and Späth 2001, Bücher 2006, Stemmler 2000, Roller 2010, and the essays collected in Galinsky 2014.

[22] Chaplin 2000: 1, with n. 3 for the uses Livy does find for the Lucretia narrative. Prominent parallels are the story of Verginia (with a direct allusion to Lucretia in 3.44.1) and of Fabia Minor (6.34.5–35.1). On Livy's use of the story-type see Kraus 1991 (Fabia Minor), Feldherr 1998: 203–12 (Verginia), and Chaplin 2010 (the continence of Scipio), with further references. On Lucretia and Verginia as *exempla* of *pudicitia*: Langlands 2006: 78–109.

monarchical excess, with the implied consequence that Lucretia's situation will not arise again; indeed, future Lucretias, like Verginia or Fabia Minor, effect political change on a smaller scale, nor do they have the same agency in becoming an *exemplum*. Finally, it is worth stressing both the political and imperfect nature of the Lucretia *exemplum*: political, because it directly pertains to the foundation of the republic, and imperfect, because Lucretia views herself as *impudica* ("unchaste"), while the audience is meant to see her as a paradigm of chastity. Lucretia thus becomes both *exemplum* and topos, a standard point of reference as well as a case study in female virtue, a moment both replicable and unique.

Lucretia, of course, is herself a literary product, and she serves, given her programmatic role for the history and for the republic, as a figure for meta-exemplarity, showcasing the complicated procedure by which an act does or does not become an *exemplum*. Such procedures might be characterized as essentially rooted in narrative, with its unique tension between the episode's importance in and of itself, and its developing relevance as the rest of the text unfolds. In prioritizing this narrative model of exemplarity, I follow Jane Chaplin in *Livy's Exemplary History*, who sees an *exemplum* as "anything from the past that serves as a guide to conduct within the text," and in consequence points out that "[f]ar from predominating, the legendary figures take their place beside unnamed and obscure individuals, as well as battle tactics, constitutional precedents, and religious affairs."[23] The two models are not unrelated, of course. Any *exemplum* aspires to participate in the "exemplary loop" Roller describes, wherein an *exemplum* succeeds in becoming a definitive description of conduct, which can then exert pressure on future imitators. Not all *exempla*, however, succeed. Lucretia is a borderline case: she becomes an *exemplum*, but not within the textual universe she inhabits. Livy's characters can re-enact her story, but they do not act in direct imitation of her. It is rather the reader who notes the differences and thereby knows to construct Lucretia as the *exemplum* she desires to be. As such, the narrative text, especially on the lavish scope of the *AUC*, becomes also a reflection of the circulation of exemplarity in the world outside the text, where *exempla* and media compete for attention and do not always receive it on their own terms. This parallelism has important consequences, not least because it blurs the lines between the text as a closed system and the "real world" as an open one. In capturing cultural processes as well as historical events, historiography arrogates, indeed constructs, for itself precisely the three-dimensionality that makes its narrative

[23] Chaplin 2000: 3.

vivid and effective. Within this closed world, however, exemplarity is without doubt a fully textual phenomenon, and it is as such that this book explores it.

Textual exemplarity is further, as Simon Goldhill has recognized, a concept porous to deconstruction: since every *exemplum* vacillates between the ideal model and the specific instance, each *exemplum* also opens up a set of destabilizing questions, which, if satisfactorily resolved, concretize the *exemplum* as definitive.[24] Goldhill is, as behooves the critic, skeptical about the possibility of such an outcome, but the particularities of Roman culture provide, as Roller and others demonstrate, sufficient evidence that the Romans could simultaneously maintain a critical distance and establish a moral resolution in regard to any particular *exemplum*.[25] The presence of a culture of exemplarity, therefore, generated also an exemplary habit, which stretched along a range of instances, some more exemplary than others. Thus, while individual *exempla* codified normative values and exerted pressure on imitators to reproduce the value in their own conduct, they were also in dynamic engagement with the interested readership, in whose evaluative judgment true exemplary status resided. In this, at least, the exemplary discourse bears considerable resemblance to the political culture of the republic itself – competitively driven by the tension between conformity and ambition.[26] Literary texts, meanwhile, participated in the discourse not only by commemorating "proper" *exempla* but also by drawing on the destabilizing set of questions such participation naturally produced. These questions evaluated what kind of *exemplum* a particular event might be, how it ought to be remembered, and above all, what quality it was that the story instantiated. Chaplin's model, which allows a broader selection of exemplary acts, thus converges with Roller's more static model at the interface of reader and text, pointing towards a habit of reading that looks for exemplary cues and therefore reveals how episodes which would normally fall outside the boundaries of the exemplary discourse nevertheless participate in it.[27]

Roman politics in themselves were a particularly effective conduit for generating *exempla*, as well as a host of competing cases from which an

[24] Goldhill 1994, esp. 70: "examples themselves are narrativized – told as narrative – and as such are open to the plays and openness of the narrative form . . . The example's narrative form always threatens to produce an excess of signification beyond the controlling lines of the case it is designed to illustrate."

[25] Roller 2001. See also my discussion of Brutus and the *imperia Manliana* in Chapter 1 below.

[26] On the dynamics of this operation in the case of C. Duilius, for whom we can reconstruct an unusually thick description, see Roller 2009a.

[27] For a similar reading, but focusing on Valerius Maximus rather than Livy: Langlands 2008.

exemplum might be paratactically rendered. Elections are a good instance of the phenomenon.[28] Electoral campaigns by definition demand that candidates conform to an implicit idea of magistracy and electability and exert their energies in convincing the voters, in their behavior if not through direct propaganda, that they were already as close to that ideal as they could reasonably be. It was then up to the voters to decide – or have decided for them – which of the candidates conformed best. The content of the rhetoric therefore constitutes the set of questions which determines which of the candidates should be elected, while the rhetorical strategies expose the values at play on that particular day. Because they are endlessly replicable, and because they were actually repeated, no single election can be an *exemplum* in and of itself, but each one was also a typical instance of the genre and exemplified, with appropriate caveats, its various counterparts. In their variety, however, electoral scenes are nevertheless collectively invested in the exemplary procedures which organized and governed political ambition.

Here, the Flamininus episode is especially illuminating. It fits Roller's pattern only partially, though, as the comparison with Lucretia suggests, this mismatch is not atypical of the genre. The exemplary action itself is difficult to determine: is it Flamininus' standing for office, or the tribunes' disruption of it? In either case, no obvious Roman value, such as *uirtus* ("bravery") or *constantia* ("endurance") is attached, even as a negative foil, though the amorphous *mos maiorum* ("ancestral custom" or "the done thing") looms large over the proceedings. Audiences there are aplenty, from the implicit voters to the explicit senators and tribunes.[29] Each of these audiences renders its own judgment on the situation, mostly in favor of the legitimacy of Flamininus' candidacy. Commemoration and imitation, however, are again problematic. The senatorial decree serves as a kind of commemoration, but it is, it seems, ad hoc in nature, and thus a long way from the honorary statue or even a specific piece of legislation. Instead, the main commemorator is Livy himself, harking bark to his sources, whether previous annalists, official documentation, or informal lore. Imitation, in cases such as Flamininus', is more a case of structural resemblance than conscious repetition, and in this it is no different from Lucretia's case, or its

28 See in particular my discussion in Chapter 3. On republican elections see: Taylor 1966, Staveley 1972, North 1990a and 1990b (with a response in Harris 1990: 291–4), Mouritsen 2001: 90–127, Yakobson 1999, and most recently Feig-Vishnia 2012. The *commentariolum petitionis* provides a unique view of contemporary Roman electioneering: Nisbet 1961, Balsdon 1963, Richardson 1971, Morstein-Marx 1998, Tatum 2007, Fezzi 2007. Lundgreen 2011: 53–120 explores elections as an arena for the resolution of conflicts of interest, an approach to which this book is highly sympathetic.

29 On internal audiences in the *AUC*, see Feldherr 1998 and Levene 2006.

relationship to that of Verginia. Moreover, both historical realities and the historiographical annalistic form guaranteed that such electoral *certamina* recurred both in the state and in its textual representation. The specifics of the situation – a premature candidacy by a future great man – is itself embedded in a series of such iterations, from Scipio Africanus to Pompey the Great.[30]

What matters more for my purposes, however, is that the episode is invested in the dynamics of exemplary discourse. The tribunes' charge can be encapsulated in Flamininus' refusal to make an exemplar of himself: by skipping the aedileship and praetorship, Flamininus failed not only to furnish *documentum sui*, a proof of his own abilities, but also to conform to the pattern demanded of a young nobleman. *Documentum* is a loaded word for Livy, featuring prominently in the programmatic statement of *praef.* 10, where he lays out his project of didactic exemplarity:

> hoc illud est praecipue in cognitione rerum salubre ac frugiferum, omnis te exempli documenta in inlustri posita monumento intueri; inde tibi tuaeque rei publicae quod imitere capias, inde foedum inceptu foedum exitu quod uites. (Livy, *praef.* 10)
>
> This is especially improving and beneficial in the study of history, to contemplate examples of every kind of behavior (*omnis exempli documenta*) set out clearly on a monument. From this you can choose for yourself and for your commonwealth which to imitate, and which, being foul from beginning to end, to avoid.

The tribunes' objection to Flamininus therefore implicates a political exchange about candidacy and its legitimacy in a much broader discourse of exemplary conduct and suggests that premature candidacy is a thing to avoid, precisely because it pre-empts and opts out of the exemplary loop. The episode is typifying in other ways, too. Throughout, the tribunes use generalizing (*nobiles homines*) and moralizing (*fastidiri, summa imis continuare*) language, and the latter invokes also Roman class consciousness as well as the tensions between the various elements of the political community.[31] The senate responds to the tribunes' generalizing with equally

30 On textual imitation: Kraus 1998. On the problems with the intertextual processes of exemplarity in historical texts: Damon 2010 and O'Gorman 2009.

31 The full text is quoted on p. 1 above. For *fastidium* in general, see Kaster 2005: 104–33, and esp. 112–21 on *fastidium* as "deliberative ranking." Kaster defines this kind of *fastidium* as applying both to one's idea of oneself as superior, and to one's idea of the object of *fastidium* as inferior and therefore repulsive. In this case, "deliberative ranking" is especially appropriate, because Flamininus is alleged to rank the levels of office themselves, thus critiquing not only the middle offices but the entire system. For the phrase *summa imis*, see Briscoe 1973: 180, and Edwards 1993: 137–72 for the Roman

gnomic force and co-opts their use of metaphor as well: where the tribunes speak of the *nobiles* as a group, the senate counters with the equally general clause *qui . . . peteret*; where the tribunes are concerned with the imbalance of high and low (*summa imis*), the senate offers level ground (*aequum esse*). Moreover, Livy goes to some effort to draw the reader's attention to the event, and the election seems to excite his imagination considerably more than the immediately preceding item, a military defeat which cost Rome an entire praetorian army, but which Livy dismisses in a few short lines. The campaign, both military and electoral, ends not only with the election of new magistrates, but also with the formulation of a principle applicable to future instantiations of the same situation, thus performing a variation on the topos of the precocious candidate or the stalwart (if frustrated) tribunes, both familiar faces on the Roman political scene. The episode thus conforms to many of the criteria of an *exemplum*, principally its dual status as something both singular and replicable.

As a heroic example of the Lucretia type, this episode may lack a little drama. But it is clear that it participates in the same literary and cultural tendency towards organizing the world in repeatable narrative topoi, which contribute to an accumulation of knowledge about the past. Such knowledge, as Jane Chaplin has argued, need not derive only from what might be termed "High Exemplarity," but also from more regular or everyday occurrences, only retrospectively found to have relevance to the present.[32] So what is Flamininus' candidacy exemplary of, and how does it do its exemplary work? In this book, I suggest that this episode and others like it exemplify the process rather than – or, better still, in addition to – the individual. In other words, what animates the episode is not the grand deed of one or more protagonists, but rather the simultaneous existence of multiple perspectives on the same structurally replicable event – the legal status of a candidacy, electoral rhetoric and the images it produces, or the behaviors of magistrates in office – and the ways in which those perspectives interact and are ultimately resolved. This resolution need not be satisfying and in fact frequently involves the prioritization of one claim over the other: in Flamininus' case, for instance, the senators privilege the laws over the tribunes' moral claim, though they notably fail to engage, or

ideas of immoral and luxurious excess it connotes. Nisbet and Hubbard 1970: 384–5, commenting on Hor. *Carm.* 1.34.12 (*ima summis*), note that "Horace's description of Fortune's actions suggests the conventional complaint of Roman constitutionalists against radical innovators." They list, e.g., Cic. *Leg.* 3.19 *omnia infima summis paria fecit* . . . and Vell. *Pat.* 2.2.3 (Tiberius Gracchus) *summa imis miscuit.*

32 See quotation on p. 10 above; cf. n. 20 above.

offer a solution to, the problem the tribunes identify, namely that rushing up the *cursus honorum* prevented the voters from properly knowing the candidates. As an *exemplum*, then, this episode holds up political as well as social values: civility, attending to the voters, respect for the senate and the laws, and the necessity of dialogue as a means to consensus. The episode is, finally, explicitly concerned with its own status as a future *exemplum*, and with the political processes which make it so. As such, it necessarily invites the reader to reflect also on the episode's validity as an *exemplum*, and of the consequences of awarding it exemplary status. For, inasmuch as magistracy was an essential and defining feature of the republican state, any evaluation of the magistrates impacted also the nature of the state. If magistrates were rapacious, so too was Rome; if they were law-abiding and loyal to their oaths, so too was Rome. If they arrogated too much power or trod too much on the people's liberty, so too was the republic in physical and ideological danger. More importantly, the episode exemplifies also the lack of any meaningful reconciliation between the two positions, and therefore the imperfect calculus of the various claims made by the participants. The element of nuance, the multiplicity of perspectives, and the incessant competition among participants, authors, and the *exempla* themselves is the very thing that the historiography of politics explores, articulates, and finally exemplifies.

Narrative, historiography, and political thought

The Roman historian Livy makes up the bulk of this book, and with good reason: the *AUC* offers the most extensive formal narrative of the Roman republic in extant Latin, and the most elaborate articulation of exemplarity as a literary mannerism. The *AUC* thus presents itself as a natural case study for illustrating how historiographical narrative and exemplary practice cohere as a literary and cultural tradition as well as a commemorative practice. This is not, of course, to say that Livy is alone in his exemplary penchant, and this book uses various episodes drawn from other authors, chiefly Cicero, to bolster and expand on Livy's view. Indeed, a secondary argument of this book is to show Livy as a politically sensitive author, for whom morality and exemplarity played a part in a necessarily political world, and whose command and presentation of the domestic material offer vivid and incisive accounts of political *mentalité*, even if his fact-finding is at times faulty.

Magistracy is ubiquitous in Roman literature, so much so that many a magistrate appears merely as part of the constitutional or literary apparatus, rather than as a meaningful actor in the plot. The episodes I treat here have instead been selected because they bring out literary articulations of the political dynamics, interests, and institutions that pertain to magistracy, and they do so in ways that rely heavily on the dynamics of exemplarity for their interest and moral lessons. Consequently, the book consists of a series of case studies, each exploring a facet of political exemplarity, the political and cultural values it negotiates, and the literary mannerisms and forms that shape the textual representation of republican political discourse. As such, the chapters are not intended to suggest a comprehensive approach to magistracy, but rather to examine some of the ways in which political theory – namely, ideas about how republican practices worked or ought to have worked – intersects with a literary theory of composition – the formal and generic conventions of the texts, of which intratextuality, topoi, and exemplarity are chief components. This selection has two obvious consequences: first, it skews away from instances where exemplarity plays a less prominent or less explicit role; second, it skews towards Livy's own preoccupations, which tend to cluster around either the annalistic description of electoral campaigns or around the exemplary tradition. The book's argument, however, attempts to explain these two biases as a product of Roman thinking itself. The progression of chapters in this book aims to show how exemplary dynamics work in the text even when exemplarity might seem to recede from the center of attention to the armature of comprehension, and part of this book's argument is that the imperfect calculus reconciling official roles, private obligations, and the demands of tradition, would apply in those cases just as well. Further, I would suggest that these preoccupations are not unique to Livy but characteristic of the historiographical tradition. As the various parallels to Livy explored in this book show, Livy's thought is often grounded in, and expands upon, impulses already present in his predecessors. His success in transmitting those ideas, for later collectors of *exempla* such as Valerius Maximus or Plutarch, is a testament to the success of his endeavor.

From a methodological standpoint, this book analyzes the language, rhetoric, and structure of a group of anecdotes, and it proceeds as a series of close readings. It treats those episodes as literary constructs meant to be read as an expression of cultural memory, articulated through narrative forms and rhetorical presentation. Republican historiography has so far been characterized by attention to the formal and rhetorical elements of the genre. Where attention has been political it has tended to focus either on the theory of politics articulated in the texts, or otherwise on the politics of the author himself. This book builds on, and yet differs from, both approaches in using the methods of historiography to illuminate written accounts of the workings of republican politics – a body of material that has been of primary, though not exclusive, interest to historians – focusing in particular on analysis of literary techniques and formal structures as a way of thinking about describing the institution of magistracy in republican Rome.[33]

In light of the above it may seem unnecessary to register my demurral from the assumption, enshrined in the *Cambridge History of Greek and Roman Political Thought*, that narrative illustrates little by way of political reflection.[34] While I do not mean to suggest that narrative provides a truer, or indeed a complete, reflection of ancient political thought, it is important to recognize what narrative is especially well-equipped to do: to convey vividly different points of view, through both obtrusive and more subtle focalizations, and to make not only thematic but also inter- and intratextual connections. In the Flamininus anecdote, for example, it is impossible to understand the political dynamic without taking into consideration the emotive and ethical vocabulary, such as *fastidiri*, *summa imis*, or *aequum*; the annalistic structure within which this episode is embedded; or the broader intra- and intertextual patterns in Livy or in other authors. Attention to such formal features necessarily privileges the author's artistic choices as an expressive medium, but such attention also focuses on how narrative can shape or reflect the ways in which such political issues are articulated, received, or preserved. Such attention to culture complements recent historical approaches to magistracy, for example that described in the recent volume *Consuls and res publica*, whose editors pronounce the study of the consulship to be "better suited to cultural history and

33 For formal readings of historiography: Woodman 1988, Kraus and Woodman 1997. The current state of affairs is captured by the essays collected in Marincola 2008 and Feldherr 2009; cf. Pitcher 2010. For politico-theoretical approaches: Hammer 2008 and Kapust 2011. Gowing 2005 and Gallia 2012 analyze the reception of the republic under the empire as a literary and cultural topos, and especially as a center of memory. The text's relationship to the politics of the author himself has been a particular focus in Caesarian studies: cf. Batstone and Damon 2006, Riggsby 2006, Grillo 2012. For a similar tack on Livy: Syme 1959 and Sailor 2006; on Tacitus: Sailor 2011.

34 Wiedemann 2005: 523 recognizes that Livy has an important contribution to make, but one insufficient to make him agree that Livy was a political thinker: "If political theory is absent from the surviving thirty-five books of Livy's history . . . it was because creating a coherent narrative structure for his material was more important to Livy than political analysis." And later on the same page: "But for a study of political thought, Livy is disappointing not so much because explicit theoretical analysis is lacking (or that his analytical categories are unsophisticated), or that literary intentions take priority, as that he is a Roman writing for Romans, and therefore takes it for granted that political and social institutions need not be described." But Livy does consistently describe the political rhythms and habits of Romans, and dismissing Livy's narrative out of hand, even as a useful source of evidence for *mentalité*, bespeaks too narrow a conception of "description."

historical anthropology than the classical 'Staatsrecht.'"[35] Historiography, and especially the anecdote, performs this very function: it animates and highlights elements of the broader cultural discourse through commemorating and articulating a range of images of the republic and its political ideology.[36]

A concomitant question to narrative's capacity to reflect political culture is its ability to transmit it, especially across the Augustan divide. In this regard, Livy is again exemplary of a broader current: a historian born under the late republic, who began to compose his work in the turbulent years before Actium, and whose *floruit* encompassed the Augustan regime, with which he shared its ideological project, literary mannerisms, and cultural sensitivities.[37] As a recorder of lived republican politics, therefore, Livy necessarily falls short of either his own annalist predecessors or of such active participants as Cicero or Sallust. Nevertheless, some archaeology of republican politics is possible in Livy, and his general sense for the rough-and-tumble nature of republican politics, its rhetorical flair, and tendency for *bons mots* is borne out even in comparison with other authors. Here too the conservative nature of the historiographical tradition increases our confidence in the transmission of the spirit, if not the specific details, of campaign, elections, and other historical minutiae.[38] The Augustan period was besides heavily invested in the republic as an ideological shield, behind whose protection the autocracy took its fledgling steps. The political transitions and upheavals made republican magistracy an appealing topic, as Romans struggled to find a model and an idiom with which to explain new modes of power. Livy himself held that republican *exempla* were

35 Beck, Duplá, Jehne, and Pina Polo 2011: 2. Lundgreen 2011 argues forcefully that negotiations between rules and principles were fundamental to the practice of Roman politics, rather than a more rigid *Staatsrecht*. Considerable attention has recently been paid to the emphatically deliberative and performative contexts of republican political culture: cf. e.g. Millar 1998, Morstein-Marx 2004 on communication and consensus, Flower 1996 and 2004 on performance and spectacle, and Hölkeskamp 2010 for an integrated view of both aspects.

36 Similar trends have been developing in the related sub-field of political oratory, on which see especially Connolly 2007 for the idea that oratorical performance contributed to the formation of a citizen-subject, while highlighting some of the fault lines inherent to that construction. For similar developments in republican historiography, see Pittenger 2008, Connolly 2009, and Roller 2009b.

37 For Livy's dates: Luce 1965 and Burton 2000. Livy's reference to Augustus' Spanish campaigns in book 28 (28.12.12 *postrema omnium nostra demum aetate ductu auspicioque Augusti Caesaris perdomita est*) in any case gives us a *terminus ante quem* of 26 BC for the third decade, though Scheidel 2009 argues, based on references to census figures, that Livy completed book 28 around 19/18 BC and wrote or revised books 1 and 3 around 28 BC. For his life and relationship to Augustus and the Augustan project: Syme 1959; Kraus 1994a: 1–7; Lowrie 2009: 157–8, 303–4.

38 For the tralatician nature of Roman historiography: Forsythe 1994 and 1999; see also Lendon 2009, for whom this procedure severely limited the artistic freedom of the ancient historian, thus guaranteeing at least some level of authenticity.

useful for his readers as they learned their history and applied its lessons to their own world.[39] Exemplarity here plays an explicitly didactic and political role, and it presents historiographical narrative as a rich vehicle for articulating the construction of political power, especially as vested in single individuals.[40] In a period when autocracy was coming to replace the old republican structures, the republic nevertheless offered the only collective past available to many citizens, while historiography offered a view into the events of the glorious past in ways that were both accessible and applicable to the brave new world that Romans found themselves entering.

History and historiography

Finally, a word on the perennial chestnut, the relationship of history and historiography. The literary approach this book takes sidelines, to a large extent, both positivist definitions of magistracy and the related issue of the semantics of authority.[41] As Robert Kaster has demonstrated in a study of Roman emotive vocabulary, however, modern categorizations of ancient words do not necessarily correlate to the ancients' own understanding of similar concepts, and *mutatis mutandis*, neither do legal or functional definitions.[42] Historical approaches, with notable exceptions, have until recently tended to isolate rather than interpellate magistracy within the

39 *Praef.* 10 *inde tibi tuaeque rei publicae quod imitere capias, inde foedum inceptu foedum exitu quod uites* ("from these you can choose, for yourself and your commonwealth, what to imitate, and from these also what – rotten from beginning to end – to shun"). The sudden apostrophe, further emphasized by the polyptotonic *tibi tuaeque* must be a deliberate move away from the impersonal *quisque* in *praef.* 9, whether or not it refers literally to Octavian or more metonymically to the common reader. Moles 1994: 152 sees the progression from the third person earlier in the preface to the second person here as "an appeal . . . so framed as to overturn the distinction between self-interest and national interest"; cf. Kraus 1994a: 14 and Jaeger 1997: 23. Hölkeskamp 2010: 106 underscores the connection between aristocratic consensus, the moral values it emphasized, and the "practical rules for the 'real-world' application of these values" in the form of traditional *exempla*. Walter 2004 sees *exempla* as loci of cultural memory but argues that the Roman "memory culture" peters out during the transition to autocracy; for *memoria*-culture, see n. 21 above.

40 On the Augustan consulship see now Hurlet 2011.

41 The bibliography on *imperium* is extensive. Brennan 2000: 12–20 and Beck 2011 summarize the *status quaestionis*, and Beck in particular advances a more nuanced view of *imperium* as a "mosaic" of competencies and regulations. See also the discussions in Staveley 1956: 90–119 and Lintott 1999: 96–7. On the semantics of *imperium* Richardson 2008 offers the most recent survey of the uses of *imperium* in Latin and traces its semantic field, especially in relation to notions of empire. On *imperium maius/minus*, see the references in Chapter 1, n. 19, with Stewart 1998, Masi Doria 2000, and Beck 2005, on the tensions between the various gradations of *imperium* in the Roman state. For the interpretative limitations of lexically centered interpretations to culture: Skinner 1979.

42 Kaster 2005: 6–8; cf. Skinner 1979 on the dangers of equating overly rigidly "terms" and "concepts," as well as of dismissing context. For change over time ("reception and distortion") in political vocabulary: Vlassopolous 2009: 14–39.

Roman landscape of authority.[43] We therefore have fairly precise knowledge of the kinds of actions any magistrate was allowed to take, and the geographical space, as well as the scope, in which law and custom allowed him to proceed. However, definitions cannot fully provide access to *mentalité*, nor to the ways in which Romans understood the relationships between themselves and authority, or how one authority was like, or different from, the other. Literature, meanwhile, as much work in recent decades has shown, remains an untapped resource precisely for those difficult-to-reach areas of study, and literary-critical approaches can therefore be complementary, though not ancillary to, historical questions on the experience of politics in republican Rome.[44]

As always, such complementarity emerges most clearly from compare-and-contrast exercises, and especially so in those few cases where literary evidence can be compared directly with its historical counterparts. The infamous *senatus consultum de Bacchanalibus* of 168 BC and Livy's account of the discovery and suppression of the cult are a case in point.[45] Livy's account undoubtedly shows much literary embroidery, and it is thought largely to depend on comic structures, motifs, and characters.[46] Livy furnishes his narrative with the *adulescens* in love, the forbidding parents, and the shrewd prostitute with a heart of gold, throws in the exotic debauchery of the Bacchic cult, and deploys the resources of the state not only to restore order and morality, but also to reward the two informers, Hispala Faecenia and Publius Aebutius. Here, the legalities encroach on the story. Livy's account of the senate's decision in 39.18–19 repeats, in a more polished style and with some abbreviation, the content of the *senatus consultum* in

43 In this they are perhaps abetted by the ancient tendency to taxonomies, especially in formal treatises, such as Polybius' sixth book, Cicero's *de Legibus*, and Varro's now lost *commentarius* for Pompey the Great on senatorial proceedings. For Polybius' views see n. 10 above. For the *de Legibus*, a largely neglected work, see Powell and North 2001 and Dyck's commentary (2004a). Varro's *commentarius* still awaits meaningful treatment.

44 Goldhill 2012: 262 is the most recent statement: "[o]ne way that literature and society interrelate is as mutually informing scripts: the scripts of social ritual are embedded in literary narrative; literary narratives provide scripts through which social life is experienced." The rise of the New Historicism ushered in a golden age for collapsing the distinctions between literature and history as terminally separate disciplines, relying especially on the anthropological practice of "thick description" (Geertz 1973, Gallagher and Greenblatt 2001: 20–31). The *loci classici* remain Greenblatt 1985 and 1997. In Roman studies this book takes its cues from Feeney 1998 and Roller 2001, among others. Searle 1995 makes an interesting case for the crucial roles of language and community in establishing a real presence and agency for abstract institutions such as government and money, thus carving out a place for literary texts as participants in political life (on which topic see also Riggsby 2006 and Connolly 2007).

45 The bibliography on the Bacchic scandal ranges over multiple sub-fields and is too large to cover here. The most recent systematic treatment of Livy's account is Briscoe 2008: 230–90, with a thorough bibliography on p. 230, to which add Nousek 2010 on Ciceronian echoes in the narrative.

46 Scafuro 1989 (reprinted in Chaplin and Kraus 2009), Walsh 1996. For the relationship of historiography and drama, see my discussion in the Epilogue.

CIL 1^2 2.581, found *in agro Taureano* (modern Tiriolo in southern Italy) in 1640.[47] The *senatus consultum* makes multiple provisions to guard against the resurrection of the cult on any large scale, demanding small numbers of worshipers, restricting places and times of worship, and preventing any permanent infrastructure, either in owning a shrine or in appointing a *magister* or priest. Any deviation from these rules required a special permit from the Roman senate, and that could only be obtained in Rome, by application to the *praetor urbanus*, and on approval of the senate by a minimum quorum of a hundred senators. These details are clearly meant as obstacles and from the point of view of the Bacchic worshiper, at least, begin and end with the *praetor urbanus*.

Between Livy and the *senatus consultum*, then, we have a fairly good idea of what the process entailed, and from one perspective at least it was no different than the many embassies magistrates regularly funneled to the senate. What is obviously missing, and can never be reliably recovered, is the experience of the individual participant, and what he or she might have thought and felt in deciding to approach the Roman authorities. It is precisely that gap that literature can fill, though of course, the results in this particular case would be to a very large degree fictional. Still, some general conclusions can be drawn, and Livy helpfully provides an approximation of the experience of an encounter between a Roman consul and his diametric opposite: a foreign woman. As the investigation into the Bacchic cult begins, the consul demands to meet Hispala Faecenia, and she is therefore summoned to the house of Sulpicia, a noblewoman and the consul's mother-in-law. When Hispala arrives to see the consular retinue in the courtyard, she comes close to fainting:

> ad cuius nuntium perturbata Hispala, quod ad tam nobilem et grauem feminam ignara causae arcesseretur, postquam lictores in uestibulo turbamque consularem et consulem ipsum conspexit, prope exanimata est. (Livy 39.12.2)
>
> Hispala, who was already disturbed by the summons, given that she was being called before such a noble and harsh lady while ignorant of the reason, after she saw the lictors in the vestibule and the consular retinue and the consul himself, almost fainted.[48]

[47] Briscoe 2008: 282–7 (e.g. 285 "Livy simplifies the provisions given in the Tiriolo inscription"). The last two clauses of the *senatus consultum* as given in Livy 39.19.5 deal with granting *priuilegia* to Hispala. Although these clauses are problematic, Briscoe argues that the technical language makes it "very likely that we have an authentic citation of a *senatus consultum* . . . not a piece of pseudo-legalism and archaism invented by a later writer" (2008: 288, with full discussion at 235–6 and 287–90).

[48] I translate *prope exanimata* as "almost fainted" for the sake of English idiom. *Exanimare* properly means "to deprive of air or life," or "to terrify greatly" and here I take it to connote the physical effect of the shock Hispala experiences upon realizing she is due to see the consul. Briscoe 2008:

Her fear does not easily subside. When the consul addresses her, panic renders her unable to speak for some time: 39.12.5 *hoc ubi audiuit, tantus pauor tremorque omnium membrorum mulierem cepit, ut diu hiscere non posset* ("When she heard this, the woman was seized by such great panic and trembling throughout her body that for a long time she could not open her mouth"). Hispala's fear might well have been founded in her perception of guilt over harboring the secret of the Bacchants, but her response seems equally grounded in the shock and awe of encountering a figure of such high authority and symbolic value. The cause of her fear is the consul himself, whom Livy presents as the rhetorical climax and ultimate focus of Hispala's gaze; the effect is emphasized by the polyptoton in *consularem et consulem*, as well as by *consulem ipsum*'s late position in the sentence, immediately before the verb *conspexit.* Further, her response suggests that consuls were quite a different category to patrons, despite the fact that, her gender notwithstanding, Sulpicia, the *nobilis et grauis femina*, was herself part of the senatorial elite, and her situation was as equally removed from that of Hispala as was the consul's. Livy goes out of his way to mark Hispala's terror as relating to the human paraphernalia of office, rather than to the person himself: *lictores*, *turbam consularem*, and *consulem ipsum* leave little room for the personal identity of the office-holder and instead project the grandiose image of the Roman official. Hispala's experience, although extreme, could not have been entirely dissimilar to that of petitioners or assembly goers or soldiers, all of whom encountered the trappings of office in situations where the consul, praetor, or tribunes stood to exercise over them an abstract power made real through lictors and *fasces*, written laws and edicts, long years of tradition and precedent, and the ability to speak and be heard in public. In other words, historiography, as the textual product of a literary imagination, constitutes the flesh on the historical bones, by which it is informed, and which it in turn enriches.[49]

It is possible, however, to make a broader ontological and epistemological claim for the relationship between historiography's representation of the past and the actuality of those events. There is no denying that the Roman historians worked within generic constraints whose priority was not always accurate transmission, and even more crucially that sometimes faithful reconstruction simply was not possible despite the historian's best efforts. All of the authors with which this book deals, who range from the late

262 points out that "normally *examimare* alone is used to refer to the sense of 'terrify to the point of fainting.'" For the qualifying *prope* I have found only one parallel, in Frontin. *Str.* 4.6.3, referring to the effect of cold on the body.

49 In this I follow, at least partially, Woodman 1988.

republic to the early empire, were removed from most of the events they wrote about by long stretches of time, different locations, and in some cases even a change of regime. Despite those handicaps, the examples in this book will show a remarkable amount of consistency in terms of how processes and principles are represented. They further share a general sense of how republican deliberation played out, in which arenas, and before which audiences.[50] That some of these authors – Cicero, Sallust, Claudius Quadrigarius, and to a lesser extent Livy – witnessed and participated in either specific events or the workings of the republican system suggests further that this consensus is rooted in some common culture. So, while the historian must allow ample room for inaccuracies, schematizations, simplifications, elaborations, and so on in the representation of events, these texts ultimately provide good evidence about how that system actually worked, even if the view is blurred by distance and time.[51]

Contrariwise, literature too has its own rules of operation, which interact with, but need not be determined by, the material it represents. In what follows, therefore, the phrase "as a literary construct" might be assumed whenever I speak of "the republic" or of "Rome," because the existence or absence of such correspondence between facts and texts has no immediate bearing on the usefulness of the literary creation as a vehicle for cultural thought.[52] Even if fictional to some degree, historiography and its literary constructions nevertheless participated in a cultural discourse about republican politics and did so in such a way as to afford an opportunity for self-reflection. It is that discourse itself, and not its evidentiary value for the history of republican constitutionalism, that is the topic of this book.

[50] For a stronger encapsulation of this view than mine, see Lendon 2009: 56 "for when historical accounts are compared with other evidence (the speeches and letters of Cicero for the late Republic, and inscriptions particularly under the empire) they fit together too well to allow the conceit that Latin history writing was something akin to modern novel writing." I see no mutual exclusivity between the two assumptions that the historiographical text is subject to literary critical method and that it is essentially an intentionally truthful, though perhaps inaccurate or erroneous, vehicle for the transmission of historical knowledge.

[51] I am grateful to Matthew Roller for helping me clarify and articulate my thoughts on this topic.

[52] Note, most recently, Roller 2004: 7: "Thus the ideological salience of Horatius' story is not compromised by the recognition – even in antiquity – that it is fabulous. On the contrary, this and many other narratives were socially efficacious because they manifest a narrative structure in which action, judging audiences, commemoration, and imitation are all present and all work together. Each element presupposed and implies the others; it is the ensemble that gives meaning to each part." For a perspective on the same issue from the field of political science, see Shenhav 2006, esp. 254: "The gaps between 'political narrative' and 'political reality' lead to their mutual shaping, deliberately or not."

Overview

This book has three contributions to make, in more or less ascending order of originality: first, to the study of Livy himself as a theoretician of exemplarity, and therefore an author in possession of a robust apparatus to support his textual choices; second, to the study of magistracy as a textual phenomenon, which is animated by, but not always and not necessarily congruent with, its historical counterpart; and third, to the study of exemplarity as a meta-cognitive tool that unifies political and literary theory. These three themes are naturally interrelated, so this book primarily offers a strong formalist reading of Livy and other authors, in a series of close readings meant to illustrate the wide variety of magisterial presentation in the text.

Two important themes likewise dominate: the authority of the magistrates and the ways in which it was portrayed, especially when a particular anecdote explores the tension between intention, consequence, and its ethical ramification; and the electoral processes which turned individuals into holders of public office, together with their exemplary capacities. These two themes relate also to exemplary types: authority appears chiefly in *exempla* already elaborated and situated within the exemplary tradition – such as Brutus' execution of his sons or the Roman defeat in Caudium, both of which operate as familiar reference points within Latin literature. Elections, meanwhile, function as both a legal and an ideological mechanism for producing office-holders and thereby also project multiple competing images of what magistracy is and what its holders should be like. Notionally, therefore, the chapters fall into two groupings, with Chapters 1 and 2 focusing on the authority of the magistracy as an exemplary subject, while Chapters 3 and 4 step back to observe the processes of election as an object of exemplary formation. Beyond this broad division, other minor themes also recur throughout: the magistrate's assertive agency over people and events, the tension between acting and being, and the effects of magistracy on narrative, and of narrative on magistracy. All the chapters, however, have in common a focus on the literary tools deployed in making the episodes meaningful and impactful: allusion and intertext, rhetorical analysis, structure, verbal play, cultural resonances, and other such tools of the writer. These tools and their effect change from writer to writer, and the chapters are therefore centered thematically rather than methodologically – that is, on aspects of magistracy rather than on literary techniques – but I have tried throughout to show that various techniques can be put to use in aid of similar effects.

As a rule, the book moves from the surface of political exemplarity to its deeper structures, or from the more to the less explicit. Chapter 1, on magisterial power and the politics of affection, introduces two of the book's important themes, which is that images of magistracy in narrative are deeply relational, that is, that they are both context-dependent and are constructed by dialogue and negotiation rather than imposed from above as a discrete legal phenomenon, and that magistracy thereby lends itself especially well to meta-exemplarity and self-reflection. The chapter's main concern is the tension between kinship and *imperium*, which derives simultaneously from the expectation of piety and obedience towards one's parent and his *patria potestas*, as well as from the ethical choices necessitated by the exercise of political *imperium* over parents and children. Magistracy gives these episodes – the *imperia Manliana*, Brutus' execution of his sons, and others – a distinctive color, making them not only *exempla* of *seueritas* or *fortitudo*, but also specifically magisterial versions of these exemplary types; the *exempla*, in other words, are what they are because the persons in them are magistrates rather than *priuati*. The ethical choices made have necessary ethical ramifications, chiefly that they reflect upon and invite the reader to consider the state of the republic itself.

Chapter 2, by contrast, treats a single extended episode from Livy's ninth book, the Roman defeat at Caudium and its immediate aftermath, in order to explore the varieties of consular experience that the episode documents: military leadership, both failed and successful; deliberation and counseling, both in the field and in the senate; the failure and resurrection of personal charisma; agency and command; and, at the heart of the episode, the consul's role as a representative of Rome. In its length and variety, Caudium offers a productive field for demonstrating not only the breadth of magisterial experience, but also narrative's capacity to showcase competing images of magistracy, using the artistic tools of Livian storytelling. Like the previous chapter, Caudium too is a story of ramifications from consular action, and it is possibly even more explicit in its articulation of how magisterial action reflects and impacts Rome at large. Caudium is, further, a traditional *exemplum*, but my interest here is more in its internal dynamics than in how it relates to comparanda or historical phenomena. Indeed, the chapter's main purpose is to introduce Livy's sustained treatment of the theme over a larger scope than in Chapter 1, as well as establishing how rich a vein magistracy offers for the study of exemplary formation.

With Chapter 3 the focus moves from magistrates performing the task for which they are appointed to the processes, rhetorical and electoral, by which magistrates were elected. Underlying both this and the following chapter is the idea that elections by definition are a creative process, in which candidates and opponents must not only articulate their own qualifications for the office but also define what the office was or meant. This notion is compelling especially for a society like Rome, in which public office lacked a prescriptive constitutional definition, and where a lively debate on related issues of political definitions and rhetorical labeling persists consistently through the sources. In other words, both chapters revolve, to some degree, around the theme of electoral credentials, but whereas Chapter 3 focuses on the exemplary nature of military leadership, Chapter 4 is interested in the broader context of those images, which is to say the electoral campaign itself. Chapter 3 takes on a more specific case, the conduct of elections in openly militarized contexts, a situation which puts considerable pressure on the Roman division between home and abroad (*domi militiaeque*) and pins down the magisterial role within more constrained parameters. At the center of the chapter is a speech by Fabius Maximus Cunctator, in which he attempts to define magistracy (here the consulship) as possessing a specific set of military skills. To illustrate this, Fabius recurs to *exempla*, both immediate, such as Hannibal, and earlier, such as the duel of Manlius and the Gaul. Here, the generation of *exempla* not only becomes a by-product of the electoral mechanism but in Livy also becomes an explicit literary technique, as voters are asked to match up candidates to idealized images offered by, and checked against, the precedents of history.

Chapter 4 finally moves to the least openly exemplary set of episodes, to show that the same operations apparent in the more explicit *exempla* apply here as well. To do so, it focuses on electoral narratives, in which normal procedure is disrupted for one of many reasons, and on the candidates' displays of assertive agency, a quality in which they compete directly with the author of the text. What concerns all of the actors in this chapter is the question of precedent, often articulated as a question of exemplarity and using loaded words like *documentum*. Here the political life of the republic is most lively, although most of the episodes fall under the rubric of extended annalistic notices. Together, however, this dossier of instances shows a consistent pattern, which must be as much textual as it was historical, and suggests that certain political sequences became almost topical in their varied repetition.

Overall, the book's project is to chart magistracy as a textual and meta-exemplary phenomenon, in which magistracy stands not isolated but embedded in a landscape of power relations, modes of knowledge, and methods of communication. The themes central to this project – elections, agency, emotion and the performance of *imperium* – all highlight the deep tensions which shaped magistracy, and Roman politics more broadly, in their literary representation. The resulting image, as this book goes on to show, is neither static nor determined by a single set of parameters. Instead, it is driven by context and constructed by dialogue, responds to and is changed by circumstances, and reflects not only literary mannerism and methods of composition but also political ideology – all of which contribute in turn to a richer sense of the burdens of magistracy.

CHAPTER 1

Magisterial authority and the politics of affection

If the foundation of Rome was marked by Romulus' fratricide, the birth of the republic was bracketed by the death of children *ante ora parentum*.[1] The expulsion of the Tarquins was famously triggered by the virtuous Lucretia's suicide, committed with her husband and father bearing witness, while the people were galvanized into action through Brutus' careful manipulation of their emotions:

> elatum domo Lucretiae corpus in forum deferunt, concientque miraculo, ut fit, rei nouae atque indignitate homines. pro se quisque scelus regium ac uim queruntur. Mouet cum patris maestitia, tum Brutus castigator lacrimarum atque inertium querellarum auctorque quod uiros, quod Romanos deceret, arma capiendi aduersus hostilia ausos. (Livy 1.59.3–4)
>
> They carried Lucretia's body from her home to the public square and already stirred people up, as happens, because of the wonder and the novelty and the indignity of the thing. Each one complained on his own account about the crime and violence of the royal family. Not only did sympathy with the father's grief move them but Brutus also admonished them for their tears and useless complaints and charged them to take up arms, as befits men and Romans, against those who dared hostile deeds.

The men of Collatia immediately join Brutus, and the crowd sets off to Rome, where Brutus delivers another speech, recounting again the story of Lucretia, and recalling in addition to the atrocities of the king also the turbulent domestic drama of the royal house: 1.59.10 *indigna Ser. Tulli regis memorata caedes et inuecta corpori patris nefando uehiculo filia, inuocatique ultores parentum di* ("he recalled the unworthy death of king Servius Tullius, and his daughter driving her impious chariot over her father's body, and the gods, summoned to avenge parents"). His words again inflamed the crowd, and they demanded the exile of the royal family and the abrogation

[1] The formula is Vergilian (e.g. *G.* 4.477, *Aen.* 5.553); for analysis of its function, O'Sullivan 2009, with particular focus on the meta-poetic tensions such deaths invoked.

of the king's *imperium*. The motif of female sexual violation as a marker for political instability is developed further later in Livy and is often deployed as the trigger to end a tyranny of some kind.[2] But the foundation of the republic also triggers another instance of a father forced to watch his children's death. Having been found guilty of conspiring to restore the king, Brutus' sons are condemned to death. Serving as consul, their father has no choice but to preside over their execution. The two episodes thus form a ring composition (private grief: public revolution :: public revolution: private grief), centered on the foundation of the republic, affirming both his public role as guardian of the state and his personal aversion to dynasticism. Lucretia's death triggers revolution; Brutus' sons die to maintain the product of that revolution.

The Brutus episode can be read in multiple ways, most conventionally as a parallel to the execution of the young Manlius Torquatus, a classic *exemplum* both of paternal *seueritas* ("sternness") and of public duty prevailing over personal bonds and affection. This focus, however, exploits only half of the *exemplum*'s rhetorical force. The most striking feature of Brutus' grief is its emphatic tension with the demands of the consulship: 2.5.5 *poenae capiendae ministerium patri de liberis consulatus imposuit* ("the consulship imposed on the father the task of exacting punishment from his children"). Were Brutus not father, the execution would have been a routine trial, no less dramatic perhaps, but without the moral dilemma introduced by ties of family. Filicide, in this context, is problematic not only for its own moral quandaries, but also because it replicates to some degree the perversion of family bonds under the monarchy to which Brutus himself had drawn particular attention. Tullia's abuse of her father's body finds a complement in Brutus' execution of his own sons. Thus, the emotive response Livy clearly expects of his audience is, I suggest, not only the result of the tragic plot but also used as an interrogative device: just as familial indignation led to political change, so too it grounds a similar inquisition of the ethical dimensions of republican ideology. Put otherwise, the fact that Brutus is both consul and father is simultaneously comforting and disquieting; comforting because justice is seen to be done, and disquieting because that justice seems also cruel and unfeeling, making insupportable demands in the name of ideology.

[2] Prominent parallels are the story of Verginia (with a direct allusion to Lucretia in 3.44.1) and of Fabia Minor (6.34.5–35.1). On Livy's use of the story type see Kraus 1991 (Fabia Minor); Feldherr 1998: 203–12 (Verginia); Chaplin 2000: 1–2 and 2010 (the continence of Scipio), with further references. On the story's afterlife in European republicanism: Matthes 2000. For the underlying theory, see my discussion on pp. 11–13 above.

Filicide, while an extreme case, points to the larger problem explored in this chapter – the emotional tension caused by the encounter between magistracy and paternity and its valorization in the exemplary tradition.[3] This tension need not be acute, and in some of the episodes analyzed the issue is more a matter of manners and decorum than justice and ideology.[4] What unifies the episodes, however, is a sense that the interaction between paternity and magistracy inflects the episode in distinctive ways and consequently projects an image of magistracy that is different from what we see in other contexts. These episodes have traditionally also been used to prove the "incontestability of consular *imperium*," and more broadly the superiority of *imperium* to other forms of *potestas*.[5] This chapter is, however, not interested in the ultimate historical result of these encounters, which collectively confirm the legal superiority of *imperium* and the priority of public duty, but rather in the dialectical processes these episodes enact, the moral questions they raise and leave largely unanswered, and the image of the magistrate they thereby project.

Pietas and the production of an *exemplum*

In 232 BC C. Flaminius, a tribune of the plebs who would win notoriety as the commanding consul during the battle of Trasimene, promulgated an agrarian law allocating individual allotments to Roman citizens in the *ager Gallicus*.[6] The law was eventually passed, over strong senatorial resistance. Cicero (*Inu. rhet.* 2.52) and Valerius Maximus (5.4.5) both record a unique event: at some point in the proceedings Flaminius' father intervened to stop a *contio* in which his son was promoting the legislation. The differences

3 On paternity as a political metaphor, specifically for the emperor, see Roller 2001: 233–47.

4 For the social utility of such mild emotionality: Kaster 2005: 4–6.

5 Beck 2011: 87; cf. Masi Doria 2000: 240–1; Lacey 1986: 130–2. *Patria potestas* as a legal construct has been extensively studied: Crook 1967, Saller 1994, and Cantarella 2003 are good starting points, with Frier and McGinn 2004 for legal cases. On the father's *ius uitae necisque*, see the references in n. 35 below. Dixon 1997 discusses the problem with assuming either continuities or changes between Roman "family feelings" and their modern counterparts. Along with Roller 2001 and Saller 1994, however, I am comfortable in seeing these texts as using paternity to connote a relationship that is predicated, at least in part, on affective bonds, and certainly on the tension between affection (*caritas*) and severity (*seueritas*). I make no claim, though, for the legal or historical accuracy of the historiographical descriptions.

6 The episode is treated briefly in Botteri 1983; Harris 1986: 89; Gardner 1993: 80. There is considerable debate over the date of this legislation. Broughton (*MRR* 1.225) accepts Polybius' dating of 233/2 (2.21.8) over Cicero's date of 228 (*Sen.* 11), an opinion which goes back to Niccolini 1934: 87–9. The most recent discussions are Feig-Vishnia 1996b and Elster 2003: 171–5, both with a survey of the *status quaestionis* and further bibliography. On the law itself and its effects on Roman policy in Gaul: Develin 1976; Eckstein 1987: 10–11; Feig-Vishnia 1996a: 25–34.

between the two versions are instructive, not because the authors differ on points of detail, but because Cicero's version, being a rhetorical exercise, parses the *exemplum* in ways markedly different from Valerius Maximus' embryonic narrative. Both authors, however, share a basic dialectic between the sacrosanctity of the tribunate and the father's exercise of *patria potestas*; moreover, their expression of this dialectic reveals that it was a profoundly uncomfortable one, putting in tension two deeply held values while seeking some imperfect calculus by which to reconcile them.

Cicero uses this case as a formal illustration of argument construction in cases in which the outcome depends on the definition of a particular word or concept, in this case, *maiestas*:[7]

> cum est nominis controuersia, quia uis uocabuli definienda uerbis est, constitutio definitiua dicitur. eius generis exemplo nobis posita sit haec causa: C. Flaminius, is qui consul rem male gessit bello Punico secundo, cum tribunus plebis esset, inuito senatu et omnino contra uoluntatem omnium optimatium per seditionem ad populum legem agrariam ferebat. hunc pater suus concilium plebis habentem de templo deduxit; arcessitur maiestatis. intentio est: "maiestatem minuisti, quod tribunum plebis de templo deduxisti." depulsio est: "non minui maiestatem." quaestio est: maiestatemne minuerit? ratio: "in filium enim quam habebam potestatem, ea sum usus." rationis infirmatio: "at enim, qui patria potestate, hoc est priuata quadam, tribuniciam potestatem, hoc est populi potestatem, infirmat, minuit is maiestatem." iudicatio est: minuatne is maiestatem, qui in tribuniciam potestatem patria potestate utatur? ad hanc iudicationem argumentationes omnes afferre oportebit. (Cic. *Inu. rhet.* 2.52)

> When there is disagreement about what to call something, because the meaning of a word must be defined by words, it is called a *definitive statement*. Let me offer the following case as an example of this type: Gaius Flaminius, who as consul managed things badly in the Second Punic War, when he was a tribune of the plebs brought an agrarian law before the people, in a seditious manner, without the agreement of the senate, and completely against the will of all the best people. His father dragged him down from the platform as he was presiding over the Plebeian Council; he is charged with acting against the people's interest. The charge is: "You have acted

[7] *Maiestas* first became the subject of law by the *lex maiestatis* of L. Appuleius Saturninus in 100 or 103 BC; Cicero cannot therefore refer to a case that was actually tried under those terms. For discussion of the meaning of *maiestas* see Bauman 1967: 1–15, and for the development from *perduellio* see pp. 16–33. On Hermagorean rhetorical theory, from which the term *constitutio* derives (Gk. *stasis*; in his later works Cicero tends towards *status* rather than *constitutio*, as does Quintilian at *Inst.* 3.6.18), Thiele 1893 remains seminal, but see also the briefer accounts in Clarke 1968: 26–7 and 67–9; Kennedy 1994: 97–101 (*stasis* theory) and 117–21 (its relevance to the *de Inuentione rhetorica*); and Connolly 2007: 69–70. For the dialogic and dialectic tendencies encouraged by *stasis* theory, Braet 1987.

against the People's interest, inasmuch as you dragged a tribune of the plebs down from the platform." The defense is: "I did not act against the People's interest." The question is: "Did he or did he not act against the People's interest?" The argument: "Clearly, I have used the power that I have over my son." The refuting of the argument: "But since he weakened tribunician power, that is the power of the People, with paternal power, that is, with a private power, he has acted against the People's interest." The question being judged is this: "Did he act against the People's interest, because he used paternal power against tribunician power?" It is towards this question that all arguments must be directed.

Several items about Cicero's procedure are worth noting, but above all the fact that he provides neither the outcome of the case nor his own judgment on the matter. This is not to say that he did not have an opinion, but rather that, whatever the outcome of any putative court case, Cicero's interest here is in the formal architecture of the argument. This focus has important consequences because it foregrounds not the resolution of the case but the plausibility or arguability of both the prosecution and the defense, without which the case fails as an instructional vehicle. As Kunkel correctly points out, this episode is revealing about the nature of *tribunicia potestas*: it is not a private power ("private Gewalt"), but rather an official power ("öffentliche Gewalt"). But to pronounce further that "[i]m Konflikt mit den *patria potestas* geht *tribunicia potestas* vor," while technically correct, risks oversimplification, since, for Cicero, both sides stand to argue a plausibly convincing case about the rights and wrongs of Flaminius' father's actions.[8] In other words, Cicero does not deploy the example in order to establish the priority of one authority over the other – that is the task of the prosecutor – but rather to show the structure of possible arguments.[9] The exercise works only because the use of *patria potestas* on a tribune of the plebs can, but need not be, judged as *maiestas imminuta*.

The procedures Cicero goes on to outline confirm his central interest in the dialectic rather than in the letter of the law. For both prosecutor and advocate, Cicero prescribes the same course of action. The first order of business is to establish a definition, which must be short (*breuis*), clear (*aperta*), and in accordance with general opinion (*ex opinione hominum*). He provides examples for both sides. The accuser defines *maiestas* as follows:

8 Kunkel and Wittman 1995: 570–2.

9 Cicero is explicit on that score: *Inu. rhet.* 2.53 *ac ne qui forte arbitretur nos non intellegere aliam quoque incidere constitutionem in hanc causam, eam nos partem solam sumimus, in quam praecepta nobis danda sunt* ("And lest anyone think by chance that we do not understand that another type of question may apply in this case, we put down only that part for which we must supply rules").

maiestatem minuere est de dignitate aut amplitudine aut potestate populi aut eorum, quibus populus potestatem dedit, aliquid derogare. (Cic. *Inu. rhet.* 2.53 "to diminish *maiestas* is to take something away from the dignity or greatness or power of the people or of those to whom the people gave power"). The advocate retaliates with: *maiestatem minuere est aliquid de re publica, cum potestatem non habeas, administrare* (Cic. *Inu. rhet.* 2.55 "to diminish *maiestas* is to manage something in the state, when you do not have the power [*sc.* to do so]"). Neither of these definitions as yet addresses the case, except in their attempt to circumscribe the definition within conveniently narrow parameters. It is, further, in these definitions that Cicero is primarily interested, and in how they determine the construction of a court argument. The fact that the case involves a tribune and his father provides simply the content of the form, although it is equally clear that Cicero finds the case appropriate and interesting enough both to choose in the first place and to dwell on.

The next step is to establish the validity of the definition by adducing other examples and reasons, on which Cicero does not elaborate. Finally, he says, both sides must show either how the accused fits in with their definition (the prosecution), or how he does not (the defense). It is here that *patria potestas* becomes relevant, since what the case is trying to establish is whether or not dragging a tribune down from the platform constituted *maiestas*. *Patria potestas* is adduced as a different sort of power under which the father's action acquires legal legitimacy.[10] Again, Cicero does not commit either way, though his presentation of the facts of the case suggests a slight slant in favor of the elder Flaminius; for the third step is the arousing of the emotion through the use of commonplaces (*communes loci*). The prosecution strives to rouse *indignatio* by showing the *atrocitas*, *indignitas*, and *culpa* (2.53) of the action, while the defense needs to show the action was done *ex honestatis et ex utilitatis partibus* (2.54). Flaminius, Cicero has already told us, was promulgating an agrarian law and was doing so against the wishes of the senate and all the *optimates* (*inuito senatu, contra uoluntatem omnium optimatium*), and divisively (*per seditionem*).[11] Cicero thus focalizes the account through the eyes of the defense and thereby casts

[10] Dion. Hal. *Ant. Rom.* 7.17.4–6 reports a *lex Sicinia* of 492 BC, according to which a tribune could not be interrupted while making a speech to the people. Russell 2013: 102 argues that the episode is fictitious, and the *lex* anachronistic, but the prohibition real and evident in the late republic (e.g. Cic. *Sest.* 79, and various other incidents, including this one). Curiously, if the law was applicable, neither Cicero nor Valerius Maximus makes explicit mention of it, though it would have neatly cut through the rhetorical argumentation.

[11] The phrase *senatu inuito* recurs in almost all of the sources. Livy 21.63.2 further adds that the fraught relationship of Flaminius with the senate stemmed from his actions during his tribunate and first

the father's action as reasonable in the circumstances. Regardless of Cicero's personal feelings, however, we are left with a hypothetical case which Cicero found interesting, instructive, without a foregone conclusion, and above all, not *prima facie* fatuous. His own opinion, it appears, makes credible the idea that, regardless of what legal outcome such a case might have produced, the defense had a plausible case to make, and, moreover, a case with its own moral force.

Valerius Maximus repeats Cicero's basic narrative, though his version of the episode takes no interest in the legal niceties of the case.[12] Instead, he is entirely invested in showing the moral value of Flaminius' obedience to his father:

> apud C. quoque Flaminium auctoritas patria aeque potens fuit: nam cum tribunus plebis legem de Gallico agro uiritim diuidendo inuito et repugnante senatu promulgasset, precibus minisque eius acerrime resistens ac ne exercitu quidem aduersum se conscripto, si in eadem sententia perseueraret, absterritus, postquam pro rostris ei legem iam referenti pater manum iniecit, priuato fractus imperio descendit e rostris, ne minimo quidem murmure destitutae contionis reprehensus. (Val. Max. 5.4.5)

> Paternal authority was equally powerful with C. Flaminius as well; for, when he as tribune of the plebs was promoting a law to make individual allotments in the *ager Gallicus*, with the senate unwilling and fighting back, he resisted the senate's prayers and threats very keenly and was not frightened off even by the army that was raised against him should he persist. Later, when he was standing on the *rostra* and practically bringing the law to a vote, his father asserted authority over him; broken by private authority, Flaminius came down from the *rostra*, reproved with not even the slightest murmur by the bereft assembly.

The implicit dialectic here is the same as the one laid out by Cicero, between the tribune's sacrosanctity and *patria potestas*, but Valerius Maximus adds one layer of interpretation. Whatever the plebs might have felt about the father's action, the spectators clearly appreciate the reason for Flaminius' acquiescence, as shown by their silence.[13] The reason they pause, we know, is because Flaminius is displaying *pietas*, reverence towards his father, which was one of the central values of Roman morality. The story appears under the rubric *de pietate erga parentes et fratres et patriam* (5.4.1–7), and Valerius'

consulship. This was the reason for Flaminius' assumption of the consulship outside Rome and his later sacrilegious conduct before Trasimene.

12 On Valerius Maximus' use of Cicero, especially for Flaminius before Trasimene (1.6.6): Bloomer 1992: 29–40.

13 For Valerius Maximus' brand of situational exemplarity: Langlands 2011.

main concern here is to emphasize the son's obedience. Of all the *exempla* under the same rubric, the issue of obedience to a parent arises only here and in the story of Coriolanus, which heads the group (5.4.1). The other *exempla* revolve around courage in saving a father from death in battle (Africanus, 5.4.2), audacity in preventing a father's prosecution or avenging a father's condemnation in court (Torquatus, 5.4.3 and Cotta, 5.4.4, respectively), and protecting a father from tribuncian intervention during his triumph (Claudia the Vestal, 5.4.6). Thus the stories of Coriolanus and Flaminius stand out in emphasizing a different facet of *pietas* – passive obedience to parental command rather than showing active aggression (i.e. *uirtus*) protecting one's father.[14] But the grouping of these different examples together – some displaying great heroism – demonstrates the esteem in which filial obedience was regarded.

The comparison with Coriolanus is instructive, since of all of the *exempla* Valerius Maximus lists under this heading, it is the one that most explicitly connects *pietas erga parentes* with *pietas erga patriam*. Structurally, the two episodes are inverted parallels: Coriolanus is a military leader, who conquers his rage at the sight of his mother's face (5.4.1 *quam ubi filius aspexit, "expugnasti" inquit, "et uicisti iram meam"*). Flaminius, on the other hand, is engaged in peacetime activities, and his father's actions have the more vigorous vocabulary attached to them (*manum iniecit, priuato fractus imperio*), while actual military threats come from the senate (*exercitu aduersum se conscripto*).[15] In both episodes, Valerius Maximus implies, *pietas* maintains social and political stability and prevents civic strife. But the harmony *pietas* imposes should not detract from the fact that the episode derives its animating spirit from the basic clash of social and political authorities. Instead, the narrative is focused on how the dialectic between father and tribunes is resolved by the application of an exemplary value, *pietas*, which displaces any interpretation of the father's action, whether seen

14 On *uirtus* as active aggression, see Roller 2011: 188; on *uirtus* as a community-based moral value, Roller 2001: 20–6. McDonnell 2006 argues for *uirtus* in the Roman republic as primarily aggressive and bellicose, but see the caveats in Kaster's 2007 review.

15 Though the phrase *manum inicere* here can simply be translated as "to lay hands on" (*OLD* s.v. "manus" 15b), *manus iniectio* appears as early as the Twelve Tables as a legal procedure: *RS* 2.588, cf. Berger 1953: 542 and 577. Especially relevant here might be Tab. 1.2 (Warmington): *si caluitur pedemque struit, manum endo iacito* ("if the defendant delays and drags his feet, let the plaintiff lay his hand upon him"). Corbeill 2005: 162 argues that in these cases, where the defendant had the opportunity to disrupt the legal process through self-help, the bodily gesture itself compelled his cooperation. The usage here is all the more apposite because *manus* was also the term which indicated the power of the head of the family over its members (Berger 1953: 577, s.v. "manus"). The phrase *priuato fractus imperio* is without parallel in extant Latin, but for private *imperium* see *TLL* s.v. 576.6ff. and for the verb *frango* see *TLL* s.v. 1246.9ff.

as demeaning the people's authority, threatening its *libertas*, or violating tribunician sacrosanctity.[16] The point is rather Flaminius' pious obedience to his father; he is willing to abandon his political program and lose standing and dignity in order to acquiesce to his father's command – as any devoted son ought.[17] *Pietas* here is not only a private virtue, but also a guide to political conduct. It is because he demands and deserves *pietas* that the father intrudes into a political process in which he has no official authority. It is also because Flaminius shows due *pietas* that he avoids the audience's open censure.[18] The episode thus clearly shows how a social virtue, *pietas*, offers a way out of a conflict of values that is difficult to resolve in practice. What Cicero omits, and Valerius Maximus adds, is the younger Flaminius' own preference: the legal dispute hides beneath it an affective relationship, which has its own set of consequences and ramifications, the most important of which is the awkward demands it placed on Flaminius and his attempts to negotiate his conflicting obligations. The two accounts, then, promise resolution of an uncomfortable situation, which not only rises from the demonstrable friction between two forms of authority in the state but also engages two different codes of morality and sympathy.

Paternity, *imperium*, and the exercise of *uerecundia*

In 213 BC a Fabius Maximus (*RE* 103) took over his father's command in Apulia, while his father, the famous Cunctator of the Second Punic War (*RE* 116), stayed on to serve as his son's legate. One story about father and son comes down to us in three authors: Claudius Quadrigarius, Livy, and Valerius Maximus. All three narrate the same basic story, though Quadrigarius differs from the others in one detail – for him, the father is *proconsul*, while for Livy and Valerius Maximus he is simply a legate, a high-ranking adviser to the consul.[19] Whatever the father's rank, all three begin

[16] For tribunician sacrosanctity as part of oratorical performance in the late republic: Steel 2010.

[17] For a fuller discussion of *pietas* in the household: Saller 1994: 102–32.

[18] Roller 2001: 26–7 distinguishes between "enacted" *pietas* and "dispositional" *pietas*, that is between a performance of the value *pietas* and an inclination towards being *pius*. Part of the confusion for the audience, internal and external, stems from the suggestive gap between Flaminius' enacted *pietas* and a broader sense that he is, nevertheless, not *pius*.

[19] Broughton (*MRR* 1.265) accepts Livy's designation of the father as legate over Quadrigarius' *proconsul*. The confusion probably stems from the fact that father and son held the command in consecutive years, and both held it as consuls (cf. *MRR* 1.258 for the father's consulship). Thus, the Cunctator's new position can be taken as either a prorogation of office (proconsul) subordinated to the consuls of the year, or as a new position entirely (legate); cf. Staveley 1963: 474. On the question of absolute and relative *imperium* (*imperium maius*): Last 1947; Ehrenberg 1953; Lintott 1999: 96–7; Brennan 2000: 12–20; and most recently Beck 2011.

with the father approaching his son, the consul, on horseback, and yet despite being in the presence of a political superior he does not dismount as protocol demands.[20] None of the lictors is willing to order the old man to dismount until the consul notices and orders one of them to do so.[21] The father dismounts and praises his son (explicit in Quadrigarius, implicit elsewhere) for enforcing proper conduct. Here are the three versions:

(1) posuimus igitur uerba ipsa Quadrigarii ex annali eius sexto transscripta: "deinde facti consules Sempronius Gracchus iterum Q. Fabius Maximus, filius eius, qui priore anno erat consul. ei consuli pater proconsul obuiam in equo uehens uenit neque descendere uoluit, quod pater erat, et, quod inter eos sciebant maxima concordia conuenire, lictores non ausi sunt descendere iubere. ubi iuxta uenit, tum consul ait: 'quid postea?'; lictor ille, qui apparebat, cito intellexit, Maximum proconsulem descendere iussit. Fabius imperio paret et filium collaudauit, cum imperium, quod populi esset, retineret." (Quadrigarius *apud* Gell. *NA* 2.2.13 = *HRR* F 57 = Beck and Walter 142 F 56 = *FRHist* F 57).

And so we have quoted the very words of Quadrigarius, transcribed from the sixth book of his annals: "Then Sempronius Gracchus was made consul for the second time, along with Q. Fabius Maximus, the son of the previous year's consul. The father, a *proconsul,* approached the consul on horseback and did not wish to dismount, since he was his father; the lictors did not dare order him to dismount, because they knew of the great harmony which existed between them. When he came closer, the consul said: 'Well then?' The lictor who was waiting on him quickly understood and ordered Maximus the *proconsul* to dismount. Fabius obeyed the command and praised his son at the same time, since he maintained the *imperium* which belongs to the people."

(2) pater filio legatus ad Suessulam in castra uenit. cum obuiam filius progrederetur lictoresque uerecundia maiestatis eius taciti anteirent, praeter undecim fasces equo praeuectus senex, ut consul animaduertere proximum lictorem iussit et is ut descenderet ex equo inclamauit, tum

[20] On the principle of "subordinate-greets-first," though without reference to this episode, Hall 1998. It is further worthwhile noting that being on horseback also puts Maximus senior on a higher vantage point than his son. For the cultural prominence attached to a magistrate's posture, see Livy 9.46.9; Val. Max. 2.5.2; Gell. *NA* 7.9.6, all on Gnaeus Flavius the scribe, whose sitting asserts the prestige of office faced with class snobbery (see my discussion in the Epilogue). Note also the prominence of the *sella curulis* among magisterial insignia: Schäfer 1989.

[21] Valerius Maximus designates this lector the *proximus lector*, who is the lictor closest to the consul, and by consequence the furthest from anyone approaching him; to reach the *proximus lictor* therefore highlights how close the father gets to the son before anyone thinks anything of it. On whether the *proximus lictor* was an official position: Shackleton-Bailey 1996: 175.

demum desiliens "experiri" inquit "uolui, fili, satin scires consulem te esse." (Livy 24.44.9–10)

The father joined his son in camp near Suessula as legate. When his son approached, and the lictors preceded him [i.e. the consul] in silence because of their reverence for his [i.e. the Cunctator's] *maiestas*, the old man rode past eleven sets of *fasces*, until the consul ordered the Proximate Lictor to pay attention, and the lictor called for him to dismount. Then at last the father leapt down and said: "I wished to test, son, whether you were sufficiently aware that you are consul."

(3) idem a senatu legatus ad filium consulem Suessam missus, postquam animaduertit eum ad officium suum extra moenia oppidi processisse, indignatus quod ex undecim lictoribus nemo se equo descendere iussisset, plenus irae sedere perseuerauit. quod cum filius sensisset, proximo lictori ut sibi appareret imperauit.[22] cuius uoci continuo Fabius obsecutus "non ego" inquit, "fili, summum imperium tuum contempsi, sed experiri uolui an scires consulem agere: nec ignoro quid patriae uenerationi debeatur, uerum publica instituta priuata pietate potiora iudico." (Val. Max. 2.2.4)

The same person was sent as legate to his son the consul at Suessa; after he noticed that he was approaching his station outside the walls of the city, aggrieved because none of the eleven lictors ordered him to dismount, angrily he kept his seat. When the son perceived this he gave an order to the Proximate Lictor that he [i.e. the father] should wait on him. Fabius immediately complied and said: "Son, I did not disdain your highest office, but I wished to test whether you knew how to act the part of a consul; I am not ignorant of what is owed to the reverence due a father, but I judge that public institutions come before private piety."

The chain of transmission here is difficult to establish with precision. Although Quadrigarius is one of Livy's sources in the third decade, Livy does not acknowledge any specific source, either for this episode or for book 24 as a whole. The lack of precise citation, however, should not obscure the obvious parallels between all three episodes, nor the differences in both style and emphases.[23] The episode has, as Hans Beck points

[22] The text is that of Briscoe's 1998 Teubner edition. Here is the relevant portion of the *apparatus criticus*: *quod... imperauit* P : om. α : *quod... lictori <ut patrem iuberet ut ex equo descenderet et> sibi... imperauit* Shackleton-Bailey (1996). Shackleton-Bailey's emendation, as he explains it, is based entirely on comparison with Livy's account of the same episode.

[23] For stylistic comparison between Livy and Quadrigarius on this episode: Courtney 1999: 151–2. For Livy's treatment of his Roman sources in the third decade, see now Levene 2010: 126–35; *FRHist* 3.318 "draw[s] the negative conclusion that Claudius was not Livy's source . . . " Valerius Maximus' debt to Livy is pervasive in the *Facta et Dicta*, as demonstrated by the index entry for "Livy" in Bloomer 1992: 281.

out, been "widely cited to illustrate the inherent contradiction between *imperium* and *patria potestas*" and as such it "served to illustrate the incontestability of consular *imperium*."[24] Indeed, all three iterations emphatically reaffirm the priority of *imperium populi*, as embodied in the consul, over *patria potestas*. However, the episodes also show more subtle nuances at work and develop the tension between *imperium* and paternity in ways that go beyond the purely hierarchical ranking. Such ranking has, of course, considerable importance here, not least because father and son are unequal not only in their official rank and their familial roles but also in their social standing. The elder Fabius was, at this point, fresh from his fourth consulship, a former dictator, and the restorer of the state. His son was a relative nobody, whose election seems to have been due to his father's prestige rather than solely his own merits.[25] Beck's final observation on this episode, that it "illustrates that the exercise of *imperium* was determined by nuances of time and space that make a holistic approach difficult," applies beyond the legal focus on the intricacies of *imperium*.[26] We might, therefore, expect these episodes not only to establish the relative priority of the two forms of authority but also to illuminate the ways in which each author deploys language and plot to evoke the moral and evaluative tensions which result from this dialectical tension.

Before looking at these examples, we might first contrast them with the quite different version in Plutarch's *Life of Fabius*:

> οἱ δὲ Ῥωμαῖοι τά τ' ἄλλα τῷ Φαβίῳ προσεφέροντο λαμπρῶς, καὶ τὸν υἱὸν αὐτοῦ Φάβιον ἀνέδειξαν ὕπατον. παραλαβόντος δὲ τὴν ἀρχὴν αὐτοῦ καὶ διοικοῦντός τι τῶν πρὸς τὸν πόλεμον ὁ πατήρ, εἴτε διὰ γῆρας καὶ ἀσθένειαν εἴτε διαπειρώμενος τοῦ παιδός, ἀναβὰς ἐφ' ἵππον προσῄει διὰ τῶν ἐντυγχανόντων καὶ περιεστώτων. ὁ δὲ νεανίας κατιδὼν πόρρωθεν οὐκ ἠνέσχετο, πέμψας δ' ὑπηρέτην ἐκέλευσε καταβῆναι τὸν πατέρα καὶ δι' αὐτοῦ προσελθεῖν, εἰ δή τι τυγχάνει τῆς ἀρχῆς δεόμενος. καὶ τοὺς μὲν ἄλλους ἠνίασε τὸ ἐπίταγμα, καὶ σιωπῇ πρὸς τὸν Φάβιον ὡς ἀνάξια πάσχοντα τῆς δόξης ἀπέβλεψαν. αὐτὸς δ' ἐκεῖνος ἀποπηδήσας κατὰ τάχος, θᾶττον ἢ βάδην πρὸς τὸν υἱὸν ἐπειχθεὶς, καὶ περιβαλὼν καὶ ἀσπασάμενος, "εὖ γε," εἶπεν, "ὦ παῖ, φρονεῖς καὶ πράττεις, αἰσθόμενος τίνων ἄρχεις καὶ πηλίκης μέγεθος ἀνείληφας ἀρχῆς. οὕτω καὶ ἡμεῖς καὶ οἱ πρόγονοι τὴν Ῥώμην ηὐξήσαμεν, ἐν δευτέρῳ καὶ γονεῖς καὶ παῖδας ἀεὶ τῶν τῆς πατρίδος καλῶν τιθέμενοι." (*Fab.* 24.1–4)
>
> And the Romans offered Fabius other marks of glory and also made his son Fabius a consul. When the son entered office and was arranging some of

[24] Beck 2011: 87. [25] Plut. *Fab.* 24.1, with Roller 2011: 203.

[26] Beck 2011: 90–1. By holistic approach, Beck means one that assumes "a holistic quality of consular power, in the sense that it prevails everywhere and over everyone, even the *potestas* of a father" (90).

> the matters pertaining to the war, his father, either because of his age and weakness or in order to test his child, mounted his horse and proceeded towards him through the crowd of bystanders. The young man saw this from a distance and would not tolerate it, and so sent a lictor with orders for his father to dismount and approach him on foot, if he happened to require something from his office. The command offended everyone else, and they looked silently at Fabius to imply that this treatment was unworthy of his reputation. But he himself swiftly leapt from his horse, practically ran to his son, and embracing him said: "Son, you have both spoken and acted well, and shown understanding of whose people's officer you are, and what a great office you have received. In this way, both we and our ancestors increased Rome, holding parents and children in second place to the good of the homeland."

In outline, Plutarch follows the same basic plot as the Latin episodes, but the social cues he includes are very different. For example, Plutarch dwells on the reason for Fabius' being on horseback in the first place – either due to age and infirmity, or through a desire to test his son. The idea of testing is explicit in both Livy and Valerius Maximus, both of whom use the same phrase, *experiri uolui*. Neither age nor infirmity is an issue for any of the Latin authors, though, and, despite Livy's use of the word *senex* to describe the elder Fabius, they all agree on his capability for wartime service. The son, on the other hand, is here more brusque and assertive in his conduct: he both sees his father's action and moves to censor it before the father can approach him. In all three Latin episodes, by contrast, both son and father wait until they are almost facing each other before any action is taken. The reason for this delay is attributed to the lictors and their interpretation of the situation, which is then supported or rebuked by the consul or the elder Fabius. Further, while the lictors form the only audience mentioned in the three Latin authors, Plutarch introduces a crowd of bystanders, who show active disapproval of the younger Fabius' treatment of his father, which demeans the very glory that ensured his election in the first place. The elder Fabius, in validating his son's action, thus also corrects the crowd's evaluation of the scene rather than using the exchange as a lesson for his son. What is striking, however, is that despite the changes in Plutarch's version, the moral quandary of the episode remains the same. The disapproval of the bystanders effectively communicates the implicit expectation that familial bonds should soften the exercise of *imperium*, while Fabius' concluding justification reasserts the patriotic value of maintaining respect for *imperium* despite the presence of affective bonds.

Of course, one of the main details Plutarch omits is that the elder Fabius was also his son's legate, and possibly a proconsul in his own right. This allows him to suggest the more pathetic characterization of old age and infirmity, which considerably facilitates the emotive response of the crowd. In the Latin examples, on which we can now focus, the elder Fabius' possession of rank is explicit, so that any emotive response they evoke focuses more urgently on his dual role as father and officer. We can see this emphasis as early as Quadrigarius, who states that Fabius remained on horseback *quod erat pater* ("since he was the father"). The lictors, for their part, know that father and son enjoy *concordia maxima* ("the greatest harmony," punning on the family's *cognomen*), and therefore do not dare to order him to dismount. We are not given the consul's sentiments, but the lictors' response certainly assumes that he would prefer to maintain harmony rather than demean his father. They do not realize their mistake until the consul himself intervenes. The vocabulary here is telling. The elder Fabius is consistently referred to as *pater*, by both the narrator and himself, right up until he dismounts from his horse. Even then, his point of view maintains its paternal character. He addresses his son, who until that point had been referred to consistently as *consul*, as *filium*, even as the praise he offers (*collaudauit*) explicitly centers on the upholding of *imperium* and its ranks. Thus, the narrative operates on two levels: the plot explicitly engages in ranking the authorities of father and consul, while the focalization undermines that ranking by imposing the father's point of view. The mechanism for resolution is likewise important. The reason why Fabius submits to the inverted relationship between himself and his son is that the inversion is entailed by the son's possession of *imperium*, *quod populi esset*. As a political norm, adverting to *imperium* saves the father from any lowering of his own station, even as he conforms to the proper conduct of a citizen before public office.

Livy's narrative of the same episode is more condensed. The father rides past eleven lictors, who precede the consul as he, too, approaches his father.[27] The lictors are silent because of their reverence for greatness, *uerecundia maiestatis*, presumably but not necessarily the father's.[28] The word *maiestas* itself, with its derivation from *maior*, already suggests a play

[27] Hall 1998: 423 (discussing Laelius' arrival at Scipio's house in Cicero's *Rep.* 1.18) notes that the social superior's movement towards his interlocutor might "not [be] placed too starkly in the role of social subordinate visiting a patron." The consul here is described specifically as *obuiam progederetur*, and his movement might attempt to alleviate the awkwardness of the situation.

[28] On *uerecundia*, see Kaster 2005: 13–27 and Chapter 4: 166–7 below.

on relative status, but the introduction of *uerecundia*, a social emotion, emphasizes the awkwardness of the situation, a sentiment which can only derive from a collective recognition that multiple claims to dignity and face must be simultaneously negotiated. As Robert Kaster has observed, *uerecundia* "animates the art of knowing your proper place in every societal transaction and basing your behavior on that knowledge."[29] The lictors, experiencing *uerecundia*, are silent for fear that any intervention on their part will pre-empt, and consequently decrease, the *maiestas* of their betters. But there is another important element to *uerecundia* here. The lictors are silent also because they do not know on whose side they are supposed to intervene, if at all. The *uerecundia* "script," in Kaster's terminology, entails gauging your own social place and signaling it to others, while inviting them to display their own status in a way that does not impinge on yours. *Verecundia*, in other words, "draws a line for the self to observe, in settings where no such line is drawn by formal or external authority, where he or she must improvise a performance as a well-socialized person."[30] For the lictors, at least, that external authority is the consul, whose orders they act on just as soon as he articulates them, which is not before his father has passed the eleventh lictor. Part of the reason this little drama takes so long, however, must be because neither the father nor the son is exercising his own *uerecundia*. The contrast with Plutarch here is glaring: the son acts immediately, the crowd finds him too forward, and the father restores harmony by asserting that the son's aggression is appropriate to his rank and to the Roman spirit. In Livy, on the other hand, silence dominates until the last moment.[31] It is also worth noting that, unlike in Quadrigarius' version, the lictors do not show a failure of understanding (cf. *cito intellexit* in Quadrigarius) but rather respectfully wait for orders. Once the son does assert himself in his public *persona*, his father can respond in kind, justifying his behavior as a test (*experiri uolui*). What matters, however, is that all the actors are carefully maneuvering around a single, meaningful problem, which they are trying to negotiate successfully. The father's recourse to his son's status as consul, whether or not we take it as a genuine historical detail, is a rhetorical appeal to a constitutional reality, which acts here to re-establish harmony. But it is easy to imagine, as the elder Fabius seems to, an equally plausible case where his son holds himself back in deference to his father's status and years.

29 Kaster 2005: 15. 30 Kaster 2005: 15.

31 On silence, one of Livy's favorite rhetorical devices, see Dutoit 1948.

Valerius Maximus paints the scene with more emphatic brush strokes. Far from being reluctant to dismount, the father is annoyed (*indignatus*) and angry (*plenus irae*) that none of the eleven lictors ordered him to do so. The son notices his father's approach and tells the *proximus lictor* to order him to dismount. Fabius' indignation signals his disapproval of any alternative to the traditional hierarchy of *imperium* over paternity. But the *uerecundia* script in Livy suggests that Fabius' indignation arises not only from his son's failure to assert his authority properly, but also from the awkward position in which this failure puts his father. The elder Fabius' concern that his actions might be misunderstood as contempt (*non . . . contempsi*) fits well with Livy's use of *uerecundia* – accurately recognizing his own place, Fabius feels affronted when his son fails to recognize the superiority of his own consular position and thereby forces his father into over-asserting himself. His final explanation makes this dynamic explicit: he is not aggrieved at being treated as inferior to his son; rather, the opposite is true – he deems *publica instituta* as more binding (*potiora*) than the private pieties of *patria ueneratio*. And yet, in casting his actions as a test (*experiri*), Fabius reveals a not-so-latent paternalism, for it presumes not only that the father is in a position to evaluate his son's performance but also that he is at liberty to test him in a decidedly ostentatious manner.[32] Thus, the problem here is not ignorance of what is due to whom, but rather a problem of character and context: Fabius could have easily stood on his paternal rights, as the son seemed to be expecting him to do. While the *exemplum* is undeniably one of subordinating personal bonds to public hierarchies, it is also an *exemplum* of the social process entailed in rearranging affective bonds to fit with the demands of public office. The prominence of *uerecundia* suggests the presence of a fear of getting it wrong, and likewise an assumption that this fear is realistic. That this fear is not "a dread or gut-wrenching anxiety, much less terror or panic" but instead a "mild and strategic sort of fear" should not belittle its importance as an organizing principle in the production of these *exempla*.[33]

32 That this kind of latent power struggle flowed both ways is shown in Val. Max. 2.2.4, an earlier example under the same rubric, and featuring an earlier pair of Fabii (probably Gurges and Rullianus [*RE* 112 and 114, respectively], though Valerius Maximus conflates the two generations): the consul, concerned for his father's safety in a crowd of hostile Samnites, invites his father to walk between himself and the lictor, a position forbidden to anyone but *filio dumtaxat et ei puero* ("to a son and only while still a boy"), so as to maintain the consul's dignity. The father correctly refuses. The refusal might stem from two reasons: first, from an acknowledgment that to accept would diminish his son's authority, but also because to accept would mean walking *in loco filii*, that is, a lower and less authoritative position.

33 Kaster 2005: 16.

Exemplary choices in the *imperia Manliana*

The previous two sections have charted some of the ways in which the exemplary tradition employs the dialectical tension between magisterial *imperium* and the dual resonances of paternity as both authoritative and affective or emotive. At the center of this tension is a literary exploration of social ambiguity, which helps to figure each of these episodes as an open question in need of resolution, as well as to highlight the mutual moves – physical as well as rhetorical – required to achieve harmony. The episodes further trace a range of responses to any assertion of paternal rights over magisterial *imperium*: the awkwardness of the Fabii example, or, in the accounts of Flaminius, the competing attempts to characterize the situation as one of either filial *pietas* or a type of paternal *atrocitas*.[34] In this section I want to look at the most extreme manifestation of this paradigm, filicide, the execution of an adult son by his father.[35] As before, my interest lies in the emotive cues that the *exempla* send, and, since they feature prominently in the *AUC*, in the larger pattern they form within Livy's narrative. Both of the *exempla* I use, the *imperia Manliana* and the execution of Brutus' sons, are standard *exempla* of the Roman subordination of private interests to that of the state.[36] But Livy also pays close attention to the emotional burdens demanded by the executioner's double role as both father and consul. This attention is deliberate, not least because it directs the audience in evaluating the execution as a didactic lesson. The emotionality both fathers show, I suggest, is an extreme form of the social awkwardness explored in the previous section. However, unlike the previous cases, here the prioritization is a foregone conclusion, and the emotional response serves as a tragic reminder of the parent's loss. As such, it invites the reader to explore the kind of ideology which requires such difficult decisions.

The execution of the young Manlius Torquatus is traditionally dated to 340 BC, during the Latin wars. Concerned for discipline in the army against a tough enemy, the consuls issue an edict that no one should break

[34] For *atrocitas* as a rhetorical device: Cic. *Inu. rhet.* 2.53 *per quem ipsius facti atrocitas aut indignitas aut omnino culpa cum indignatione augeatur* ("through which [i.e. commonplace] the atrocity and indignity of the deed itself, or at least its guilt, should be increased along with our indignation"). *Atrocitas* is thematic in the *imperia Manliana* (8.8.1 *atrocitas poenae*); both *indignitas* and *indignatio* are thematic for the Fabii in Val. Max. 2.2.4.

[35] The bibliography on *ius uitae necisque* is extensive. See, e.g., Crook 1967: 113; Saller 1994: 114–23; Shaw 2001; Cantarella 2003, and Gaughan 2010: 23–52; along with Frier and McGinn 2004: 193–211. On the *seueritas* inherent in consular behavior: Hölkeskamp 2010: 117–18, 120.

[36] See Litchfield 1914: 27–43 on the Brutus/Manlius nexus, as well as discussion in n. 62 below.

ranks.[37] It so happens (8.7.1 *forte*), Livy narrates, that the consul's son leads a sortie that encounters the Tusculan cavalry. As they are all known to each other, words are exchanged, and the Latin leader, Geminus Maecius, challenges the young Torquatus to a duel. Having won the fight, Torquatus carries the spoils back to his father the consul, who, instead of praising the youth for victory, finds his son guilty of breaking military discipline and flouting the authority of the consuls and executes him.[38] The tragedy, and with it the moral force of the *exemplum*, derives from the two different ways in which father and son manage their respective roles, and from the start it is clear that a large part of the younger Torquatus' failure to obey orders is his inability to distinguish clearly between his father's two *personae*. Upon returning to the camp, the younger Torquatus rushes *ad praetorium ad patrem* (8.7.12) and there details how his achievement forms another link in the family's exemplary tradition: 8.7.13 *ut me omnes, inquit, pater, tuo sanguine ortum uere ferrent* ("so that everyone might say, father – he said – that I was truly born of your blood"). The way in which Livy narrates the father's response emphasizes the multiplicity of roles he plays, in contrast to the son's unitary focus. Livy opens by styling Torquatus emphatically as *consul*, and his immediate action is turning away from his son (8.7.15 *filium aversatus*) and towards the camp (8.7.14 *contionem classico aduocari iussit*).[39] The physical movement, even before he speaks, signals to both son and reader Torquatus' attempt to re-establish his consular *persona*.

However, despite the emphatic opening, the family affection designated by the opening picture of *pater* and *filius* remains in operation. The family model, which gives the son his primary impetus, is central throughout this episode. The son enters the duel because Maecius' taunts make him forgetful of his father's orders and the consular edict (8.7.8 *oblitus itaque imperii patrii consulumque edicti*), a phrase which again stresses the parallel

37 Livy 8.6.16 *per haec ne quo errore milites caperentur, edicunt consules ne quis extra ordinem in hostem pugnaret.* For the recurrence of the edict in single combat narratives: Oakley 1998: 131 (*ad* 7.10.2). For the importance of obtaining the commander's permission to engage in a duel, see Oakley 1985: 406, with the important corrective in Feldherr 1998: 96 n. 47.

38 Livy 8.7.1–22; Zonaras 7.26.3–5. Fragmentary accounts in: Dion. Hal. *Ant. Rom.* 8.79.2 and Dio fr. 35.2. See Oakley 1998: 436–8 for discussion of sources and Livy's structuring of the episode. Oakley suggests that "traces of an overwrought annalistic version, in which Torquatus is made first to decorate his son and then order his execution" may be found in the Greek sources; however, as Oakley himself recognizes, a Roman writer would hardly have imagined that a Roman general would "honour a man for breaking ranks" (438). Still, the center of the episode is consistently the execution of Torquatus' son at the hands of his father. The fact that the Greek sources have Torquatus first decorate and then punish his son suggests that the paternal role was central to their view of the story, and the tragedy was bound up in the fact that the father was ascendant and the consul a secondary role.

39 On the detail of the *classicum*, Oakley 1998: 444.

and dual roles within which the son interprets his actions. The phrase *imperii patrii* is itself evocative, especially in relation to the family tradition of the Torquati: the *cognomen Imperiosus* had been attached to the family since at least 363 BC[40] and, more importantly, the father himself was an *exemplum* of a heroic duelist, a status which the son actively seeks to imitate.[41] This, of course, is his fatal mistake: in his eagerness to repeat his father's *exemplum*, he forgets to follow it to the letter, since Roman duels called for a strict protocol whereby the duelist asked for and received the consul's order to fight *extra ordinem*. His forgetfulness immediately precludes him from the imitative feat to which he aspires.[42] The phrase *imperii patrii*, however, also mediates two phases in the reader's view of Torquatus the father. In 8.6.16 we hear of the consuls' edict: *edicunt consules ne quis extra ordinem in hostem pugnaret*. The phrase is repeated at 8.7.8 (*consulumque edicti*), where it is juxtaposed with *imperii patrii*. The consular edict is then picked up by Torquatus the consul, who finally conflates it with consular *imperium*: 8.7.15 *tu, T. Manli, neque imperium consulare neque maiestatem patriam ueritus, aduersus edictum nostrum extra ordinem in hostem pugnasti* ("you, Titus Manlius, fearing neither consular orders nor the *maiestas* of your father, fought the enemy outside the ranks against our edict"). Thus, to a significant extent, the son's forgetfulness determines the way in which the *exemplum* is constructed, not only as a failed attempt at repetition, but also in establishing the parameters according to which the son is judged and found guilty. His offense is construed not only as against the consular edict, but also, and equally forcefully, as a betrayal of the family's honor. We might finally note that the son's inability to separate his father's two roles manifests itself also in his terminological confusion. He sees *imperium* as a quality of his father, inscribed in his character by the cognomen *Imperiosus*, rather than as a quality of the consular office he holds. It is the father who eventually corrects him, assigning the adjective

40 The grandfather, L. Manlius Capitolinus Imperiosus, was *dictator claui figendi causa* in 363 BC (*MRR* I.117, s.a. 363). The *cognomen* is attested in Livy (7.3.4) and on the *fasti consulares* ([–] *Imperiossus*): Degrassi 1954: 42–3. Regardless of whether the *fasti* accurately reports the earlier Manlius' *cognomen* or retrojects it based on a later tradition, for Livy, *Imperiosus* is an inherited *cognomen*.

41 On Manlius and the Gaul: Oakley 1998: 113–23 and Courtney 1999: 114–50, both with further references. On the *imperia Manliana*: Oakley 1998: 436–51. Kraus 1998: 270 n. 15 points out the linguistic parallels between father and son. Feldherr 1998: 105–11 aligns the duel of the young Torquatus with a theology of *imperium*, arguing that the youth fought without contact with the authority of either magistrates or the gods; he was thus supporting neither familial tradition nor the interests of state.

42 Kraus 1998: 269–70. For the procedure whereby the combatant first asks the consul's permission, Oakley 1985: 406 (republican practice), Feldherr 1998: 96 n. 47 (Livian insertion), and my discussion in Chapter 3.

consulare to the noun *imperium*, and setting it against *maiestas patria*, a more precise breakdown of the power dynamics.

The family model is a preoccupation of the episode as a whole as well. The consuls are concerned for discipline because the Latins are so very similar to the Romans: 8.6.15 *lingua, moribus, armorum genere, institutis ante omnia militaribus congruentes* ("being alike in language, customs, type of weapons, and above all in their military institutions").[43] Such similarity between peoples activates for Livy the notion of civil war (8.8.2 *fuit autem ciuili maxime bello pugna similis*), in which fathers, sons, and brothers are pitted against each other. The name of the Latin leader whom the young Torquatus fights also suggests the closeness of the two sides. The name *Geminus* styles him "double" or "similar," as well as "twin" – all with the semantic range connoting likeness and perhaps even kinship.[44] Even more forcefully, his name suggests the duplication of the father's *exemplum* which the son attempts to enact and highlights the fact that his death is entailed by his failure to repeat *exactly* his father's action.[45] In the context of a Latin war, however, and especially with the comparison to a civil war, the son's failure multiplies. He fails not only in forgetting to ask permission, but also in choosing his rival. His father's opponent was a Gaul, and the duel was meant to establish the family's symbolic role as Gaul-fighters through its descent from Manlius Capitolinus.[46] The son instead chooses a Latin cavalryman, who is both known to him and his equal in rank and birth.

As a duel, then, it has better parallels in Roman dueling history than the one his father wages with the Gaul, most prominently the pre-republican

43 Lipovsky 1981: 113–14 suggests that Livy "palliates Manlius' offense," in having the consuls merely worried about the similarity of the enemy, in comparison with Dionysius of Halicarnassus, who at 15.4.5–6 has them issue the edict to instill fear and quell a mutiny. However, although Livy changes the intent behind the edict, the result of the execution remains both fear (8.7.20 *metu*) and an increase in obedience (8.8.1 *oboedientiorem duci militem*). For this type of oblique allusion in Livy, see Levene 2010: 126–63.

44 The name Maecius is attested as both Italian and Roman, which, combined with the *cognomen* Geminus, emphasizes the similiarity, indeed the identity, between the warring sides: *RE* 14: 232–8. The *nomen* is epigraphically attested on lists of Italian *magistri* from Delos, dated to *c.* 112 BC (*ILS* 9417 [Maicius] and *CIL* 1^2.2236 = *ILS* 9237 [Maecius]), and as the name of one of the Roman tribes, the *tribus Maecia*, added to the rolls in the census of 332 BC (Livy 8.17.11; Taylor 1960: 53–4).

45 Kraus 1998: 269–70.

46 Livy 7.10.3 *si tu permittis, uolo ego illi beluae ostendere . . . me ex ea familia ortum quae Gallorum agmen ex rupe Tarpeiae deiecit* ("if you permit, I wish to show this beast that I am of that family who hurled a troop of Gauls from the Tarpeian rock"). Cf. Kraus 1998: 269–70. The evocation of Capitolinus highlights, perversely, the downward trajectory (*deiecit*) of the exemplary link: Capitolinus defeats a whole *agmen*, Torquatus fights one Gaul, and his son misses the point altogether. The torch is instead passed to Valerius Corvus, a better and more precise imitator (Livy 7.26.2–7). The Torquati do, however, carry on their tradition of paternal severity: Feeney 2010; Flower 2006: 63–6 with further references.

duel between the Horatii and Curiatii.[47] The link here is corroborated by a verbal echo as well. When the elder Torquatus ends his speech, he uses the formulaic phrase *i, lictor, deliga ad palum* (8.7.19. "go, lictor, tie him to the stake"), a variant of the formula *i, lictor, colliga manus* ("go, lictor, tie his hands"), which Livy uses in 1.26.8, when the *duumuir* pronounces Horatius guilty of killing his sister.[48] Structurally, this is a reasonably straightforward parallel for the *imperia Manliana*, as a public officer passes judgment on a returning duelist, and it lends the proceedings a legal cast. It is worth noting in this context that the king, Tullus Hostilius, shies away from the severity of the punishment and urges Horatius to appeal (1.26.8 *auctore Tullo, clemente legis interprete "prouoco" inquit*), though, unlike Torquatus, he has nothing personal at stake. Indeed, Horatius is eventually acquitted, and the decisive factor is his father's speech, in which he announces that his daughter was justly killed (1.26.9 *iure caesam*). The speech, too, puts the legal pronouncement to good rhetorical effect:

> i, lictor, colliga manus, quae paulo ante armatae imperium populo Romano pepererunt. i, caput obnube liberatoris urbis huius; arbore infelici suspende; uerbera uel intra pomerium, modo inter illa pila et spolia hostium, uel extra pomerium, modo inter sepulcra Curiatiorum; quo enim ducere hunc iuuenem potestis ubi non sua decora eum a tanta foeditate supplicii uindicent? (Livy 1.26.11)
>
> Go, lictor, tie his hands, which earlier under arms saved the empire of the Roman people. Go, cover the head of this city's liberator. Hang him from a barren tree. Flog him, within the city's boundary, among the spears and spoils of the enemy, or perhaps outside the boundary, among the tombs of the Curiatii. For where can you take this young man where his decorations will not protect him from the great vileness of this punishment?

As an intertext for the young Manlius' duel and execution, Horatius' speech highlights two important points, both confirming the trajectory of exemplary failure. The first emphasizes again the young Manlius' failure to live up to his exemplary precedents. His duel achieves nothing within the context of the war (8.7.8 *uinceret an uinceretur haud multum interesset*), especially by contrast with the family's paradigm. The second point, however, focuses on the father rather than the son, since Livy establishes a trajectory of *exempla*, from Horatius to Fabius Rullianus (8.30.1–35.12),

[47] Livy 1.24–6; Solodow 1979; Feldherr 1998: 123–44; Oakley 2010.

[48] The Horatius trial is related also to the actual case of Rabirius Postumus, accused of *perduellio* in 63 BC. Livy echoes Cicero's phrases closely: compare *i, lictor, conliga manus; caput obnubito, arbori infelici suspendito* in *Rab. Post.* 13 with Livy 1.26.11 (quoted in text). On the trial: Watson 1979. On the relationship between Livy's trial and that of Rabirius: Bauman 1969 and Solodow 1979.

where the father intervenes in a legal dispute to shield his son from harmful consequences, despite the son's manifest guilt.[49] But the young Manlius' insistence on interpreting his act as a repetition of his father's *exemplum* precludes the father from assuming the merciful role which the Horatius intertext makes available to him, since to insist on upholding this family's traditions entails also accepting the family's tradition of paternal severity.[50]

Indeed, the father's speech makes it clear that offense against *consulum imperia* is at the heart of the matter. His son's life or death is weighed against the integrity of the consular orders which the son violates: 8.7.19 *aut morte tua sancienda sint consulum imperia aut impunitate in perpetuum abroganda* ("the authority of the consuls must either be confirmed by your death or be annulled forever by your escaping punishment"). Further, the father states, he has been made to choose between the republic's interest and his own:[51]

> quando . . . quantum in te fuit, disciplinam militarem, qua stetit ad hanc diem Romana res, soluisti meque in eam necessitatem adduxisti, ut aut rei publicae mihi aut mei [meorum] obliuiscendum sit, nos potius nostro delicto plectemur quam res publica tanto suo damno nostra peccata luat; triste exemplum sed in posterum salubre iuuentuti erimus. (Livy 8.7.15–7)
>
> Since you, as far as you were able, weakened military discipline, on which the Roman state has relied to this day, and have led me to this necessity, that I must be forgetful either of the state or of myself, we should rather incur damages ourselves than have the state pay for our failings with such a great loss to itself. We shall be a grim but salutary example to the youth of future generations.

The father's vocabulary parallels his actions and his son's: the son's forgetfulness of authority imposes on the father forgetfulness (*obliuiscendum sit*) either of himself or of the state.[52] This forgetfulness is characteristic not only within the immediate plot but also within the larger intratextual frame of reference: the Latins are forgetful of their defeats and the Roman kindnesses towards them (8.5.10 *adeo et cladium ueterum uestrarum et beneficiorum nostrorum erga uos obliti estis*), a forgetfulness which triggers the

[49] On the Rullianus narrative as a "companion piece" to the *imperia Manliana*: Lipovsky 1981: 113–30; Chaplin 2000: 108–13. Cf. Masi Doria 2000: 15–125 for the juridical aspects of the procedure.

[50] On the severity of the Torquati as an annalistic stereotype: Oakley 1998: 86; Feeney 2010. Especially relevant is the severity of the first *Imperiosus* (Cic. *Off.* 3.112; Livy 7.4.1–5.9; Val. Max. 5.4.3; cf. Oakley 1998: 83–95), the father and grandfather of our two Manlii. Like the *imperia Manliana*, the episode is coupled with a *deuotio*, though not of the Decian type, thus further bolstering the theme of typological repetition.

[51] Compare, e.g., Plut. *Aem.* 35–6 (Aemilius Paulus) and Livy 5.21.14–15 (Camillus) for individual leaders requesting that potential damage to the state revert onto them and their family.

[52] There was a Torquatus family tradition regarding *damnatio memoriae*: see Flower 2006: 63–6.

Latin war; Horatius, meanwhile, reviles his sister for her own forgetfulness of her brothers and her homeland (1.26.4 *oblita fratrum mortuorum uiuique, oblita patriae*). In all these examples, and especially in Torquatus' case, forgetfulness threatens the individual's ability to fit in with his or her family and consequently places them, as it does the Latins, in opposition to the Roman state. Vice versa, the younger Torquatus' crime against the state implicates his family, which forces his father to bring to bear both his official powers and his paternal authority on his son's punishment.[53] Finally, these intratexts also make clear the consequences of disobedience and, therefore, the proper *officium* of a son, soldier, daughter, or ally towards the figure of authority, embodied in the consuls (or, before them, the king and the *duumuirs*). More importantly, the speech highlights the son's failure to recognize the state's authority vested in the consuls. The father's prioritization of state over self makes up for the son's failure to do so, and the consul's verdict exacts the punishment.[54]

But the father's speech adverts also to the alternative scenario, in which he might have championed his son against the accusation:

> me quidem cum ingenita caritas liberum tum specimen istud uirtutis deceptum[55] uana imagine decoris in te mouet; sed cum aut morte tua sancienda sint consulum imperia aut impunitate in perpetuum abroganda, nec te quidem, si quid in te nostri sanguinis est, recusare censeam, quin disciplinam militarem culpa tua prolapsam poena restituas. (Livy 8.7.18–19)
>
> For myself, not only the inborn affection of a father towards his children inclines me towards you, but also this example of your valor, even though it is tarnished by a false idea of glory. But since the authority of the consuls must either be confirmed by your death or be annulled forever by your escaping punishment, you too, if you have a drop of my blood in you, would not refuse, I think, to restore by your punishment our military discipline, which has collapsed through your fault.

Although the father's formal stance does not change, he concedes both affection for his son and a grudging admiration for his valor. Further, the

53 The phrase *qua stetit ad hanc diem Romana res* alludes to Ennius' famous line *moribus antiquis res stat Romana uirisque* (*Ann.* 467 = 156 Sk.; Oakley 1998: 445). In light of this allusion, it is remarkable that Torquatus the father does not directly appeal to *mos* or precedent to support him.

54 On the limitations to the consul's military *imperium*: De Martino 1958–72, vol. 1: 417–20; Lintott 1999: 98–9. It is important to note that this power applied strictly to soldiers. Citizens outside the *pomerium* enjoyed the same rights of *prouocatio* as those within the city, but as Lintott (p. 98) points out "it was hard to control a Roman magistrate with *imperium* in the field." On the legal problem of the father's *ius uitae necisque*, Harris 1986: 82–8 points out that in the majority of filicide cases the execution is carried out through magisterial *imperium*, and not *patria potestas*.

55 Oakley 1998: 448 emends *deceptum* to *deceptae*, modifying *uirtutis* rather than *specimen*.

punishment is now cast as an opportunity to restore *disciplina*, itself a proof of the son's kinship to the father, and a chance to bring into alignment the two exemplary strands his duel has bifurcated. This admission, little though it affects the outcome, finally brings to the fore the affective bonds between father and son, bonds which are invoked further by the closing formula *i, lictor*. Thus, the dialectic between the roles of father and consul here takes on a symbolic value that is slightly different from what we have seen with the Fabii or with Flaminius. The *imperia Manliana* episode is based on the premise that the father is able to exercise his consular role despite the affective bonds of family. However, the emphasis on memory and forgetfulness hints also at more complicated processes required in order to dissociate the two roles completely. At the end, the father proves not only unable but unwilling to do so, since the overlap of the two roles achieves also the generation of a new type of *exemplum*: one that is both *triste* and *salubre*.[56] On the level of focalization, context, and exemplary patterns, this episode suggests the unity of the state and the family and decries the oblivion that separates one from the other.

Brutus and the ethics of republicanism

When Manlius Torquatus executes his son, he takes up a place in a tradition of filicide that reaches back to the dawn of the republic. As I mentioned briefly at the opening of this chapter, the foundational act of political filicide sees Brutus execute his sons for supporting the Tarquins against the nascent republic. The father in this case is also Rome's first consul, and he is faced with the awful necessity of having to choose between the two roles, and thereby, symbolically, between two political regimes. To choose the role of father is to privilege affective bonds, the life of the child and the death of certain values, while to choose the consul's role is to privilege the republic's interest, the death of the child, and life for a new form of exemplary conduct, which values the state above the needs of the individual. Placed at this critical juncture of the republic's development, and against the background of monarchical tyranny on the one hand, and monarchical clemency on the other, the trial and execution of his sons

56 The effects of the *exemplum* are varied. As an army, the soldiers' discipline and resolve are improved (8.8.1 *fecit tamen atrocitas poenae oboedientiorem duci militem; et . . . cum descensum in aciem est, ea seueritas profuit*). The soliders, however, also respond to the execution with complaint and lamentation (8.7.21 *conquestu, lamentis, exsecrationibus*) and further give the *exemplum* its distinctive label, *imperia Manliana*, commemorating the episode through its emphasis on the family rather than the consular office.

require Brutus to transform them into a distinctively republican *exemplum*. This mythical story had much currency during the late republic, with the tragedian Accius composing a *Brutus*, perhaps as early as 133 BC, on which Livy's narrative must rely to some extent.[57] In the even more turbulent times of Caesar's dictatorship, Cassius of Parma, one of Caesar's assassins, likewise composed a *Brutus*, thus cementing the tragedy as a symbol of resistance to tyrannical rule.[58] Not much survives of either tragedy, but a short fragment of Accius' version suggests that the foundation of the consulship concluded the play: *Brutus*, fr. 3 Klotz (= Varro, *Ling.* 5.80) *qui recte consulat, consul cluat* ("let him who dispenses good advice be called consul").[59] The tragedy itself can help us little in exploring the interaction of paternity and political office, but it establishes not only a close connection between them, but also a foundational connection between filicide and the origins of the consulship. Just as Rome itself began with an act of murder, so too did the republic: Brutus' response to the execution, I shall argue, establishes also an ethics of consular conduct that is distinctly republican in ideology.

Shortly after the expulsion of the kings, the nascent republic was threatened by a conspiracy of noble youth (Livy 2.3–4). The sons of the consul Brutus were among the conspirators, and their father found himself in the unenviable position of having to preside over their execution:

> damnati proditores sumptumque supplicium, conspectius eo quod poenae capiendae ministerium patri de liberis consulatus imposuit, et qui spectator erat amouendus, eum ipsum fortuna exactorem supplicii dedit. stabant deligati ad palum nobilissimi iuuenes; sed a ceteris, uelut ab ignotis capitibus, consulis liberi omnium in se auerterant oculos, miserebatque non poenae magis homines quam sceleris quo poenam meriti essent. (Livy 2.5.5–6)
>
> The traitors were convicted and their punishment set, which was the more notable since the consulship assigned the office of exacting the punishment to a father over his own children. And the man who should have been removed [from the proceedings] were he a spectator, him fortune made

57 On the date of the *Brutus*: Boyle 2006: 123. The play was restaged in 57 BC (Cic. *Sest.* 118–23) and was scheduled for performance in 44 BC, when it was replaced with Accius' *Tereus* (Cic. *Att.* 16.2.3, 16.5.1, *Phil.* 1.36). T. P. Wiseman has argued forcefully for the reliance of Roman historiographers on dramatic performances; see the essays collected in Wiseman 1994 and 1998. Feldherr 1998: 165–212 highlights the dramatic elements in Livy's narrative of the Tarquins; cf. Scafuro 1989 and Walsh 1996 on the comic underpinnings of Livy's narrative of the Bacchic scandal.

58 Boyle 2006: 158–9. Only one line survives, quoted in Varro, *Ling.* 6.7, 7.72 (*nocte intempesta nostram deuenit domum*), though even this is sometimes attributed to Accius.

59 The last word of the fragment is problematic. *Cluat* in Klotz's edition is Palmer's emendation of the manuscript *ciat*; Warmington's *Remains of Old Latin* Loeb edition prints *siet* following Niebuhr. Whichever reading is accepted, the connection between counseling and consuls remains clear.

> the executioner. Youth of the noblest families stood tied to the pole; but the children of the consul drew everyone's eyes, as if the others were of no consequence, and men did not pity them more for their punishment than for the crime by which they had merited it.

Livy sets his scene in such a way that both the consul and his sons are at the center of attention. The father's dual roles as father and executioner make the event more notable (*conspectius*), while his children, meanwhile, focus everyone's attention on themselves, and thereby also on their relationship to the consul (*consulis liberi*). The peculiar sympathy the audience feels for them likewise collapses the political and affective relationships: the pity they feel is not so much for their impending death, but rather for having betrayed the state, and with it their father, in the first place. In this extreme case of treason, the office of the consul must disrupt the relationship of the father and his children, and negate any feelings of natural affection. Outside the text, we can safely assume, treasonous children were a rarity, but within the plot of the *AUC* up to this point, dynastic plots and treachery have so far been almost normal: the execution, as I have argued at the opening of this chapter, closes off a cycle that began with Tullia's depraved abuse of her father's body.[60] The execution is therefore also a marker of the new regime's inversion of the behavioral norms of the monarchy, and the disruption of paternal bonds carries with it a double irony: the republic was founded to avenge Lucretia's violation, and it requires now a disruption of a similar order. As the foundational figure of the new republic, Brutus will be unable to avenge his sons, and his controlled restraint is emblematic of the new rule.[61] The audience's sympathy, however, is marked, and it is pointed at the sons, and not at their father, despite the fact that they form an equal

60 A historical case of a *priuatus* father executing a treasonous son is the senator A. Fulvius, who in 63 BC executed his son for setting out to fight for Catiline (Dio 37.36; Sall. *Cat.* 39.5; Val. Max. 5.8.5, with discussion in Harris 1986: 85). See also [Quintilian] *Minor Declamations* 322, on a son murdering a father who suspected him of tyranny, and more generally 258, 285, 314, 315, 317, with Gunderson 2003.

61 Matthew Roller points out to me that the execution of Brutus' sons is a quintessential rejection of any dynastic aspirations of political inheritance. Against this we can balance Livy's description of the Roman kings as elected, as well as the Roman practice of inheritance by adoption, a later favorite trick of the principate. An interesting variation of the tension between heredity, tyranny, and republicanism can be seen in Dion. Hal. *Ant. Rom.* 5.8–13, in which Brutus executes his sons, and following that the nephews of his fellow consul Collatinus. In both trials Brutus' actions are unequivocally cruel (5.8.1 σκληρὰ καὶ ἄπιστα), and he himself is unfeeling (5.8.6), refusing to relent despite interventions by the crowd in the first trial in defense of the sons, and by Collatinus in defense of his own nephews, claiming to do so by the same power by which Brutus ordered their execution (5.9.3 ἐπεὶ σκαιὸς εἶ καὶ πικρὸς ἐγὼ τὰ μειράκια ἀφαιροῦμαι τῆς αὐτῆς ἐξουσίας ἧς σὺ κύριος ὢν). In response, Brutus accuses his colleague of being himself a traitor, and Collatinus is forced to forsake his office and depart into exile. The juxtaposition of the two trials highlights Brutus' severity and self-sacrifice in the name of the republic, but it also raises some interesting

share of the spectacle. By opening with the image of explicitly pitiable sons and their sympathetic father, with ideology for the moment left behind, the scene invites the reader to share the spectators' sense of pity.

We might briefly compare here the famous treatment of this scene in the *Aeneid*, which is markedly less sympathetic:

> uis et Tarquinios reges animamque superbam
> ultoris Bruti, fascisque uidere receptos?
> consulis imperium hic primus saeuasque securis
> accipiet, natosque pater noua bella mouentis
> ad poenam pulchra pro libertate uocabit,
> infelix, utcumque ferent ea facta minores:
> uincet amor patriae laudumque immensa cupido.
> (Verg. *Aen.* 6.817–23)

> Do you see the Tarquin kings and the haughty spirit of Brutus the avenger, and the rods he received? He will be the first to accept the power of the consul and the savage axes, and the father will summon his sons, scheming new wars, to their punishment, in the name of lovely freedom, wretched, however later generations will relate these deeds: the love of country will win out, and the immense desire for praise.

If Brutus desires praise, Vergil's text offers it only with considerable qualification. Although Anchises commemorates the two actions for which Brutus was known – the foundation of the republic and the execution of his sons – his spin on the story is at best jaundiced. Brutus is throughout given negative epithets, in contrast with *pulchra libertas*, in whose name he acts. His spirit is *superba*, an epithet regularly associated with the *Tarquinios reges* immediately preceding in 817, and which is here ironically transferred to Brutus himself. The enjambement in lines 817–18 further highlights the connection, as the reader, primed to read *superbam* with *reges*, is surprised to find Brutus lurking in the next line. His axes, further, are savage (*saeuae*), a quality ranged against Aeneas and his men from the opening of the poem.[62] *Infelix*, which can also mean "infertile," pointedly

questions of Collatinus, who was unable to sacrifice even once-removed relations, even at the expense of removal from the state. For a historical instance of a father managing public grief at the loss of a child, see Wilcox 2005 on Cicero and Tullia. I'm grateful to Chuck Oughton for drawing my attention to the juxtaposition in Dionysius and its relevant consequences.

[62] On the Tarquins' *superbia* as incompatible with republican ideology: Bruno 1966; Baraz 2009: 383–7. On the specific connotations of *superbia* here: Christenson 2002: 49–50, who also points out that Brutus is associated with Manlius Torquatus, the next figure in the procession, marked *saeuumque securi* in 824. On *saeua*: *Aen.* 1.4 *saeuae memorem Iunonis ob iram* ("because of the mindful wrath of savage Juno"). On the long process of reconciliation: Feeney 1984.

suggests Brutus' loss of his sons.[63] The section closes with Brutus' motivation: not freedom or love of country alone, but also an immense desire for praise, a civic-minded value, that could, as Sallust had already warned, come dangerously close to ambition.[64] Livy, by comparison, treats Brutus much more generously, assuming genuine paternal emotion in the place of stark ambition, and restoring authenticity to Brutus' love of country. For Valerius Maximus, likewise, the situation is simple, since Brutus is able to strip off his paternal *persona*: 5.8.1 *exuit patrem, ut consulem ageret, orbusque uiuere quam publicae uindictae deesse maluit* ("he put away the father, so he could act the part of consul, and preferred to live bereft than to fall short in redressing the public grievance"). *Orbus* is the sole word suggesting an emotional response, and if Livy draws Brutus' emotional complexity more richly, he does so through his simultaneous expression of duty and affection.

This nexus is articulated most explicitly when Livy shifts his attention to Brutus himself (Livy 2.5.8):

> nudatos uirgis caedunt securique feriunt, cum inter omne tempus pater uoltusque et os eius spectaculo esset, eminente animo patrio inter publicae poenae ministerium.
>
> They beat the stripped youths with the branches and executed them, while for the whole time the father himself, his face and expression became a spectacle, his paternal spirit conspicuous amidst the performance of public punishment.

The consul's face displays paternal sentiment even as he discharges his public duty, and his sorrow and affection are a *spectaculum* to match the execution. The confluence of sentiments, brought on by the performance of conflicting roles, is important. Catiline, for example, allegedly orchestrated the death of his own son, and this cruelty was a hallmark of his mad and tyrannical disposition.[65] Here, however, paternity helps to soften

[63] On *infelix*, see Austin 1971 ad loc.; cf. *OLD* s.v. 1 "(of plants, soil), yielding nothing useful, unproductive."

[64] Sallustian *ambitio*: *Cat.* 11.1–2 *sed primo magis ambitio quam auaritia animos hominum exercebat, quod tamen uitium propius uirtutem erat. nam gloriam honorem imperium bonus et ignauos aeque sibi exoptant; sed ille uera uia nititur, huic quia bonae artes desunt, dolis atque fallaciis contendit.* ("But first ambition rather than avarice engaged the spirits of men; because of the vices it was closest to virtue. For good men and bad both equally long for glory, office, and command; but one strives for them by the true path, and the other, who lacks noble arts, strives through treachery and deceit"). Cf. Earl 1961: 14 and, on the problem of *uera uocabula*, Batstone 1988.

[65] Sall. *Cat.* 15.2 *pro certo creditur necato filio uacuam domum scelestis nuptiis fecisse* ("it is taken as certain that he cleared his house for impious marriage by the killing of his son"). The speech of Cato the Younger (52.30–1) cites the story of the execution of the young Torquatus (though with the wrong

the consul's otherwise grim countenance: it transforms an act of magisterial coercion into an act of patriotic self-sacrifice, thus distinguishing the assertion of consular authority from tyrannical abuse. Vergil's *saeuae secures* lose some of their sharpness precisely because Brutus does not abrogate his paternal feeling, and with him, the audience too can engage in cathartic sympathy.

The priority of state over individual and family is well known from Cicero's philosophical works. According to Cicero, love of country is the most important of a man's obligations (*officia*), because the *patria* embraces all other forms of social relationship (*Off.* 1.58):[66]

> sed si contentio quaedam et comparatio fiat, quibus plurimum tribuendum sit officii, principes sint patria et parentes, quorum beneficiis maximis obligati sumus, proximi liberi totaque domus, quae spectat in nos solos neque aliud ullum potest habere perfugium, deinceps bene conuenientes propinqui, quibuscum communis etiam fortuna plerumque est.
>
> But if there is any contention and ranking, as to which offices should be attended to especially, first come homeland and parents, to whom we are obligated through the greatest benefits, and then children and the whole household, who look only to us and have no other recourse, then our kinsmen, with whom we live on good terms, who in most respects have the same fortune as us.

Cicero's formulation neatly orders a Roman man's view of his world: first those to whom one is obligated, and then those who are obligated to that person, in descending order of magnitude of the obligation. This formulation applies to all Roman men, magistrates and *priuati* alike; as such it does not reveal very much about attitudes to consular powers *per se*. It does, however, neatly explain why Brutus was in the end able to execute his children: like the younger Torquatus, their betrayal is doubled, not only of their *patria*, but also of their *parens*.

name and date) as justification for the execution of the conspirators: *apud maiores nostros A. Manlius Torquatus bello Gallico filium suom, quod is contra imperium in hostem pugnauerat, necari iussit, atque ille egregius adulescens inmoderatae fortitudinis morte poenas dedit; uos de crudelissumis parricidis quid statuatis, cunctamini?* ("among our ancestors, A. Manlius Torquatus, during the Gallic war, ordered his son be killed, because he engaged the enemy against orders, and that excellent youth paid with his death the price of his excessive bravery; and you dither in deciding on the cruelest of murderers?") Sallust probably conflated the father and son, both named Titus. The *praenomen* Aulus is attested for the Manlii Torquati, e.g. the father is Titus Manlius L.f. A.n. Imperiosus Torquatus (cf. *MRR* 1.135).

66 The idea of *patria* for Cicero is complicated by his national affiliations, both to his native Arpinum, and his adopted *patria*, Rome. Farrell 2001: 18–26 emphasizes the linguistic aspects of the *duae patriae* question, while Connolly 2007: 77–113 explores the idea of naturalized citizens as a rhetorical motif. See also Feldherr 1997 and Dyck 1996 ad loc.

The complex interplay among *parens*, *pater*, and *patria* is expressed by Livy's internal audience, whose pity seems to be mixed with surprise. Precisely when their father has guaranteed not only freedom for Rome but also glory for their house, the sons choose to cast their lot with a wretched exile, albeit a former king (2.5.7). The phrase through which Livy expresses this sentiment plays precisely on these concepts (Livy 2.5.7):

> illos eo potissimum anno patriam liberatam, patrem liberatorem, consulatum ortum ex domo Iunia, patres, plebem, quidquid deorum hominumque Romanorum esset, induxisse in animum ut superbo quondam regi, tum infesto exsuli proderent.

> in that very year they were of a mind to betray their liberated homeland, their father its liberator, the consulship born of the Junian house, the senators, plebs, and whatever belonged to Roman gods and men to a once haughty king, now a hostile exile.

The list of accusatives plays heavily on the connection between private and public institutions:[67] the list goes from *patriam* to *patrem*, mentions the consulship in conjunction with a specific family, and moves from private to public through the word *patres*, which itself conflates public ("senators") and private ("fathers") meanings. The sons, it is heavily implied, were in a position to enjoy the considerable glory their father's action had won, which is sharply contrasted with the fortunes of the exiled king. As such, the phrase *consulatum ortum ex domo Iunia* is especially poignant in this context, since it is the consulship that imposes the role of executioner on the father. Brutus' sons, too, spring from the *domus Iunia*; hence their father, conceived of as the progenitor of the consulship, is faced with a choice between offspring.

The close interaction of public and private agrees well with Cicero's formulation in *de Officiis* 1.58. The idea that the good of the community encompasses and surpasses the good of the individual citizen is the underlying principle of the execution, as well as of the audience's sorrow. This is, further, a uniquely republican notion: in a monarchy, where all power is monopolized by the king, crime and punishment are decided not solely by principles and laws but also by the king's personal decision. It is therefore not surprising that the conspirators have a different view of the new regime, or that they explain their monarchical allegiance in entirely different terms. They prefer to live under a king than under a rule of law, because laws are deaf and relentless (2.3.4 *leges rem surdam, inexorabilem esse*), whereas

[67] The sequence *liberatam... liberatorem... ortum* likewise sets up an echoing repetition, which provides an aural halo for Livy's transition from public to private.

a king was a man, with whom his friends could have a complex relationship of *gratia* and *beneficium*, as well as error and forgiveness.[68] Just as they expected, the conspirators find the new regime cannot forget offenses against it (2.3.3 *irasci et ignoscere*). The conspirators thus see the republican communality of interest between state and citizen as entirely exclusive of compassion and forgiveness. On the conspirators' terms, they were right to mistrust the new regime, and the role of Brutus as father, consul, and executioner only underlines the horrific paradoxes the republic might lead to.

This is a very pessimistic reading of Livy's narrative and might rightly lead one to ask if there is a way to exonerate Brutus' actions, and, along with them, the morality of the consular office. Cicero's formulation offers one way: the state encompasses all other obligations, so that what accrues to the benefit of the state also accrues to the benefit of the individual. Still, even this concept cannot address every misgiving: a philosophical assertion that one moral good (in this case, the benefit to the state) is absolute does not eliminate others' criticism of cruelty, even in the service of the state. What these episodes offer, however, is the deployment of emotion in the service of ideology. Brutus' misery and Torquatus' *caritas* function like a philosopher's stone: they reveal the genuine affection beneath the stern countenance, and that affection in turn enables the executions to be seen as a sacrifice in the name of the state rather than a tyrannical measure. The same is true on the milder levels at which the Fabii or Flaminius' father operate. The younger and elder Fabii, for instance, both feel discomfited by the inversion public office causes in their biological relationship. The elder Fabius' keenness to uphold that inversion marks him as a good citizen, just as the son's reluctance to advert to his office enables his father's open praise. The exemplary tradition thus reveals the tension between father and consul as constitutive of republican magistracy, and, in the episodes analyzed here, offers an image of the magistrate as someone who simultaneously causes discomfort and feels it. This mutually driven *uerecundia* is finally what separates republican magistracy from its tyrannical counterparts.

68 Livy 2.3.3 *eam tum, aequato iure omnium, licentiam quaerentes, libertatem aliorum in suam uertisse seruitutem inter se conquerebantur: regem hominem esse, a quo impeteres, ubi ius, ubi iniuria opus sit; esse gratiae locum, esse beneficio; et irasci et ignoscere posse; inter amicum atque inimicum discrimen nosse* ("Then, as they were seeking license, with the law made equal for all, they complained amongst themselves that the freedom of others was turned into their own slavery; that the king was a man, whom you could petition when there was need of law or of injury; there was place for favor, and for benefaction; he could grow angry and forgive, and he knew how to distinguish friend from foe").

CHAPTER 2

Authority in crisis: the Caudine Forks

In book 9 of the *AUC* Livy recounts the Roman defeat at the Caudine Forks in 320 BC and subsequent recovery, an episode marked not only for its artistry but also for its exemplary value both within and outside Livy's history.[1] The narrative is intricate and finely crafted with extensive symmetries of plot and structure: a Roman army is trapped and forced to sue for peace; a treaty is signed, which, upon being presented in Rome, the senate finds too ignominious and shameful to bear. The treaty is in consequence repudiated. In order to observe religious propriety and avert any divine displeasure from Rome, those who vouched for the treaty are handed over to the enemy, following which new Roman consuls defeat the Samnites.

Livy's account of the Caudine Forks and its aftermath is an episode deeply interested in magistracy and magisterial behavior, with a particularly acute focus on the consuls. As a narrative as well as an event, the Caudine Forks provides a broad cross-section of consular behavior: military leadership, both failed and successful; deliberation and counseling, both in the field and in the senate; personal charisma; agency and command; and, at the heart of the episode, the consul's role as a representative of Rome. This range of magisterial behaviors, therefore, makes the episode uniquely suitable as a larger-scale case study of narrative's capacity to showcase and explore competing images of magistracy, using the artistic tools of Livian storytelling, especially formal elements such as diction, structure, and intratextuality. The resulting images, as the previous chapter has already suggested, are relational, which is to say contextual and dialogic, and between them furnish a set of cognitive and textual definitions of consulship and public office. But the Caudium narrative is also exemplary in

[1] On Livy's episode: Lipovsky 1981: 141–51; Morello 1996: 70–111; Chaplin 2000: 32–49; and Oakley 2005a: 3–184, with further references. For the historicity of the events: Salmon 1929 and the summaries in Oakley 2005a: 25–38 and 651–4. On the background in Livy 8.38–9: Morello 1996: 71–3, and Oakley 1998: 760–70.

that the episode is an *exemplum*, a guide for future conduct, and inasmuch as it invites the reader to share a multi-dimensional experience of consularity and Romanness, and thereby to consider the role of the episode and its magisterial actors as a microcosm of the Roman state.[2]

What makes the episode so useful as a heuristic is the treaty at its heart, which sets the consuls up as noxal substitutes for the Roman state.[3] As Jane Chaplin has noted, the Caudine Forks makes for an extremely flexible *exemplum* in Livy's text. In its seven appearances, it is cited as "a practical lesson for the Romans, a false indication of Roman vulnerability for the Samnites, a negative religious omen, an exhortation to fight and not appear cowardly, an evocation of Samnite glory, an argument that soldiers who act in a craven fashion should be given a second chance, and an illustration of what not to do when trapped in a ravine."[4] Its usage elsewhere likewise suggests the polysemous reception of the events. Cicero, for example, treats the Roman consul Postumius favorably in the *de Officiis*, particularly for promoting his own extradition in the senate.[5]

> at uero T. Veturius et Sp. Postumius, cum iterum consules essent, quia, cum male pugnatum apud Caudium esset, legionibus nostris sub iugum missis, pacem cum Samnitibus fecerant, dediti sunt iis, iniussu enim populi senatusque fecerant. eodemque tempore Ti. Numicius, Q. Maelius, qui tum tribuni pl. erant, quod eorum auctoritate pax erat facta, dediti sunt, ut pax Samnitium repudiaretur. atque huius deditionis ipse Postumius, qui dedebatur, suasor et auctor fuit. (*Off.* 3.109)
>
> And indeed, T. Veturius and Sp. Postumius, when they were consuls for the second time, were handed over to the Samnites because they had signed a peace treaty with them after the Romans were defeated at Caudium and the legions sent under the yoke – for the consuls had done this without the approval of the Roman senate and people. At the same time, Ti. Numicius and Q. Maelius, who were tribunes of the plebs at the time, were handed over, because the peace was signed under their authority, so that the Samnite peace could be repudiated. And this Postumius, who was handed over, both authored and promoted his hand-over.

Cicero goes on to cite the parallel example of C. Hostilius Mancinus in Numantia in 137 BC, an event which reproduces largely the same structure

2 On Caudium as *exemplum* in Livy's narrative, see Chaplin 2000: 41–7.

3 Noxal liability refers to the responsibility of a master or father over expenses or offenses incurred by those in his *potestas*, such as slaves or children. On the relationship between consuls and fathers, see my discussion in the previous chapter. For noxal liability in Caudium: Rüpke 1990: 110–11.

4 Chaplin 2000: 47.

5 Dyck 1996: 631–2. Litchfield's catalogue (1914: 33) lists Postumius as an *exemplum* of *uirtus*, *fides*, *pietas erga patriam*, *fortitudo*, and *constantia*.

as the Caudine Forks. Indeed Livy's account, at least, may have been elaborated in order to anticipate Mancinus' defeat in the now lost books.[6] The *exempla* of Postumius and Mancinus both come after a citation of Regulus' iconic self-surrender, and all three are, counterintuitively, part of Cicero's discussion of perjury, and of the circumstances under which it counts as *honestas* ("up-rightness") rather than *utilitas* ("utilitarianism").[7] In this discussion Cicero argues against claims that Regulus ought to have perjured his oath to return to Carthage, with the implication that Postumius' oaths, too, were undertaken under the same code which governed Rome's interaction with declared enemies. His surrender to the Samnites affirms, therefore, his honest intention, which both the senate and Postumius are keen to maintain. Here, much as Livy does in the *AUC*, models from the past are used to illuminate a far from straightforward ethical point, and it is no wonder, therefore, that both Livy and Cicero choose an episode which is itself exemplary of various moral and political lessons. The flexibility of the Caudine *exemplum* stretches beyond the moral evaluation of the actors themselves, and indeed as an exemplary moment it has much potential for thinking about Roman magistracy – not only the office-holders, but also the office itself.

The young Cicero provides a somewhat farcical view of the events in the *de Inuentione* (Cic. *Inu. rhet.* 2.91.5–92.5), which nevertheless demonstrates the central importance of magistracy to the episode. There, a noble *adulescens* finds himself at the center of a hypothetical legal debate on whether or not he should be surrendered to the Samnites along with everyone else, despite the fact that his involvement consisted solely of holding down the sacrificial pig (2.91.1 *porcum sustinuit*).[8] The argument for his surrender is simply that he was a participant, and therefore liable to the same treatment as the rest of the signatories.[9] The argument against it, however, is more interesting and goes directly to the issue of agency. The

6 Oakley 2005a: 27–31 lays out the ancient connections between the two events. On Mancinus and his later fortunes, see Wikander 1976 and Rosenstein 1986.

7 *Off.* 3.108 *non enim falsum iurare periurare est, sed quod EX ANIMI TVI SENTENTIA iuraris, sicut uerbis concipitur more nostro, id non facere periurium est* ("for it is not perjury to swear falsely, but it is perjury to swear 'upon your conscience' as in the words laid down in our custom, and not do it"), with Dyck 1996: 630.

8 On the *porcus*: Gladhill 2008: 66–9, though the idea that the passage has an "underlying consideration that the boy is a *porcus*" (68) seems unwarranted.

9 2.92.5 *at enim quoniam particeps tu factus es in turpissimo foedere summae religionis, dedi te conuenit* ("But still, because you were made a participant in that most vile treaty of the highest solemnity, it is right that you be handed over"). The passive voice *factus es* picks up the *adulescens'* insistence on his lack of agency in deciding his participation in the ritual and denies that agency or passivity are relevant to the question of participation.

adulescens was there on orders from the general (2.91 *iussu imperatoris*), and his argument relies on a sharp contrast between his own position and that of the general: *non enim meum fuit officium nec mea potestas, cum et id aetatis et priuatus essem et esset summa cum auctoritate et potestate imperator, qui uideret, ut satis honestum foedus feriretur* (2.92.5 "it was not my duty nor within my power, since at that time I held no office and the general, who saw to it that the treaty was struck with sufficient honor, held all the authority and power").

The rhetorical contrast is clearly between the *adulescens*' *non meum officium nec mea potestas* and the general's *summa cum auctoriate et potestate*. Cicero's sentence structure highlights the juxtaposition further, devoting one half to each of the consul and *adulescens*, and marking the transition by the verbal polyptoton *essem et esset* (where, perhaps, the conjunction *et* primes the reader to the change in verbal ending from the first person *-em* to the third person *-et*).[10] The disavowal of responsibility is, of course, far from watertight and in an important sense does not substantially engage the initial argument: the argument for the *adulescens*' surrender is religious and moral, while the argument against is instrumental, taking the *adulescens* as a mere prop in an elaborate procedure, the responsibility for which lay entirely with those who gave the orders, rather than those who followed them. Cicero's view of Caudium in both the *de Officiis* and the *de Inuentione* focuses on what we would call "administrative responsibility," and his exemplary choices in the *de Officiis*, as well as the *adulescens*' self-defense in the *de Inuentione*, place that responsibility squarely at the feet of the magistrates on the scene. Their conduct, their ability to organize and order, and their willingness to stand by their actions allow the consuls and tribunes to transcend the *realia* of the event and become exemplary.

Consilium and the consular role

Livy neatly structures his account of the Caudine Forks around a reversal in the Roman fortunes (9.15.8 *mutatione subita rerum*). The nadir of defeat quickly turns into the zenith of victory, as the Romans meticulously turn the situation on its head, recovering their lost arms, standards, and hostages, and inflicting on the Samnites all the indignities they had meted out to

10 If Latin prose admitted elision in non-metrical passages, the *-em* of *essem* might be elided to produce the aural effect *ess-et esset*, leaving only the consul as agent and bolstering the *adulescens*' rejection of agency. On prosody and elision in Latin prose, see, e.g., Riggsby 1991.

the Romans, chiefly the passage under the yoke.[11] This tight symmetry, as Oakley has pointed out, has its central axis in the consular elections for 321 BC and in the subsequent first speech of Postumius in 9.8.1, in which the former consul speaks extensively for the first time.[12] Since the episode also begins with the consuls' decision to enter the gorge and ends with Papirius Cursus' victory in Luceria, it is evident that the consuls play a particularly important role throughout.

This sense of consular importance is borne out more fully by Oakley's observation that deliberation, especially faulty deliberation, is a key theme of the narrative.[13] The English word "deliberation," however, while capturing the spirit of indecision and the demands of choice in the narrative, occludes the tighter semantic range of decision-making in the text. In fact, deliberation in this episode, on both the Roman and Samnite sides, is precisely characterized as the taking of counsel. The Romans choose which path to follow by means of a *consultatio* (9.2.5 *ea modo, qua irent, consultatio fuit*), while the Samnites, who cannot decide what to do with the trapped Roman armies, send letters to Pontius Herennius to ask his advice (9.3.4 *per litteras consulendum censent*; cf. 9.3.6, where Herennius is *consultus ab nuntio filii*). Indeed, verbs of counsel – *consulo*, *consultare*, and their cognates – appear ten times in the episode, while the related noun *consilium* appears fourteen times, with both verb and noun divided roughly evenly between Romans and Samnites. The act of giving counsel, *consulere* or *consultare*, is, almost by definition, the proper activity of the consuls, who, according to the popular etymologies of the period, were tasked with, among other things, counseling well.[14] It should thus not be surprising that the word *consul* appears in this episode thirty-six times, divided more or less

[11] 9.15.7 *septem milia militum sub iugum missa praedaque ingens Luceriae capta, receptis omnibus signis armisque quae ad Caudium amissa erant et, quod omnia superabat gaudia, equitibus reciperatis quos pignora pacis custodiendos Luceriam Samnites dederant* ("Seven thousand soldiers were sent under the yoke, and a huge amount of plunder was captured in Luceria, and the weapons and standards that had been lost in Caudium were restored. But the thing that caused most joy was that the knights who were handed over as hostages for the treaty, and guarded by the Samnites in Luceria, were also restored"). The restoration of the hostages caps the Roman victory, just as the surrender of the *sponsores* capped the Roman defeat.

[12] Oakley 2005a: 11–12, following Bruckmann 1936: 3. Chaplin 2000: 33 locates the turn in 12.1–4, as the Romans attempt to surrender the *sponsores*, only to be rejected by the Samnites. Chaplin's and Oakley's views, however, need not be mutually exclusive, since the two points they identify bracket the portion of events when the Romans begin to disentangle the mess they have created at the Forks.

[13] Oakely 2005a: 23–4; Morello 2003.

[14] Varro, *Ling.* 5.80 explains *consul* as *qui consuleret populum et senatum* ("he who would counsel the people and senate") and offers as an alternative Accius' famous definition, on which see further below and p. 54).

equally between its two parts. Thus, the theme of deliberation reveals also a thematic fascination with the consuls, their function, and their failure or success to perform it. This interest is bolstered also by the proliferation of other counselors, who become themselves surrogate figures for the consuls: the legate Lentulus, the tribunes of the plebs, and, most successfully, the new consuls Papirius Cursor and Publilius Philo, whose election not only enables their own action but finally releases the state from the paralysis of the Caudine ambush.

Taking counsel, and doing it well, therefore emerges as a central concern in this narrative and as such helps to sharpen the story of consular failure. If, as Accius' famous fragment (fr. 3 Klotz) suggests, a consul was someone who *recte consuleret* ("counsels well"), the failure of deliberation throughout the episode points up a marked failure by the consuls to live up to their most basic definition. The failure of the consuls, further, occurs on multiple levels: military, deliberative, and in consequence, symbolic or representative. The consuls first fail to choose the right path in their *consultatio*, and once trapped they are unable to offer the army any useful counsel, so that Livy concludes the scene by noting that night found the Romans *querentes magis quam consultantes* (9.3.1 "complaining more than deliberating"). The consuls' second failure is a consequence of the first; having been thoroughly trapped, they offer no battle, although at least some of the soldiers express a desire to attempt battle despite the impossible odds (9.3.2 *omnia aequa et plana erunt Romano in perfidum Samnitem pugnanti*, "everything is flat and open to a Roman fighting a treacherous Samnite"), and even those who despair deplore the inactivity (9.3.3 *sedens bellum conficiet*, "[the enemy] would end the war without even getting up").

The Romans, therefore, struggle to find not only good advice, but also purpose and agency. I have noted already that the decision to enter the gorge is the result of a faulty *consultatio*, itself the result of an elaborate Samnite ruse, wherein the Romans are fed false information about Samnite maneuvers, which impels the consuls into an overly hasty decision. Although the consuls deliberate to decide which of the two paths available to them they might choose, the decision itself is simply narrated, without any report on the reasons or content of deliberation (9.2.9 *in eum campum . . . Romani . . . pergerent*, "The Romans proceeded to that field"). Instead, Livy fills up the space between *consultatio* in 9.2.5 and the beginning of Roman movement in 9.2.9 by giving a detailed account of both paths, as well as of the gorge itself. The creative license Livy allows himself in this topographical description has been amply treated, but it is worth noting also that this short descriptive passage fills out the consuls' debate.[15] The narrative gaze takes in both options and focuses in on the Caudine Forks, just as the consuls, presumably, discussed both options to zero in on the (wrong) one.[16]

This same state of affairs, with the narrative working around the consuls' indecision, continues as the Romans enter the gorge and both sides settle in for a long impasse. At this stage, however, the narrative focus expands to include also the Roman army, whose point of view will dominate the narrative for the entire duration of the stay in the gorge. Livy's first vignette of the Romans already delineates a tension between the inactivity of the consuls and the activity of the soliders, especially as they look to the consuls for guidance:

> sistunt inde gradum sine ullius imperio stuporque omnium animos ac uelut torpor quidam insolitus membra tenet, intuentesque alii alios, cum alterum quisque compotem magis mentis ac consilii ducerent, diu immobiles silent; deinde, ubi praetoria consulum erigi uidere et expedire quosdam utilia operi, quamquam ludibrio fore munientes perditis rebus ac spe omni adempta cernebant, tamen, ne culpam malis adderent, pro se quisque nec hortante ullo nec imperante ad muniendum uersi castra propter aquam uallo circumdant, sua ipsi opera laboremque inritum, praeterquam quod hostes superbe increpabant, cum miserabili confessione eludentes. ad consules maestos, ne aduocantes quidem in consilium, quando nec consilio nec auxilio locus esset, sua sponte legati ac tribuni conueniunt militesque ad praetorium uersi opem, quam uix di immortales ferre poterant, ab ducibus exposcunt. (Livy 9.2.10–15)

> At this they halted, without any command being issued, and everyone's spirits were dazed, and it was as if their limbs were struck by some unaccustomed sluggishness. And they all looked at each other, as if maybe someone else might be of sounder mind and advice, and so they stood, fixed to the spot without a word, for a long time. But then, when they saw that the consuls' tents were being set up, and that some soldiers were getting their tools out, even though they could see that it was laughable to throw up fortifications

15 On the topography of the Forks: Oakley 2005a: 52–60, with further references. On Livy's illusory description: Horsfall 1982, Morello 2003, and more generally Horsfall 1985.

16 The second-person address, to which Livy switches as he describes the path through the Forks, is likewise evocative. As a feature of Latin historiographical style (Gilmartin 1975), the "imaginary" second-person subjunctive was common to geographical descriptions (cf. Oakley 2005a: 60–1) and as such helped to create the vivid experience (*enargeia*) of the reader in the text. The second person, however, seems to have been taken over from oratorical practice (Gilmartin 1975: 105) and here, at least, retains some rhetorical flavor, as it mimics one of the disputants arguing for – or more intriguingly, against – the decision to enter the gorge. On the technique of narrative editorializing, especially as it pertains to historiographical treatment of legal and procedural materials: Damon 1999.

> when the day was already lost and all hope was snatched away, still, lest they add blame to their woes, they each fell to digging, without encouragement or command, and fortifying a camp close to water. They even joked, with miserable honesty, about their futile work and effort, while the enemy jeered haughtily. The legates and the tribunes gathered spontaneously around the wretched consuls, who had not even summoned their council, since that was no place for either advice or help, and the soldiers turned to the command tent and demanded help from their leaders, which the immortal gods would have been barely able to furnish.

The dolorous scene vacillates markedly between the Roman soldiers' feeling of helplessness – strengthened by Livy's final remark that help was beyond even the gods – and their tendency towards self-reliance. Here it is worthwhile tracking how those two feelings map onto the consular presence in the camp. The first thing to note is that the consuls themselves, at this stage, do absolutely nothing.[17] In fact, Livy throughout highlights the absence of any of the actions they might have been expected to perform. This is most explicit in the final lines of this vignette, when the army assembles automatically and spontaneously (*sua sponte*), to demand help (*opem . . . exposcunt*) from consuls who are unable even to summon a council, mired as they are in hopelessness (*quando nec consilio nec auxilio locus esset*).[18] This demand for help, which goes largely unanswered, concludes a scene remarkable for its precise development of trapped movement. The men, who begin the scene by standing stock-still – *sistunt, stupor, torpor, immobiles* – awaken from their dazed shock when they see the consular command tent being erected (*ubi praetoria consulum erigi uidere*). The sight, along with the spontaneous actions of some of the soldiers, drives the Romans to build and fortify a proper camp, and having done so they gather around their leaders for an assembly. Despite the seeming propriety inspired by the view of consular command, however,

17 Morello's comment on this passage that "the leaders do not feature in the narrative" (1996: 79), along with her view that the consuls first appear in the surrender scene (1996: 96), is too reductive, since it ignores the fact that the consuls do feature in the text throughout, but not in a positive or successful fashion. As I go on to argue, the tension between expectation and reality in fact animates the episode.

18 *Exposcere*, a verb which appears nineteen times in extant Livy, gives the scene added poignancy. Its semantic range connotes a regular demand, as the soliders are *prima facie* doing, but stretches also to encompass a request from the gods, as in prayer (*TLL* s.v. 1172.10–26), as well as, pertinently, a demand for surrender (*TLL* s.v. 1771.20–34). The consuls are therefore cast in the two extreme points of their military activities: revered as gods, as on a triumph, and the object of a demand to surrender. This semantic range prefigures as well the remainder of the plot: first the actual surrender to the Samnites, which the consuls share with the soldiers, and then the ritualistic surrender of only the *sponsores*.

the army continues as it started, without actual command: *sine ullius imperio* ~ *nec . . . ullo . . . imperante*. The absence of *imperium* contrasts sharply with the presence of the consuls, and the final moment, when the army expectantly watches them, thus neatly dramatizes the congruency of *imperium* and *consilium* in the episode. The consuls, however, can offer neither, so the army must find its *consilia* elsewhere. Indeed, the narrative resolves finally into the historiographical topos of conversational *sermones*.[19] Although Livy qualifies the talk as complaining (*querentes*) rather than taking counsel (*consultantes*), the tight exchange nevertheless has a deliberative air, much like Livy's description of the Caudine path.

It is perhaps worth noting further in this context, that, for this portion of the narrative, the Samnites suffer from the opposite problem: their military good fortune is accompanied by an excess of counsel. After finding themselves bereft of any source of advice (9.3.4 *ne Samnitibus quidem consilium tam laetis suppetebat rebus*, "good advice was not at the ready even for the Samnites, though things were going so well for them"), they overcompensate for their initial lack by demanding more and more advice, none of which they actually accept: 9.3.10 *priore se consilio . . . altero consilio . . . tertium nullum consilium esse*. The source of this advice, crucially, is not their *imperator*, Gaius Herennius, but rather his aged father, who performs the traditional role of the "tragic warning figure" and dispenses his advice by messenger as well as in person.[20] And, of course, the Samnites settle precisely on a *tertium consilium*, sending the Romans under the yoke, thus ensuring both the survival of the Roman army and the increased enmity of the Romans. In due course they come to rue their choice (9.12.1 *et sero ac nequiquam laudare senis Ponti utraque consilia*, "too late and in vain they praised both of the old Pontius' proposals"). Despite its various flaws, however, the Samnite narrative is clearly a mirror image of the Roman, highlighting by its excesses precisely what the Romans so desperately lack.

Pontius Herennius also finds parallels in a sequence of surrogate authority figures, mostly on the Roman side, who attempt to fulfill the consular role of either offering counsel or, as is more appropriate to the military context of the episode, making decisions and exercising *imperium*. We have seen already how Livy deploys narrative techniques to achieve that effect,

19 Note the repetition of *alius* in 9.3.1–3, capped by 9.3.4 *his in uicem sermonibus qua cibi qua quietis immemor nox traducta est* ("in such discussions they passed the night, forgetful of either food or sleep").

20 "Tragic warner": Oakley 2005a: 68–9, with further references. On unheeded warnings as exemplary failure: Chaplin 2000: 78–85.

glossing over moments of crisis by fronting other voices, whether his own or those of the soldiers. This happens even in moments where it might have been reasonable to assume that the consuls and other magistrates were involved, for example the Romans' repeated failed attempts to break out, which Livy reports obliquely and in passing: 9.4.1 *cum frustra multi conatus ad erumpendum capti essent... uicti necessitate legatos mittunt* ("when the captives' many attempts to break out were contained... in defeat they were forced to send emissaries"). The plural form of the verbs must include the consuls, since it is unlikely that, even if the attempt to break out were spontaneous, any dispatch of official emissaries would have been possible without the consular imprimatur. Livy's earlier description of the scene in the camp, however, primes the reader to take the plurals, and therefore the agents of any Roman action, in a much more generalized sense, with the Romans acting still out of habit rather than under any explicit command. The consuls, in fact, do not appear at all until the emissaries return, and then only to advertise their recurrent inability to act: 9.4.7 *nec consules aut pro foedere tam turpi aut contra foedus tam necessarium hiscere possent*... ("the consuls were unable to speak either for such a shameful treaty or against a treaty so necessary... ").[21] This suppression, or perhaps arrogation, of the consular speech is part and parcel of Livy's broader technique in this first part of the episode; it continues here, as the speech of the legate Lentulus, rather than of the consuls, provides the impetus for the surrender. Ironically, Lentulus is referred to as the foremost of the legates in courage and honors (9.4.7 *princeps legatorum uirtute atque honoribus*) and was himself a former consul. Lentulus therefore highlights not only the impotence of the current pair of consuls, but also the decline in consular behavior overall.[22] The best of the Romans can now only advocate shame and surrender.

The consuls, for their part, continue in their inability to speak until, paradoxically, they are given a direct order to do so. Lentulus concludes his speech, in which he assimilates the army's situation to the Gallic siege of Rome, by ordering the consuls to do what is necessary: 9.4.16 *ite,*

[21] The focalizing adjectives *turpi* and *necessarium* trace out the consular dilemma, torn as they are between the demands of honor and pragmatism, and Postumius repeats the phraseology in 9.8.4 *cum me seu turpi seu necessaria sponsione obstrinxi*, though he refers to a *sponsio* rather than a *foedus*, for rhetorical reasons. The aristocratic Roman expectation that soldiers stand and fight is expressed instead by the soldiers themselves (9.3.2–3), who have a much clearer sense of Roman honor, though a perhaps more hotheaded interpretation of the dangers involved. On Roman expectations of soldiers: Rosenstein 1990: 92–113.

[22] We know little of Lentulus beyond his consulship in 327 BC: Livy 8.22.8, with Oakley 1998: 652 and 2005a: 77.

consules, redimite armis ciuitatem, quam auro maiores uestri redemerunt ("go, consuls, buy back the city with arms, which your ancestors bought back with gold").[23] The consuls immediately and obediently then go to negotiate with Herennius (9.5.1 *profecti . . . ad conloquium*), although they aver that they are able to enter into a *foedus* without the authority of the people (9.5.1 *iniussu populi*), and without the correct religious procedures (9.5.1 *sine fetialibus caerimoniaque alia sollemni*).[24] After a brief discussion on whether the treaty was a *foedus* or a *sponsio* (9.5.2–3, a topic that will turn out to be of crucial importance, but which also continues Livy's practice of distracting attention from consular action), the treaty is signed: 9.5.4 *spoponderunt consules, legati, quaestores, tribuni militum, nominaque omnium qui spoponderunt exstant . . .* ("the consuls signed, and the legates, quaestors, and tribunes of the soldiers, and the names of those who signed survive . . . ").[25] Regardless of whether Livy has his legal information right, and whether or not the names of the *sponsores* do survive, the sequence of events from Lentulus' speech to the signing of the treaty sets up one of the more important themes of the episode. We have seen already how the narrative is driven by consular failure, and the signing of the treaty is no different in this regard, although it remains the sole occasion on which the consuls do much of anything. However, the signing of the treaty marks also a nadir in the consuls' position, as they are forced to admit that any action they take is necessarily done *iniussu populi*, without the approval of the people.[26]

This admission is all the more striking because the legal force it carries – that the treaty is meaningless without the imprimatur of the senate and people in Rome – both cements the impression of consular impotence Livy has so far given and contrasts in important ways with the speech of Lentulus. The rhetorical force of the speech, encapsulated in its last line (*ite consules*, quoted above), derives from a compare-and-contrast exercise

23 On Veii as intertext for military deliberation, see also Chapter 3: 121–2. On the phrase *ite, consules*, see Chapter 1: 50–1; the phrase alludes to the more standard *i, lictor . . .* , an allusion which cements the inverted power dynamics between the consuls and Lentulus.

24 For consuls as agents of diplomacy: Pina Polo 2011: 58–82. Eckstein 1987 argues that the senate responded to the decisions and impressions made by the general on the ground, but that this did not extend to policy making or diplomacy.

25 On *sponsio* and *foedus*: Crawford 1973; Oakley 2005a: 31–4. For a discussion of *foedera* in Livy: Gladhill 2008: 90–132, though without discussion of Caudium.

26 On *sponsio* as a legal enactment of *uoluntas*, cf. Varro, *Ling.* 6.69 *spondere est dicere spondeo, a sponte: nam id ualet et a uoluntate* ("to swear an oath is to say 'I swear,' from 'voluntarily': for it is both binding and voluntary." Cf. Festus 441, 1–2, citing the Augustan Verrius Flaccus *sponte sua, id est a uoluntate* ("voluntarility, that is, by one's wishes"), and Flobert 1985: 146–7. For *uoluntas populi* as a political principle, see my discussion in Chapter 4.

between the present conditions and the situation of the Gallic siege of the Capitoline. Lentulus' father, we are told, was the only one set against the decision to ransom the city with gold (9.4.8 *unum non fuisse auctorem*). His son, by contrast, in giving the speech and urging the consuls to treat with the Samnites, becomes the *unus auctor* of the Caudine treaty, since his is the only voice given substantial narrative space.[27] *Auctor*, and the authorship of proposals, will in turn become one of the redeeming features of the consul Postumius, silent now, but who will later be marked as the author of the treaty (9.8.11 *uix crederent illum eundem esse Sp. Postumium qui auctor tam foedae pacis fuisset*, "they could barely believe that this was the same Sp. Postumius who was the author of such a foul peace") and earn the senate's approval as *auctor* of the proposal to surrender the *sponsores* to the Samnites (9.10.1 *mouit patres conscriptos cum causa tum auctor*, "the plea as well as its author moved the senators"). Being *auctor*, therefore, is also a marker of agency and command (*auctoritas*), which ought to have been in the province of the consuls alone, but which Lentulus usurps temporarily out of necessity.[28]

At the heart of Lentulus' speech, however, is the fundamental difference between the besieged Capitol and the besieged army at Caudium.[29] It is here also that Lentulus begins to articulate the consuls' failure to stand as a synecdoche for Rome itself.

> equidem mortem pro patria praeclaram esse fateor et me uel deuouere pro populo Romamo legionbusque uel in medios me immittere hostes paratus sum; sed hic patriam uideo, hic quidquid Romanarum legionum est; quae nisi pro se ipsis ad mortem ruere uolunt, quid habent quod morte sua seruent? tecta urbis, dicat aliquis, et moenia et eam turbam a qua urbs incolitur. immo hercule produntur ea omnia deleto hoc exercitu, non seruantur. quis enim ea tuebitur? (Livy 9.4.10–12)

> But I confess that dying for the homeland is glorious, and that I am ready to devote myself in exchange for the Roman people and legions, or rush headlong into the midst of the enemy. But here I see my homeland, here,

27 On the authenticity of Lentulus' father: Oakley 2005a: 80. The phrase *unus auctor* recalls the *unus uir* topos, of which the prime example is Camillus, whom Lentulus evokes. This *unus uir*, however, does not save the day but rather urges Roman surrender, though a more generous reading would suggest that he merely casts himself as an *exemplum* of pragmatism rather than blinkered heroism. *Vnus auctor* might also be, in context, a self-reflexive joke, since Livy reveals at least one of his sources, Claudius Quadrigarius, which makes for at least two *auctores*, if not more. On characters like Camillus or external authorities like Augustus competing with the authority of Livy see Feldherr 1998: 78–81; Sailor 2006.

28 For *auctoritas* derived *ab auctor*: *TLL* 2.6.1213.67, *OLD* s.v. "auctoritas"; *OLD* s.v. "auctor" 9 "a writer who is regarded as a master of his subject or as providing reliable evidence, an authority."

29 For a close reading of the whole speech: Morello 1996: 86–95.

all that is left of the Roman legions; and unless they are ready to rush at the enemy on their own behalf, what will they have to save by dying? The roofs and walls of the city, someone might say, and that rabble who live within the city. But surely they are betrayed by the loss of this army, not saved. For who will protect them then?

As it happens, the answer to Lentulus' rhetorical question is a Camillus-like figure, who might swoop in to rescue the city in its time of need (9.4.14 *an a Veiis exercitum Camilumque ducem implorabunt?*). The trouble, Lentulus suggests, is that such a figure does not exist, since both consuls and what is left of the Roman army are trapped here at the gorge. On one level, this argument is patently false, as the narrative goes on to show. When Rome hears of the situation at Caudium, they immediately begin to levy a new army, even if news of the ignominious surrender causes them to lose heart.[30] What this rhetoric does achieve, however, is to present the trapped Roman army as singular and irreplaceable, and more crucially, entirely congruent with the state.[31] Lentulus' speech is therefore also a negative image of the exhortatory speech, whose persuasive aim is therefore inaction and surrender, excluding by default such elements – hearths, walls, women and children (the *imbellis* and *inermis multitudo* of 9.4.13) – which might have heightened emotions and rallied the troops.[32]

Such negativity is appropriate also because inaction has been the order of the day thus far, especially for the consuls, who fall far short of either of the consular *exempla* Lentulus invokes. The first one – Camillus – has already been mentioned, and it is important here as an instance of the consul as savior, a role which Caesar had developed to a high art in his *commentarii*.[33] This image is immediately negated, not only as improbable in the circumstances, but also because of its chronological irrelevance: a Camillus would only be necessary if, and only if, this army were to

[30] 9.7.6–7 *iam et Romae sua infamis clades erat. obsessos primum audierunt; tristior deinde ignominiosae pacis magis quam periculi nuntius fuit. ad famam obsidionis dilectus haberi coeptus erat; dimissus deinde auxiliorum apparatus, postquam deditionem tam foede factam acceperunt* . . . ("The disaster was already infamous in Rome. First they heard about the siege; then a sadder message than the danger, that of the ignominious treaty. A draft was begun when news came of the siege; the preparation of relief forces was dropped, after they heard that the surrender had already been made so dishonorably").

[31] This congruence is supported by the fact that, once the Roman morale is restored in 9.10.7, they hold a draft and re-enlist the Caudine legions: 9.10.6 *in ciuitate ira odioque ardente dilectus prope omnium uoluntariorum fuit. rescriptae ex eodem milite nouae legiones ductusque ad Caudium exercitus* ("in a city burning with anger and hate a draft was held, almost entirely from volunteers. New legions were re-enlisted from the same body of soldiers, and the army was led to Caudium"). On *rescriptae* as "re-enlisted," a Livian *hapax*: Oakley 2005a: 133.

[32] On the exhortatory speech, see p. 109 n. 30.

[33] Kraus 2005: 188–90. On Caesar relative to his army and officers, see Welch 1998 and Goldsworthy 1998.

perish at Caudium in parallel with the Roman defeat at the Allia. This image of the magistrate-general, active, energetic, and heroic, is therefore a counterfactual phantasm, something that generic expectations might call for, but which the situation on the ground ultimately transcends. As such, it goes well with Lentulus' overall strategy, which must deconstruct and pre-empt the well-worn trope of an army *in extremis*, covering itself in glory or dying in the attempt.[34] This strategy, however, not only holds up topical models for consular behavior but also constructs a narrowed focus on the army and its leaders as a discrete and unique *exemplum*, a living miniature of the Roman state.

Assimilation and reintegration

It is now time to return to the gorge, and to the events following the signing of the treaty. A useful way to see how the consular *persona* is deconstructed after the treaty, and then reconstructed again, is to track the consuls themselves, from the signing and passing under the yoke to their return to Rome. The consuls' return to the camp causes a great lament, and Livy's phraseology, *redintegrauit luctum* (9.5.6 "restored the mourning"), is striking, both because it suggests that there had been a phase where such laments had ceased, and because the restoration of *luctus* is one of the few actions the consuls achieve in the gorge. In fact, negative affect has become characteristic of the consuls, since their return to the camp replays the return of an earlier *legatio*, which brought back Herennius' demands and prompted Lentulus' speech. The response then was *tantus gemitus . . . tantaque maestitia* (9.4.6 "such great weeping . . . and such great sadness"), two verbal elements which together make up *luctus*, parsed out into its constituent parts by the initial shock and reconstituted, indeed capped, by the return of the consuls.

Mourning triggers a more hostile response:

> redintegrauit luctum in castris consulum aduentus, ut uix ab iis abstinerent manus, quorum temeritate in eum locum deducti essent, quorum ignauia foedius inde quam uenissent abituri: illis non ducem locorum, non exploratorem fuisse; beluarum modo caecos in foueam missos. (Livy 9.5.6–7)
>
> The arrival of the consuls restored the mourning in the camps, such that the men barely refrained from violence against those by whose foolishness they were led to this place, by whose cowardice they would leave more shamefully

[34] Cf my discussion in Chapter 3: 118–27.

than they had come; the consuls did not have a guide to the area, no scout; like beasts, they were blindly sent into the trap.

The set of terms the men now apply to the consuls – *temeritas, ignauia, belua* – starkly reveal how far they have fallen in the army's estimation. The phrase *illis ducem locorum* is particularly suggestive, since it can be taken equally as an attack on the consuls or as self-pity by the soldiers. For the consuls, to be without a *dux* is both a technical matter – to be without a guide – but also a matter of political order: the consuls are themselves *duces*, albeit failed at their task. For the men to be without a *dux*, however, implies a more serious breakdown of authority and command and reflects well the sentiment in the Roman camp.

Nevertheless, the looming passage under the yoke begins some process of rapprochement, as the men go on to look at each other, at the arms they will be required to throw down, and imagine with increasing horror the passing under the yoke and its subsequent indignities.[35] The men's concern for *arma*, expressed from Lentulus' *redimite armis* ("buy back with arms") through to the soldiers' obsessive focus on them in the moments before the surrender (9.5.8 *contemplari arma*; 5.10 *sine ferro*; 5.10 *non stringere licuisse gladios*; 5.10 *nequiquam arma*), stands, in a sense, for their actual surrender. When the time comes for the final humiliation, however, it is the stripping away of the consuls' insignia, rather than the army's weapons, which is the focus of the narrative and of the spectacle. The soldiers are ordered out of their camp *cum singulis uestimentis inermes* (9.5.12 "unarmed and with one garment each"), and the hostages are given over, but those are mere preliminaries. Emotions begin to run high when the consuls are ordered forward, and their insignia of office are removed: *tum a consulibus abire lictores iussi paludamentaque detracta* (9.5.13 "then the lictors were ordered to leave the consuls, and their cloaks were removed"). Between them, the lictors and the *paludamenta* symbolize the consuls' *imperium* and *potestas*, and their absence cements ritually the humiliation and the inefficacy of both consuls and paraphernalia. It is this that finally wins them some sympathy from their men, who all forget their own trouble and their former loathing and avert their eyes from the unspeakable spectacle

[35] 9.5.8–9 *proponere sibimet ipsi ante oculos iugum hostile et ludibria uictoris et uoltus superbos et per armatos inermium iter, inde foedi agminis miserabilem uiam per sociorum urbes, reditum in patriam ad parentes, quo saepe ipsi maioresque eorum triumphantes uenissent*... ("and they each placed before their eyes the hostile yoke and the mockery of the victor and the haughty faces and the unarmed path among armed men, and then the wretched cohort's miserable path through the cities of the allies, the return to the city, to their parents, which often both they and their ancestors had made in triumph ... ").

(9.5.13–14 *tantam inter eos . . . miserationem fecit ut suae quisque condicionis oblitus ab illa deformatione tantae maiestatis uelut ab nefando spectaculo auerteret oculos*, "this caused such great pity that each one of them, forgetful of his own condition, averted his eyes from the disfiguring of such grandeur, as if from a foul spectacle"). The soldiers' pity is here to be expected, especially since they function as an internal, guiding audience for the reader, whose pity ought to need only the slightest of goads to be provoked.[36] The forgetfulness it occasions, however, is more interesting, not only because forgetfulness of their own principles is, arguably, what led the Romans into these dire straits, but also because it handily obfuscates the soldiers' own complicity in the deformation of the consuls' *maiestas*. Whereas the Samnites achieve this effect by physical removal of the consular marks of honor, the Romans do so by dehumanizing the consuls, and turning them, albeit metaphorically, into blind beasts.

Literally as well as spatially, this is the nadir of the consular experience – consigned by their men to a metaphorical *fouea*, a trap which literally means a pit, and therefore below level ground. They are also sent under the yoke, a procedure which required bending low to the ground, and they do so *prope seminudi* (9.6.1 "almost half-naked"), a rhetorical exaggeration which casts their loss of the *paludamentum* as worse than the men's *singulum uestimentum*. Indeed, as the Roman army leaves the gorge, Livy compares them to men returned from the dead, blinking in the light of a new day: *etsi uelut ab inferis extracti tum primum lucem aspicere uisi sunt, tamen ipsa lux ita deforme intuentibus agmen omni morte tristior fuit* (9.6.3 "although they appeared like men released from the netherworld upon seeing the light for the first time, still that same light was sadder than any death for those beholding the ugly column"). *Deforme agmen* here picks up *deformatione tantae maiestatis* in 9.5.14 and therefore begins the process of reconciling consuls and leaders, as the consular experience encompasses the whole army. The language of sight is important in accomplishing this work, since for those beholding the Roman *agmen* there is now no meaningful way to differentiate between the Roman ranks. They are all deformed, in some way, and that collective change renders them a single, undifferentiated mass. This uniformity cannot last long, however, since it is in itself an offense to the consular *maiestas*, such that, for the moment at least, the very same thing that bridges the rift between consuls and men also vitiates the consuls' authority.

36 It is interesting that the soldiers' *miseratio* prompts them to look away, thus breaking the sight lines that normally connect audience and spectacle in historiography, and transforming empathy into revulsion: Levene 1997, Feldherr 1998, and Konstan 2001: 75–104.

The process of restoration begins even before the army arrives back at Rome. The city of Capua, upon seeing the bedraggled column, recognizes the problem immediately and sets about re-establishing the army's ranks: *confestim insignia sua consulibus, [fasces, lictores,] arma, equos, uestimenta, commeatus militibus benigne mittunt* (9.6.6–7 "immediately they kindly sent their proper ensigns to the consuls [fasces, lictors], as well as weapons, horses, garments, and supplies for the soldiers"). The words *fasces* and *lictores* are usually excised by editors of the texts, because both *fasces* and lictors were not within Capua's purview to restore.[37] Indeed there is no reason to believe that the lictors were kept back in the Caudine gorge, though their *fasces* may have been surrendered with the rest of the Roman *arma*. Beyond such speculation, however, this scribal variant highlights how successful Livy is in constructing an image of the denuded consuls, and how pity for the Roman plight moves the Capuans. Indeed, the sentiment they feel, *miseratio* (9.6.5), is the very same that moves the Roman soldiers finally to pity the same consuls they had reviled, and which is likewise spurred by the sight of the separation of consuls and their paraphernalia. The analogy can be taken as political – the consuls are to the men as Rome is to Capua – but it also continues the growing sense of uniformity and lack of distinction between rank and officers occasioned by the treaty and the yoke.

The Capuans' generosity, however, is insufficient, even if it marks the beginning of the Roman recovery, since Rome itself mirrors the situation of the army in the gorge. Having begun a draft for a new army, news of the treaty causes the Romans to despair and drives them to the same emotion – *luctus* – and the same lack of leadership experienced by the army: 9.7.7 *extemploque sine ulla publica auctoritate consensum in omnem formam luctus est* ("and immediately, without any official authority, they fell to every form of mourning"). As in the gorge, mourning precedes a ritualistic removal of status insignia, in this case by the senators, who put off their golden rings and broad-striped togas (9.7.8 *lati claui, anuli aurei positi*), thus undergoing another kind of deformation in sympathy with the army. Unlike the Capuans, however, the people at Rome feel anger against the entire army, consuls as well as soldiers, regardless of administrative responsibility (9.7.9 *nec ducibus solum atque auctoribus sponsoribusque pacis irasci sed innoxios etiam milites odisse*). Thus, though the city takes on an appearance parallel to that of the army, its people feel themselves distinct enough to criticize, and, like the Capuans, they do so according to hierarchical ranks,

[37] Oakley 2005a: 99. Valerius Maximus, whose account is so close to Livy's "that it must be lifted straight from him" (p. 99) has simply *consulibus insignia honoris* (5.1.*ext*.5), which has much the same effect.

gradations which Livy lists even as he insists that they made no difference to the Romans' anger. In such circumstances, it is little wonder that the army slinks into Rome late in the day, and the men vanish into their homes. Unlike the rank and file, however, such action has greater significance for a consul in office. The entrance into the city itself is already something of a mockery of the ideal entrance, the triumph – which the soldiers themselves had lamented earlier in their trek. The real sting, however, comes when the consuls refuse to continue in office, their last action the appointment of a dictator in charge of holding the election: 9.7.12 *consules in priuato abditi nihil pro magistratu agere nisi quod expressum senatus consulto est ut dictatorem dicerent comitiorum causa* ("the consuls retired to their homes and did nothing further in an official capacity except what was explicitly required by the decree of the senate, namely that they appoint a dictator for holding the elections"). The withdrawal into the private sphere parallels that of the troops (9.7.11 *se in suis quisque tectis abdiderunt*), but it also now makes concrete what has been the case all along – this set of consuls had never really acted as a consul ought (note especially *nihil pro magistratu agere*). Indeed, blending into the common body of men means simply a diminution of the power of the consulship, not the restoration of the ability to act on behalf of the people. The remedy turns out to be, on the one hand, the election of new consuls, and, on the other, Postumius' embracing of his responsibility for the treaty, transforming it from military inefficacy to ritual potency.

Substitution and sacrifice

The second consular *exemplum* in Lentulus' speech – the *deuotio* – is of a slightly different sort, and it, too, is revealing of the Caudine dynamics. This example, too, is presented as a hypothetical scenario, and one which Lentulus asserts he would have performed himself (9.4.10 *me uel deuouere . . . paratus sum*, "I am ready . . . to devote myself"), had he not been stopped by the sight of the *patria*, embodied in the Roman legions. Unlike Camillus, who, as dictator, has something of the superhero about him, the *deuotio* is very much a consular *exemplum*, inasmuch as only a consul could undertake the ritual, whether or not he chose to devote himself or appoint another sacrifice in his stead.[38] As such, it balances the Camillus example well, and it also bolsters Lentulus' posturing as a surrogate consul, as he imagines himself undertaking (or, rather, pointedly shirking)

[38] On the *deuotio* as a consular exercise, see my discussion in Chapter 3: 113–15.

a consular exemplary legacy. But the mention of the *deuotio* here, like the use of *auctor* above, also looks proleptically to the senatorial response to the consul Postumius' second speech: 9.10.3 *Postumius in ore erat; eum laudibus ad caelum ferebant, deuotioni P. Deci consulis, aliis claris facinoribus aequabant* ("Everybody was talking about Postumius; they praised him to the heavens and made comparisons to the *deuotio* of P. Decius the consul and other great deeds"). In spite of the comparison we can distinguish clearly between the aim of each attempt: Decius is trying to ensure victory for the Romans, while Postumius is trying to find a legalistic way around an embarrassing treaty. The element of self-sacrifice is shared, but not the purpose: Decius' *deuotio* binds Rome and the consul together in an inextricable bond, while Postumius goes out of his way to dismantle that bond, the better to protect Rome from religious infamy.

This process is played out in the interaction between the main four speeches of this half of the episode, two by the consul Postumius and one each by Pontius Herennius and the tribunes of the plebs, since they offer judgment on the events and bring together some of the rhetorical strategies used by Lentulus and by the Samnites early on. The Caudine treaty is naturally the first order of business once the army returns and the new consuls are elected, and the debate on it consists in large part of the two speeches of the former consul Spurius Postumius, both arguing the same basic point: the peace was not binding on the people, because it was not made with their approval. Consequently, only the *sponsores* are responsible for it, and they, including Postumius himself, ought to be surrendered to the Samnites in order to uphold Rome's honor and repudiate the peace.[39] I have already mentioned that this proposal leads to comparison with the *deuotio Deciana*, and indeed it is part of a tradition of heroic self-sacrifice, manifested here through Roman legal sophistry. But Postumius' speech and indeed the repudiation of the treaty are geared not towards ensuring victory, as in the case of Decius, nor towards saving Rome from crushing defeat, as in the case of Camillus. Instead, Postumius' speech aims at removing an embarrassing stain on Rome's reputation, and thereby reconstituting his own *exemplum* as one of consular devotion rather than ignominy. The potential alternative course – that Rome simply accepts the treaty – is worth bearing in mind, however, not only because Postumius' interests are not necessarily congruent with Rome's, but also because there is reason to believe that, outside the historiographical tradition, Rome did not in fact

[39] This point is stated explictly on four separate occasions (9.8.5, 9.8.9, 9.9.4, 9.9.16) and, throughout Postumius' two speeches, is in fact the only item of substance he discusses.

break the Samnite treaty.[40] As such, Postumius' speeches, as might have been expected, serve above all as a mirror image to his own behavior at the gorge, and equally as a balance for the more standard consular *aristeia* of Papirius Cursor.

Postumius rises to speak wearing the same expression as he had worn when passing under the yoke (9.8.2 *qui ubi surrexit, eodem illo uoltu quo sub iugum missus erat*). The juxtaposition of the consul's hangdog expression and the upward movement of the verb *surrexit* recalls the disheartened Roman column as it left the Caudine Forks: upwardly mobile (9.6.3 *e saltu euasissent*), but still licking their wounds. If anything, however, the juxtaposition here in 9.8.2 is stronger, since *sub iugum* picks up directly on the contracted *sub* prefix of *surrexit*, making clear the spatial connections between Postumius' physical location and his mental state: to rise from below is to rise from beneath the yoke. By the end of the speech-making, however, Postumius is praised to the heavens: 9.10.3 *eum laudibus ad caelum ferebant*. Although the phrase is reasonably standard, here it is doubly poignant, first in its continuation of Postumius' upward motion, from the bottom of the pit to the heights of heaven, and second in the intratextual allusion to an early exploit of P. Decius Mus, who would, within three years, commit his *deuotio*.[41] The tension is resolved, somewhat paradoxically, in the content of the praise Postumius is offered, since it is there that he is compared (9.10.3 *aequabant*) to the *deuotio Deciana*, an act that synchronizes the two *exempla*.[42] The Decian allusion in *laudibus ad caelum ferebant*, however, is perhaps the most poignant of all, since this early exploit prefigures the Caudine Forks almost exactly: a consular error causes the Roman army to be captured at a ravine, with threatening Samnites all around.

> nam ab Saticula profectus Cornelius consul exercitum incaute in saltum caua ualle peruium circaque insessum ab hoste induxit nec prius quam recipi tuto signa non poterant imminentem capiti hostem uidit. (Livy 7.34.1–2)
>
> For the consul Cornelius, upon leaving Saticula, hastily led the army into a ravine within a hollow valley, which was was besieged all around by the enemy, and he did not see the enemy looming overhead before it was too late to turn the column around safely.

40 Oakley summarizes the arguments in 2005a: 34–8, with further references.

41 For the phrase, and its application to Decius: Oakley 1998: 348 *ad* 7.36.5.

42 The *deuotio Deciana* likewise has a strong tension between upward and downward mobility, since Decius is compared to a plague-star: 8.9.12 *haud secus quam pestifero sidere*. Curtius' leap into the chasm in the forum, which is also cast as a *deuotio*, is a more concrete instantiation of the *deuotus*' downward motion.

Fortunately for Cornelius, and unlike Caudium, there was, in fact, a way out, since the Samnites had not noticed that their camp, in turn, was visible and threatened from another hill (7.34.3 *imminentem hostium castris*). The besiegers now become the besieged, as Decius leads a small group of soldiers to capture the hill, from which they provide cover for the escape of the main column. Fury and indecision keep the Samnites from overrunning Decius and his force, though they also manage to keep the Roman forces from reuniting. In good heroic fashion, Decius inspires his men to make a dashing break for freedom in the dead of night, which they pull off almost faultlessly. In the midst of tiptoeing through the Samnite camp, however, one of the Romans knocks over a shield, which wakes the sentry. The Romans raise a shout loud enough to stupefy the Samnites, cut a path to safety, and push on to rejoin the main force, but not before taking a calculated break so as to arrive at the camp in broad daylight, the better to advertise their glory. Decius, of course, is praised to the sky (7.36.7 *Decium in caelum ferunt*) and makes a triumphal entrance to the camp (7.36.8 *castrensis triumphus*), whereupon he is praised again, this time by the consul (7.37.9 *orsusque meritas Deci laudes*). Not yet done with daring, Decius calls a halt to the proceeding, urging the consul to seize the opportunity when the Samnites are still in disarray. The army does so and the Samnites are routed.[43]

The story is everything the Caudine Forks is not. Luck does not abandon the Romans, either in the fortuitous presence of the hill, or the escape through the camp. Though the consul himself is hasty, his advisor is not the defeatist Lentulus, but rather the heroic Decius. Within this context, the later *deuotio* makes sense as part of a larger pattern of heroic substitution, which emphasizes the consul's relationship to the whole army rather than mere parts of it. As a young tribune Decius leads a cohort on a risky mission, and he is willing to sacrifice it for the safe escape of the whole army, even if that sacrifice never actually occurs. Later on as a consul, however, he will ritually and in actuality sacrifice his own person for the army, a sacrifice that proves effective. Postumius can hardly lay claim to such a legacy, and although he cannot be faulted for his pragmatism, Decius' *exemplum* makes a mockery of Postumius' self-sacrificial pretensions.

[43] A third possible intertext is the "Roman Leonidas" in Cato the Elder, *ap*. Gell. *NA* 3.7 = Cato fr. 83 P = Beck and Walter 4.7.a = *FRHist* F 76, wherein, during the First Punic War, an unnamed tribune of the soldiers leads a cohort on a suicide mission, with the consul's blessing, to relieve a beleagured Roman army. On the tribune as heroic exemplum: Popov-Reynolds 2010: 173–83; on the fragment, *FRHist* 3.121–4. Caudium, too, can be seen as a variant of the Thermopylae-scenario, on whose treatment in Livy see Chaplin 2010.

Decius urges his small force, unlike the cowed Roman army at Caudium, to fight even against impossible odds, falling in line with standard Roman rhetoric but also showing a foretaste of his consular abilities – so much so, in fact, that he is received in the camp with the honors due a consul (7.36.8 *omni honore tribunum consuli aequantibus*). He therefore provides a paradigm of consular behavior, years before he will attain the office itself. Postumius, meanwhile, attempts to recuperate what he can, but even this effort comes up short against the people's overly generous praise.

Decius, undoubtedly, was a unique sort of military tribune, while the tribunes of the soldiers at Caudium continue the anti-heroic theme of the whole episode. They do not figure very prominently at the gorge itself, but they do attempt to intercede their veto when the people prepare to vote for Postumius' proposal of surrender and repudiation.

> cum omnes laudibus modo prosequentes uirum in sententiam eius pedibus irent, temptata paulisper intercessio est ab L. Liuio et Q. Maelio tribunis plebis, qui neque exsolui religione populum aiebant deditione sua, nisi omnia Samnitibus qualia apud Caudium fuissent restituerentur, neque se pro eo quod spondendo pacem seruassent exercitum populi Romani poenam ullam meritos esse, neque ad extremum, cum sacrosancti essent, dedi hostibus uiolariue posse. (Livy 9.8.13–5)
>
> Just when everyone was praising and moving to vote on the proposal, the tribunes of the plebs, L. Livius and Q. Maelius, attempted to intercede the veto. They argued that the people would not be released from its religious obligation by handing them over, unless all other such advantages the Samnites had at Caudium were also restored; and that they had saved the army of the Roman people by acting as guarantors of the peace and deserved no punishment; and finally, that they could not be handed over to the enemy, since they were sacrosanct.

The intervention of the tribunes is not in itself remarkable, and the force of their rhetoric likewise deflates as they progress from religious propriety and ethics to legalistic self-preservation. Nevertheless, their presence lends the whole affair a greater complexity, not least because the identity of these tribunes as *tribuni plebis* conflates the tribunes of the plebs with the tribunes of the soldiers, the type of tribune likely to have served with the legions, and the one Livy explicitly mentions as signing the treaty.[44] The conflation has

[44] *Tribuni militum* signing the treaty: 9.5.4. Tribunes of the plebs normally stayed within city limits to ensure their *auxilium* was available to the citizens, though they were occasionally dispatched on special business (e.g. Lintott 1999: 124). Cicero, *Off.* 3.109, gives their names as Q. Maelius and Ti. Numicius rather than Maelius and Livius; on the textual problem of Minucius/Numitius/Numicius: Dyck 1996: 632.

various consequences, not least the conflation of people and army, but it highlights in particular the problem of defining magisterial behavior, even in cases where the distinctions between two offices were historically and legally clear. A historiographical "howler" thus opens up a broader political question by importing a new set of magisterial topoi and *exempla*. Consuls and tribunes ranged against each other are a historiographical cliché, but there are more topical concerns at work. Principally, the blurring of the distinction between *plebis* and *militum* in the designation of the tribunes, as well as their insistence on their sacrosanctity, evokes the function of the tribunes as a champion of the people, both in the sense of someone meant to protect them against the atrocities of the rich, and in the sense of someone meant to speak with their voice. For consul and tribunes to face off in this context highlights the disjunction between the consul and the people, as both sets of magistrates interpret the same gesture in two mutually exclusive ways.

What is especially striking, however, is that the tribunes' rhetoric is echoed by no other than Pontius Herennius, the Samnite *imperator*, in a speech he gives upon rejecting the surrender of the Roman *sponsores*, and in which he lectures the Romans at some length about honor, faithfulness, and consular decorum.

> populum Romanum appello; quem si sponsionis ad Furculas Caudinas factae paenitet, restituat legiones intra saltum quo saeptae fuerunt. nemo quemquam deceperit; omnia pro infecto sint; recipiant arma quae per pactionem tradiderunt; redeant in castra sua; quidquid pridie habuerunt quam in conloquium est uentum habeant; tum bellum et fortia consilia placeant, tum sponsio et pax repudietur. (Livy 9.11.3–4)

> I call upon the Roman people: if any of them repents of the agreement made at the Caudine Forks, let him send the legions back into the ravine in which they were penned. No one will have deceived anyone; everything will be as if nothing happened. Let them receive the weapons they have surrendered at the treaty. Let them return to their camp. Let them have whatever it was they had then the day before they came to conference. Then let them decide for war and harsher counsels. Then let the treaty and the peace be repudiated.

The apostrophe of the Roman people is already evocative of tribunician language, since *appello* was a regular verb for appeal to tribunician help by Roman citizens.[45] Whereas the tribunes' remark on restoring to the

[45] *Appello* as tribunician verb: *OLD* s.v 2c; cf. e.g. Livy 3.56.5 *tamen et tribunos appellauit et, nullo morante arreptus a uiatore, "prouoco" inquit* ("still he both called upon the tribunes, and when he

Samnites their earlier advantages is a general statement of principle, Pontius breaks down this statement into its specific constituent parts, rewinding events to a point where the Romans can choose for themselves a different ending. Pontius' rhetoric is, of course, not without self-interest: he does not, for instance, propose to restore events to a point earlier still, before the Romans were fed the false information which led them into the Caudine gorge. His proposal does, however, offer the Romans a chance to reassert themselves in the typical Roman mold, fighting a way out from a difficult situation. This reassertion of national character becomes all the more important in light of the rhetorical congruence between Herennius and the tribunes, which itself continues the Caudine theme of Samnite arrogation of Roman action. The surrender of the *sponsores*, therefore, is a halfway house that satisfies neither side, because it cannot ultimately undo the damage done at Caudium.

The congruence between Pontius' rhetoric and that of the tribunes, however, is typical more broadly of a rhetorical reciprocity between Pontius and the various magistrates of Rome. For example, for Pontius the Roman repudiation of the speech is treachery of a particularly Roman sort (9.11.6 *nunquamne causam defiet cur uicti pacto non stetis?*, "will you ever lack for a reason not to abide by a pact you made in defeat?"), and his examples are the hostages held by Porsenna, of which Cloelia is the most famous, and the now iconic Roman attempt to ransom the city from the Gauls. Pontius' choice of example, as well as his phraseology – 9.11.6 *auro ciuitatem a Gallis redimistis* ("you have redeemed the city from the Gauls with gold") – picks up, albeit unknowingly, on Lentulus' closing phrase, 9.4.16 *ite, consules, redimite armis ciuitatem, quam auro maiores uestri redemerunt* ("go, consuls, redeem the city with arms, which our ancestors redeemed with gold"). The irony, however, is pointed. The surrender of the *sponsores*, focused heavily as it is on Postumius, is merely another attempt to ransom the city, this time with the body of its magistrates. The old consuls thus set out to reconstitute the synecdochal relationship between magistrate and people, so that the new consuls in turn can wage a war of revenge on the Samnites. In so doing, these doubled consular actions begin to dispel the ethos of surrender valorized in Lentulus' speech, although the Romans significantly refuse to return to the gorge itself, thus leaving the surrender, the yoke, and even the treaty, as a live problem at the heart of the episode.

was snatched by the bailiff with no delay, he said 'I appeal'"; and 8.33.8 *tribunos plebis appello et prouoco ad populum* ("I call upon the tribunes, and appeal to the people"). On tribunician *auxilium* see now Arena 2012: 49–54.

Symmetry and the consular resurgence

From a narrative standpoint, it is not surprising that the episode of the Caudine Forks ends in a resounding Roman victory. Knowing themselves to be free of religious taint and with the treaty repudiated, the Romans are free to launch a vengeful war, which they accomplish with great success. At the head of the campaign are the two new consuls, Q. Publilius Philo and L. Papirius Cursor. Immediately, they embark on a two-pronged campaign, with Cursor besieging Luceria, where the Roman hostages are held, and with Philo lying in wait for the Samnite forces returning from Caudium. This campaign restores to the Romans most of their losses, as well as their lost dignity, and it suitably ends with Cursor returning to Rome in triumph, which Livy doubles by a passage of extended praise, known today as the *laus Cursoris*. More importantly, the campaign provides closure not only in material terms, but also in terms of magisterial prestige. If Postumius and Veturius bring the Romans low by their blundering inefficacy, by the end of the *laus Cursoris* confidence is so much restored that the episode formally ends with an image of the consul utterly in control:

> equites etiam aliquando ausos ab eo petere ut sibi pro re bene gesta laxaret aliquid laboris; quibus ille "ne nihil remissum dicatis, remitto" inquit, "ne utique dorsum demulceatis cum ex equis descendetis." et uis erat in eo uiro imperii ingens pariter in socios ciuesque. Praenestinus praetor per timorem segnius ex subsidiis suos duxerat in primam aciem; quem cum inambulans ante tabernaculum uocari iussisset, lictorem expedire securem iussit. ad quam uocem exanimi stante Praenestino, "agedum, lictor, excide radicem hanc" inquit "incommodam ambulantibus," perfusumque ultimi supplicii metu multa dicta dimisit. (Livy 9.16.15–18)

> The cavalrymen once dared to ask him to release them from some work as reward for good service. He said to them: "So that you do not say you've not been let off anything, you're free from patting your horse upon dismounting." And there was a great force in this man as much in command over the allies as over citizens. A Praenestine praetor was late, out of fear, to move his unit from the reserve to the front line. Cursor had him summoned, as he was walking about before his tent, and ordered his lictor to brandish his axe. When the Praenestine stood in shock at this order, Cursor said, "Come then, lictor, cut out that root – it's inconvenient to passers-by." Then he fined the man and sent him away, thoroughly stricken by fear of the ultimate punishment.

As often in Livy, the two seemingly unrelated vignettes interact in a number of ways. The consul, Cursor, is clearly the center of narrative attention, and it is his *bons mots* that Livy sets out to transmit as an illustration of *uis imperii.* But these two vignettes also implicate the consul in a set of relationships, social and legal, in which he asserts his command over two different types of subordinates. The Roman *equites* are members of the Roman aristocracy, of a class just below the consul's own senatorial rank, and clearly comfortable with the aristocratic idea of reward for good service (*pro re bene gesta*). Cursor, for his part, although he does not give them what they want, dismisses them in a jocular tone, and one which presumes a care, even if a comic one, for their bad opinion of him (*ne . . . dicatis*). The *Praenestinus praetor*, however, despite holding the highest office in his home town, sees quite a different face of the consul, even if Cursor maintains his jocular tone.[46] What is added is the theatrics of *imperium*, complete with an axe-wielding lictor, and a thinly veiled threat of eradication. The two vignettes, therefore, trope the consul's behavior in two related contexts. The first is within Roman society, as the consul *qua* Roman aristocrat interacts with men who are normally his peers, and whose relationship to him changed for the duration of his time in office. The second, on the other hand, shows the consul as a representation of Rome and its attitude towards its subordinate allies, an institutional façade that remains (or ought to remain) consistent even as the individuals behind the consular mask change.

The two halves, further, relate in a more formal symmetry, of which the contrast between cavalry and infantry is only one element. In the first half, physical movement is delineated only vaguely, but the impression left by the consul's words is of his own stillness and their movement. The point of his joke, as Oakley well brings out, is that his concession is so small as to be meaningless, but the repetition of the prefix *de-* in *demulceatis* and *descendetis* focuses the attention on their downward movement.[47] The consul's rhetorical condescension causes a physical descent in his audience, asserting the consul's authority not only over his army's actions but also on their spatial relationships with him.[48] With the Praenestine praetor, the movement dynamic is reversed, and it is the consul who is moving while the praetor stands, presumably in imitation of his slowness to action in battle. Here too, the consul instigates downward movement (*dimisit*), though mostly by "dressing down" rather than actual descent; his threat

[46] Roman readers may have found the discrepancy in rank between the Roman consul and the Praenestine praetor all the more amusing given the mismatch between the Roman and Praenestine *cursus*; cf. Oakley 2005a: 181. There is a parallel acount in Dio fr. 36.24, although Dio (or his excerptor) omits the story about the *equites* (Oakley 2005a: 175–6).

[47] Oakley 2005a: 180 ad loc.

[48] On the intertwining of affective and spatial relationships, see my dicussion of the Fabii in Chapter 1: 38–45.

of eradication, of pulling out (and up) a root fixed in the ground (*excide radicem*), likewise entails the lictor's reaching down, again demonstrating the sympathetic movement of political subordinates.[49]

Livy rounds off the encomium with a more robust moral: 9.16.19 *haud dubie ille aetate, qua nulla uirtutum feracior fuit, nemo unus erat uir quo magis innixa res Romana staret* ("and there is little doubt that in that age, than which none was more bountiful in virtue, there was not one man on whom the Roman state leaned more heavily"). The line combines allusions to two famous lines of Ennius, *moribus antiquis res stat Romana uirisque* (156 Sk., "the Roman state relies on men and ancient customs"), and *unus homo nobis cunctando restituit rem* (363 Sk., "one man by delaying restored the state to us").[50] Albeit an appropriate gesture to round off the encomium, the allusion does more than elevate the register, since it introduces also shades of other famous men to bolster Cursor's reputation. The *unus homo* line in particular calls to mind Fabius Maximus as well as Camillus, to whom Livy makes regular reference throughout the episode, and the image of the state leaning on its famous men looks proleptically to the subsequent Alexander digression, with its celebration of Rome's many commanders against Alexander the Great's singularity.[51] The allusion further introduces a gnomic element to the *laus Cursoris*, transforming it from topical praise to a universalizing *exemplum*.

The newly robust image of magistracy at the end of the episode, however, is the climax of a process of restoration, which begins with the repudiation of the treaty and works its way towards resolution over a sequence of battles. Two scenes are particularly worth examining, as the Roman army finally releases its pent up anger and exorcises the ghosts of Caudium. The first of those is the first set battle of the campaign, with the Samnites dithering about which of the consular armies they ought to follow, and deciding to try their luck with Publilius Philo. This setup is already reminiscent

49 For this episode as a variant on the *imperia Manliana*: Elliot 2009b: 652–3.

50 Oakley 1998: 445 *ad* 8.7.16 and 2005a: 182 ad loc. For the extensive use Livy makes of Ennius for his characterization of Cursor: Elliot 2009b, though she reads the episode as distinctively "Manlian" in color.

51 9.17.5–7 *sed clariorem tamen eum facit quod unus fuit, quod adulescens in incremento rerum, nondum alteram fortunam expertus, decessit . . . recenseam duces Romanos, nec omnes omnium aetatium sed ipsos eos cum quibus consulibus aut dictatoribus Alexandro fuit bellandum . . .* ("but what made him more famous still was that he was alone, and died as a young man at the height of his power, not having yet suffered a change of fortune . . . But let me count out the Roman leaders, not from every age, but those actual ones with whom as consuls or dictators Alexander would have waged war . . . "). On the formal connections between the Alexander digression and the Caudine Forks: Morello 2002: 72–6. On political ideology in the Alexander digression: Viparelli Santangelo 1978 and Morello 2002: 74–83.

of Caudium. The division of the Roman forces throws the Samnites into confusion (9.12.10 *distendit ea res Samnitium animos*), and they can neither go to Luceria, lest they be caught out with an enemy at their back, nor stay where they are. Unlike the Romans in the same situation, the Samnites decide to offer battle and lead out their forces. The Roman response is emphatic and overwhelming.

> aduersus quos Publilius consul cum dimicaturus esset, prius adloquendos milites ratus contionem aduocari iussit; ceterum sicut ingenti alacritate ad praetorium concursum est, ita prae clamore poscentium pugnam nulla adhortatio imperatoris audita est; suus cuique animus memor ignominiae adhortator aderat. uadunt igitur in proelium . . . nihil illic imperatoriae artis ordinibus aut subsidiis locandis fuit; omnia ira militaris prope uesano impetu egit. (Livy 9.13.1–3)

> The consul Publilius, thinking that he ought to address the troops before the battle, ordered an assembly summoned. But just as they rushed to the command tent with great eagerness, not a word of the consul's exhortation could be heard over the din of those demanding battle. Each soldier, mindful of his shame, was his own goad. They therefore rushed into battle . . . there was no need for any art of command, for placing ranks or reserves. The anger of the army drove everything before it in an almost maddened rush.

In comparison with the army at Caudium, the morale of the army is much improved. The Caudine apathy and stillness is replaced by enthusiasm for battle and a wide-awake eagerness (*alacritate*). The consul, likewise, is a considerably more energetic figure. The soldiers at the gorge had rallied around the *praetorium* spontaneously; here, the rush on the command tent (*concursum est*) is the result of a consular order (*aduocari iussit*). Nevertheless, the recovery is still incomplete. Despite the consul's attempts at assertion, his voice and presence are still overwhelmed by the excited soldiers. Thus, not a word he says is heard over the din or makes it into Livy's text, and the soldiers rush into battle (*uadunt*) not only without a consular speech, but also without any meaningful acts of command. Not only is there no need for *ars imperatoria* in the mad rush (*prope uesano impetu*), each of the men also becomes his own *adhortator*, thus doing individually what the consul was meant to have done collectively. The men's flocking to the consul mimics their rush to battle, with *in concursu* and *cursu* in 9.13.2 (elided in the block quotation above) picking up *concursum est* in 9.13.1, so that the army's actions towards their commander, although enthusiastic, are nevertheless assimilated to their action towards the enemy forces. Indeed, the army's anger (9.13.5 *ira*) assists them in victory but renders the consul useless in the event.

The situation changes, however, by the time the Romans fight their next set-piece battle near Luceria. While Publilius Philo has been engaged with the Samnite forces, Papirius Cursor leads his own army to Luceria. Livy's phrase, *exercitus alter cum Papirio consule* (9.13.6) reflects the same dynamic as the pre-battle assembly, with the army as subject and the consul as an ancillary figure. Philo's arrival at Luceria, for which he is both named explicitly and the subject of the clause (9.13.10 *priusquam alter consul uictore exercitu aduenit*; 9.13.11 *artiora omnia aduentus Publili fecit*), marks also a rise in the agency and authority of the consuls, as together they begin both to manage the siege and to force the Samnites into offering battle. The arrival of envoys from Tarentum, demanding the cessation of hostilities and threatening retribution, further enables the turn from two individual consuls to a united Roman front. Whereas before their arrival the Samnites were preparing for battle *cum Papirio* (9.13.12), upon their arrival Papirius stalls for time by consulting his colleague: 9.14.2 *cum collega se communicaturum respondit*. The consuls proceed by making a show of consultation while Papirius completes his battle preparations, and although Papirius takes on all the speaking parts, for the remainder of the engagement the two consuls work as a single unit.

The presence of the Tarentines also changes the dynamics of the battle and allows the consuls to engage in pre-battle chatter which replaces the battle exhortation; thus, Papirius tells the envoys that the omens are favorable and the gods approving before leading out his forces.[52] The Samnites, seeing the Romans lined up for battle (9.14.6 *instructos repente ad pugnam*), announce that they will abide by the Tarentines' wishes and refuse to give battle. A decisive rout follows, but, unlike the previous iteration, the battle begins with confident commanders, whose voice is clearly heard (in both direct and indirect discourse), and with the army arrayed in its proper ranks. Anger is still the main goad, as well as the memory of their shame, but, interestingly, the soldiers themselves interpret their emotions and conduct as virtuous, even as they descend into fury. Thus, as they charge at the Samnite camp, Livy tells us that it was not only *uirtus* but also *ira* goading them forward (9.14.9 *nec uirtus modo insita sed ira etiam exulceratos ignominia stimularet animos*, "it was not only inherent prowess but also anger that goaded their spirits, suppurating with ignominy"). The

[52] 9.14.5 *"auspicia secunda esse, Tarentini, pullarius nuntiat; litatum praeterea est egregie; auctoribus dis, ut uidetis, ad rem gerendam proficiscimur." signa inde ferre iussit et copias eduxit* . . . ("'The chicken-keeper announces, Tarentines, that the auspices are favorable; favorable omens have been attained most successfully, besides; with the gods as our leaders, as you see, we go forth to accomplish something.' He then ordered the standards to be carried out, and led forth his forces . . . ").

soldiers themselves, however, shout out that here is not another Caudium, with its unmanly errors and deceit (9.14.10 *haec Furculas nec Caudium nec saltus inuios esse, ubi errorem fraus superbe uicisset*), but rather *Romanam uirtutem, quam nec uallum nec fossae arcerent* (9.14.10 "Roman courage, which neither wall nor trench can ward off"). This verbal rejection of Caudium as a determining model for Roman behavior applies particularly to the change from the old set of consuls – whose *error* led the army into the gorge, and whose *fraus*, as the Samnites would have it, led them back out again – to the new, who restore the army to its old prowess.

The Roman fury burns so hot that the slaughter is indiscriminate, and it falls to the consuls to restrain the army.

> caedunt pariter resistentes fusosque, inermes atque armatos, seruos liberos, puberes impubes, homines iumentaque; nec ullum superfuisset animal, ni consules receptui signum dedissent auidosque caedis milites e castris hostium imperio ac minis expulissent. itaque apud infensos ob interpellatam dulcedinem irae confestim oratio habita est, ut doceretur miles minime cuiquam militum consules odio in hostes cessisse aut cessuros; quin duces sicut belli ita insatiabilis supplicii futuros fuisse, ni respectus equitum sescentorum qui Luceriae obsides tenerentur praepedisset animos, ne desperata uenia hostes caecos in supplicia eorum ageret perdere prius quam perire optantes. laudare ea milites laetarique obuiam itum irae suae esse ac fateri omnia patienda potius quam proderetur salus tot principum Romanae iuuentutis. (Livy 9.14.10–16)
>
> They cut down equally those who resisted and those in flight, armed and unarmed, slaves and free men, grown men and boys, man and beast, and not a single living thing would have survived, had the consuls not given the sign for retreat and dragged the soldiers, who were still eager for slaughter, from the enemy camp with commands and threats. A speech was given immediately, to men furious at the interruption of their sweet revenge, so that the soldiers would learn that the consuls did not cease their anger at the enemy any more than any of the men, nor would they. They would have been leaders just as insatiable in punishment as they had been in war, except that consideration for the six hundred cavalrymen still hostage at Luceria restrained their spirits, for fear that if the enemy despaired of clemency, they might blindly execute their prisoners, wishing to kill them before perishing themselves. The soldiers praised these words, rejoiced that the consuls resisted their anger, and professed that everything must be borne rather than endanger the well-being of so many leading members of the Roman youth.

The madness itself recalls the earlier iteration, where the army rushed forward *prope uesano impetu*, and the soldiers' anger at being held back recalls also Livy's verbal assimilation of consul and enemy with *concursum est.* In this case, however, the consuls crucially succeed not only in pulling the army back, but also in turning rage into joy (*laetari*), a capacity for emotional manipulation which has so far been utterly lacking (contrast *redintegrauit luctum* in 9.5.6, an emotional affect that is contingent on the consuls but not caused by them). In fact, this is the first time a magistrate in office has managed to convince anyone of anything in the episode, a marker of the restoration of *consilium* now enabled by the new consuls. The other instances of successful persuasion – Lentulus and Postumius – have the magistrates as their object rather than subject, compelling them either to sign the treaty or to surrender the *sponsores*. This new persuasive tone is encouragingly inclusive, since, rather than seeking to separate out portions of the army or the population, as Postumius does, this consular speech aims at securing the hostages. The distinction is sharper still in comparison with Lentulus' speech, a more pragmatic call to preserve the city and the army by bowing to necessity. Here, too, necessity enforces pragmatism, but it is of an entirely different sort, victorious rather than defeatist.

Although such communicative prowess is matched by a decisive military success, the dynamic between consuls and army continues to retain a hint of antagonism. Thus the consuls must drive their own soldiers out of the enemy camp (*e castris hostium . . . expulissent*), a description more apt for defending their own camp against enemy attack. The consuls do so *imperio ac minis* ("with commands and threats"), a *hendiadys* that suggests, perhaps, that the force of *imperium* alone was insufficient. This assertion of magisterial rights is successful to a point – it achieves its immediate end of withdrawing the Roman forces, but it is clear that the consuls feel a need to explain themselves immediately (*confestim*), which they do by giving the explanatory speech on the hostages. This post-battle speech reverses some of the salient features of Philo's *contio* in 9.13: the soldiers are not eager to hear the speech but must be placated, and, rather than arouse an already-present fervor in the troops, this speech soothes their spirits. Finally, here at last the consuls speak about themselves, constructing an image of military leaders (*duces*) who match their troops in sentiment and ferocity (*minime cuiquam militum . . . cessuros*). Where they differ is in self-control, the consuls able to keep in mind the larger picture, which the men applaud, proclaiming eventually to feel much the same. Thus, at the end of the battle of Luceria, consuls and army find themselves at last in some precarious harmony, aiming at a common goal and operating under the traditional hierarchies and values disrupted at Caudium. It is only now, therefore, that true revenge can be exacted, and events come to a swift conclusion. Within a few lines, paucity of resources necessitates the surrender of Luceria, the restoration of the hostages, and in neat poetic justice, the sending under the yoke of seven thousand Samnite troops, but especially Pontius Herennius, expiating specifically the *consulum ignominia* (9.15.8 "shame of the consuls"), rather than that of the whole people.

As an episode, the Caudine Forks is neatly bound both structurally and narratologically. The narrative, as already mentioned, is divided into two and disposed chiastically, with one *peripeteia* casting the Romans low, and another restoring them to victory. Structurally, the episode is bounded on the one side by the opening of the book and the consular year (9.1.1 *sequitur hunc annum nobilis clade Romana Caudina pax* . . . , "the treaty at Caudium, famous for the Roman defeat, followed in this year"), and on the other by the lengthy Alexander digression, in which Livy meditates on the outcome of a hypothetical clash between Rome and Alexander the Great.[53] But even within the episode, there are various closural elements. Working backwards from the end, Livy offers the reader the *laus Cursoris*, with its two vignettes and gnomic allusion. That is itself introduced by the notice of Cursor's triumph, and though there is no mention of Philo, there is mention of a problem of transmission: 9.16.11 *inde ad triumphum decessise Roman Papirium Cursorem scribunt qui eo duce Luceriam receptam Samnitesque sub iugum missos auctores sunt* ("from there Papirius Cursor went to Rome for his triumph, or so write those who believe that Luceria was surrendered and the Samnites sent under the yoke under his leadership"). Livy's opinion, one may deduce, is in favor of Papirius Cursor, both because the *laus Cursoris* then unfolds, and because that is indeed the version he has been narrating so far. Nevertheless, this bifurcation of the tradition is given some treatment, separated from the *laus* by a description of a military operation against the Satricani. In a sense, then, the narrative space between the surrender of Luceria and the end of the episode is taken up with a sequence of digressive material, first the problem of the sources, then the Satricani, then the *laus Cursoris*, and only then a transition to the Alexander digression. All this digressive material, however, has in common a focus on magisterial activity, its forms, and the problems of representing it in textual form.

The source problems begin earlier still, since the sending under the yoke of Pontius Herennius is itself of dubious authority. Livy finds it *quibusdam in annalibus* (9.15.8), and indeed it seems too good to be true, so much so

[53] On the digression, see n. 51 above, as well as Kraus 1994b.

that Livy is less than surprised to find such variations (9.15.9 *id minus miror*). This kind of archival digression is not atypical of Livy, and here it extends beyond the Samnite general to the Roman consuls. The name of Papirius Cursor seems securely attested, but of greater interest to Livy (9.15.9 *magis mirabile est*) is the identity of the magistracy – whether Cursor was consul, or only the *magister equitum* to a L. Cornelius *dictator*. That there was a discrepancy is beyond doubt, as the *Fasti Capitolini* indeed record three different dictatorships for the year 322 BC, for two of which Cursor serves as *magister equitum*, and for one of which the dictator is a Lucius Cornelius Lentulus, a name already redolent of the Caudine surrender.[54] The doubt proliferates, extending temporally to the next year – did Papirius win another consulship, or was there a confusion with another Papirius? – as well as affecting Livy's narrative for this year. For, if there was a mistake, and Cursor was merely a *magister equitum*, then the glory ought to go to the dictator:

> id magis mirabile est ambigi Luciusne Cornelius dictator cum L. Papirio Cursore magistro equitum eas res ad Caudium atque inde Luceriam gesserit ultorque unicus Romanae ignominiae haud sciam an iustissimo triumpho ad eam aetatem secundum Furium Camillum triumphauerit an consulum – Papirique praecipuum – id decus sit. (Livy 9.15.9–10)

> It is more surprising that it is not certain whether Lucius Cornelius, dictator, with L. Papirius Cursor as his master of the horse, did these deeds at Caudium and then at Luceria, and alone avenged the Roman humiliation, and, in my opinion, with the best justified triumph since Furius Camillus; or whether the consuls – and especially Papirius – deserve the commendation.

The two versions are, as Livy presents them, mutually exclusive, and they cannot be resolved by reference to the *fasti* entry, which records both the consulship of Philo and Cursor and the dictatorship of Cornelius Lentulus with Cursor as *magister equitum*. Livy's elaboration here, however, does more than just offer an alternative version of what happened in the aftermath of Caudium; it also requires a reassessment of the events in the gorge, both because *ad Caudium* becomes a shorthand for referring back to the events in the gorge, and because as Postumius reminds the senators, nothing was done *ad Caudium* by human counsels – an aphorism extended

[54] In this I follow Oakley 2005a: 167–9 ad loc., as I do in accepting these notices as essentially correct, on the principle of *lectio difficilior*: "the very extraordinary nature of the notices in *F[asti] C[apitolini]* strengthens their credibility" (p. 169). However, whether or not we accept them as correct has little bearing on Livy's knowledge, and within the economy of the episode what matters more is the existence of the discrepancy than its prosopographical resolution.

here to apply to the narrative as well.[55] Whether or not the dictator is the same Lentulus as the legate who supported the surrender, the name certainly evokes him, though Livy is noticeably coy about the attribution: he gives only *nomen* and *praenomen* here, and only *nomen* and *cognomen* in 9.4.7 when introducing the legate.[56] It is up to the reader to connect the dots. If we accept the identification, however, another detail becomes pertinent, and that is Livy's mention of Furius Camillus, another avenging dictator to whom the epithet *unicus* is expansively applied.[57] Camillus, to recall, was also the *exemplum* of choice in Lentulus' speech, which relied heavily on differentiating Caudium from the Gallic siege: then, the ignominy of ransom bought time enough for the arrival of Camillus, but now, there is only the ignominy of the yoke. Camillus' reappearance here adds another layer to Lentulus' speech – if he is indeed a second Camillus, then the surrender at the gorge was merely buying time for his own revenge – and it explains as well the odd submission of the consuls to his advice.

Whatever the implications of the Lentulus scenario, however, one effect it is sure to have is to destabilize retrospectively the careful and intricate narrative of consular behavior Livy has constructed, and it is worthwhile asking, in conclusion, why Livy felt the need to admit it into the narrative. The most generous answer to Livy *qua* historian is simply that the discrepancy existed, therefore it ought to have been narrated and kept to the end so as to maintain the unity of the narrative.[58] Nevertheless, such a deep confusion over the identity of the magistrates, which Livy himself finds surprising, threatens to destabilize the artistic integrity of Livy's narrative and to cast serious doubt over the *laus Cursoris* which follows shortly after the discrepancy notice. As we have seen, however, the alternative scenario retains some of Livy's structure and does not in fact require a complete dismantling of the episode, since Lentulus' putative dictatorial appointment is not incompatible with the election of the new consuls, Philo and Cursor. Thus, in some sense, the source discrepancy both generalizes the episode to apply to more magistracies and refocuses attention on the specific role of the consuls. The *laus Cursoris*, with its concluding vignettes of the Roman

[55] 9.9.10 *nihil ad Caudium, patres conscripti, humanis consiliis gestum est.* For *ad Caudium* referring back to events in the gorge, note also 9.12.9 and 9.15.7, and in a stricter geographical sense 9.10.7 (where it can also have a symbolic meaning) and 9.27.2. The phrase does not occur elsewhere.

[56] On the identification: Oakley 1998: 652 *ad* 8.22.8.

[57] On Camillus *unicus* see Oakley 1997: 455 and Kraus 1994a: 128, both *ad* 6.6.17 *imperatore unico.*

[58] On the discrepancies: Oakley 2005a: 167–9. See also Morello 2002: 75–6, who argues that such counterfactual scenarios are part of a larger strategy framing book 9.

equites and the Praenestine praetor, leaves the reader on a specifically consular note, but it comes also at the end of an extended meditation on the scope and effective exercise of *imperium*, whether by consuls, tribunes, or, for a fleeting moment, a dictator. The Caudine Forks, as a historical as well as a historiographical event, puts the consular role under tremendous pressure, where the effects on the state of consular failures and successes find expression in the intricate structures of the text.

CHAPTER 3

Elections and the generation of exempla

At the end of 215 BC Q. Fabius Maximus Cunctator (*consul suffectus* 215: *MRR* 1.254) came to Rome to hold the elections. When the first results arrived, however, the consul found his successors, Titus Otacilius and M. Aemilius Regillus, not to his liking, despite a close personal connection to one of them – Otacilius was married to Fabius' niece (24.8.11).[1] Never one to shirk duty in the service of the state, Fabius stopped the elections to deliver a lengthy diatribe calling on the voters to retake the vote and elect other, more suitable, candidates. The voters consented, the vote was retaken, and new consuls duly chosen.

As a political event, the episode is typical of the personal animosities which came to characterize the Roman aristocracy, though Fabius' rhetoric is nevertheless striking in its *ad hominem* specificity. Brusquely dismissing Regillus as weighed down by his flaminate, he goes on to disparage Otacilius at length for his uninspiring record: we have had you as leader in minor affairs, he says, and you have given us no cause to trust you with greater (24.8.13 *in minore te experti, T. Otacili, re sumus; haud sane cur ad maiora tibi fidamus documenti quicquam dedisti*). In these troubled times, the ship of state required a firmer hand at the helm (24.8.12–13).[2] This familiar metaphor is made more pointed by the context: Otacilius had command of a Roman navy, without much success (24.8.14–15). For all his disparagement, however, Fabius is here interested in more than personal invective. He is invested, and heavily so, in ensuring the election of a consul who

[1] On the sometimes hostile relationship between the Fabii and the Otacilii, see Pinsent 1964. On the politics of this election: Patterson 1942: 325–7; Develin 1985: 159–61.

[2] 24.8.12–13 *quilibet nautarum uectorumque tranquillo mari gubernare potest; ubi saeua orta tempestas est ac turbato mari rapitur uento nauis, tum uiro et gubernatore opus est. non tranquillo nauigamus sed iam aliquot procellis summersi paene sumus; itaque quis ad gubernacula sedeat summa cura prouidendum ac praecauendum uobis est* ("any sailor or passenger can navigate when the sea is calm; but when a harsh storm rises and the ship is snatched by the wind and the churning sea, then there is need of a real man and a helmsman. We are not sailing in the calm, and we have been nearly drowned in several storms; and so, you must take the utmost care and precaution as to who should sit at the helm").

would be up to the specific military task demanded of him, continuing Rome's recovery from the nadir it had reached with the defeat at Cannae. His speech opens with just such an admonition:

> si aut pacem in Italia aut <id> bellum eumque hostem haberemus in quo neglegentiae laxior locus esset, qui uestris studiis, quae in campum ad mandandos quibus uelitis honores adfertis, moram ullam offerret, is mihi parum meminisse uideretur uestrae libertatis; sed cum in hoc bello, in hoc hoste nunquam ab ullo duce sine ingenti nostra clade erratum sit, eadem uos cura qua in aciem armati descenditis inire suffragium ad creandos consules decet et sibi quemque dicere: "Hannibali imperatori parem consulem nomino." (Livy 24.8.1–2)

> If we had either peace in Italy or a war and an enemy which left a greater space for negligence, the man who caused any delay in your enthusiasm for bestowing honors on the field upon whomever you wish, I would have thought him too little mindful of your liberty; but since in this war, against this enemy, under not one leader has there been an error which did not result in an immense defeat for us, it behooves you to apply the same care in electing the consuls as you do when you form the battle line under arms, and for each to say to himself: "I name a consul who is a match for the commander Hannibal."

On the face of it, this is precisely the kind of electoral rhetoric one would expect to find in a state as militarily preoccupied as the Roman republic: direct, substantive, and focused on merit and competence for the particular task that would occupy the consul during his year in office. Fabius even specifies the index by which decisions should be measured – Hannibal – and following this passage goes on to list *exempla* for the kind of men who ought to be elected: heroic figures equal to the confrontation.[3] I will return to Fabius' exemplary standards later in this chapter, but his invocation of martial heroism as a measure of consular suitability arises from another important dimension of the speech, its delivery at a time of crisis – within two years the war will be brought to Rome's very gates. At moments like this, the conventional distinction between home and war, or, as the Romans put it, *domi militiaeque*, comes under considerable pressure. This issue, indeed, underlies the very first sentence of the speech, when Fabius acknowledges that, current circumstances notwithstanding, his intervention would normally impinge on the people's *libertas*.[4]

[3] On Roman patterns of election during the Hannibalic war as driven by the military emergency: Patterson 1942.

[4] Note that the idea of *libertas* here is formulated as the people's ability to elect whom they will (*quibus uelitis*), an issue that will preoccupy us again in Chapter 4.

This pressure is, at least in part, created by Fabius himself. Recalled from active duty near Puteoli, Fabius proceeded directly to the Campus Martius, bypassing the city: *ex itinere praeter urbem in campum descendit* (24.7.12). This detail already bodes ill for the elections, since *ex itinere* is a common descriptive for marching armies (cf. *OLD* s.v. "iter" 2), while *in campum*, properly referring to the *campus Martius*, the site of consular elections, connotes also the field of battle. Fabius' omitting to pass through the city also enabled him to retain his military auspices. This fact considerably complicates the election, because Fabius not only stepped up to demand a new vote but also concluded the day by reminding all and sundry of the powers he still possessed. When Otacilius tried to retaliate by claiming that Fabius' actual motive was his desire to remain in office (24.9.1 *continuare consulatum uelle*), Fabius dispatched his lictors to warn him that he, Fabius, had not entered the city and, therefore, the axes – the symbol of his coercive authority – remained in his *fasces*.[5] Fabius' action is nothing short of intimidation, but it is based on the fact that while these elections appear to be held at home *(domi)*, they are in actuality held by a consul in possession of military *imperium*. Thus, the Fabius episode exposes the division between the civic and military functions of the state (which is to say between the citizen-body and the soldiery), a division it both interrogates and threatens to collapse, as Fabius addresses the voters as precisely the same people who would fight as soldiers.[6]

This division is manifested in the text in a number of ways, primarily through the distinction between affairs "at home" (*domi*) and affairs "at war" (*militiae*), a principle to which annalistic history in particular was naturally sensitive, because any breach of the division involved disruption of the schematic structures of the annalistic year.[7] The annalistic structure, however, as well as Roman political practices, also appear in the text in an inverted form, where the *domi/militiae* divide has already been collapsed by extreme circumstances, causing an army to function as a substitute for the city. This situation, known as the army-as-city topos, offers another perspective on the problem of magisterial *personae* and qualifications. The *exempla* produced through the topos are a modified version of the problem

5 24.9.1–2 *lictores ad eum accedere consul iussit et, quia in urbem non inierat protinus in campum ex itinere profectus, admonuit cum securibus sibi fasces praeferri* ("the consul ordered the lictors to approach him, and, because he had not entered the city, having gone straight to the Campus from his march, he cautioned him that he was still preceded by *fasces* with the axes").

6 Fabius is, after all, addressing the *comitia centuriata*, the Roman people in its military guise (Lintott 1999: 55–61).

7 On the annalistic structure, especially as based on the consular year: Rich 2009. On the historiographical sensitivity to disruptions in the annalistic rhythm: Rüpke 1990 and Levene 1993.

Fabius presents to the assembly – the relationship between the merits of a magistrate and the task they are expected to perform. Both the topos and the *domi militiae* merism it collapses recur to the same political reality – the considerable overlap in personnel between the citizen body, the soldiery, and the officer ranks. The *comitia centuriata*, for example, represented the citizen body in its military guise and as such elected the magistrates who would lead it in battle. On the other hand, the complicated structures of *imperium* and *prouocatio* likewise shifted when a person moved from one sphere to the other: while the people remained the same, the relationships between them altered significantly.

This chapter explores the construction of the magisterial (in this case, primarily consular) *persona* as a military figure and focuses in particular on how a specific context – electoral rhetoric – and a specific mannerism – the production of *exempla* – together fashion an image of the magistrate as a stereotype or embodiment of a Roman ideal. The electoral process, in other words, generates a set of *exempla*, which themselves produce a set of idealized images of magistracy and magistrates. In this, the chapter builds on some of the ideas introduced in the previous chapter on the Caudium episode, namely the magisterial experience in situations of military urgency. The episodes analyzed in this chapter, likewise, move along the range of relationships between army and city, from the structured divide between a war abroad and an election at home, to the more extreme conditions elaborated by the army-as-city topos which increases the tension between civic habits and military circumstances. But whereas Caudium offers a more informal view of the generation of consular exemplarity, the electoral mechanisms explored here offer a more consistent focus on what a magistrate ought to be. Each of these circumstances, this chapter will argue, showcases a particular tendency in the generation of exemplarity and engages the central questions of how one man can fit within two separate, yet overlapping, ideological structures, and what rhetoric and which kinds of *exempla* might be used to negotiate these conflicting expectations.

Electoral rhetoric and the problem of criteria

Fabius' speech illustrates one way in which electoral rhetoric generates *exempla*.[8] He offers a set of circumstances – the sequence of Roman defeats

[8] On the extent to which substantive issues of politics played a part in Roman electioneering: Yakobson 1999: 148–83. On the relevance of military success or failure in particular: Rosenstein 1990.

against Hannibal and the need to prevent their recurrence – as the determining criterion in electing a consul: whoever the Romans proceed to vote for must be the kind of man who is on a par with Hannibal. The invective against Otacilius and the dismissal of Regillus offer the two further criteria that would logically demonstrate such competence: the man must be unencumbered by domestic concerns, and he must have proof of, at least, a more than mediocre career. But whether or not the speech, as Otacilius protested, was aimed at assuring Fabius' own electoral success, it lacks any positive description of what parity with Hannibal precisely consists of. Instead, Fabius relies on exemplarity to demonstrate his point for him. I will return to his actual examples – a sequence of chronologically receding duels – in the next section of this chapter, but even so it is easy to see how strong an emphasis he places on exemplarity as a guide for conduct: Trasimene and Cannae are sad examples to recall, he concludes, but they offer a *documentum* for the avoidance of similar outcomes: 24.8.20 *Lacus Trasumennus et Cannae tristia ad recordationem exempla sed ad praecauenda similia [utiles] documento sunt.*[9]

The large scope of Livy's work allows him to develop his penchant for both exemplarity and typological characterization in complicated and far-reaching narrative structures, which the last two sections of this chapter will explore in more detail. The rhetorical move whereby a substantive issue – in this case, military competence – is used to highlight a particular quality of the magistrate is not unique to Livy, however, and can be seen in more discrete episodes as well. A relatively simple example is Pliny the Elder's account of the painting of the siege of Carthage used by L. Hostilius Mancinus in 146 BC:

> non dissimilem offensionem et Aemiliani subiit L. Hostilius Mancinus, qui primus Carthaginem inruperat, situm eius oppugnationesque depictas proponendo in foro et ipse a<ds>istens populo spectanti singula enarrando, qua comitate proximis comitiis consulatum adeptus est. (*HN* 35.23)
>
> L. Hostilius Mancinus, who had first broken into Carthage, likewise offended Aemilianus by putting a painting of its site and siege in the forum, while he stood by it explaining the details to the watching people. With this affability he obtained the consulship in the next elections.

From Pliny's account, this ingenious display did not take place during an actual canvass for the consulship, though it is difficult to imagine that

[9] Compare Fabius' use of *documentum* in 24.8.13 to refer to Otacilius: *haud sane cur ad maiora tibi fidamus documenti quicquam dedisti.* The verbal repetition confirms the apotropaic thrust of Fabius' speech – to elect Otacilius is to ignore the *documenta* of the past.

Mancinus did not have just such an outcome in mind when he set up shop in the forum. Nevertheless, even this brief sketch points up two main issues: first, that Mancinus explains military events to the people; and second, that Pliny elides the substantive talk on the capture of Carthage in favour of noting Mancinus' affability (*comitas*), supposedly the quality by which he won the consulship.[10] The two elements of the anecdote are inextricable: Carthage fell in 146 BC; Mancinus won the consular election that same year to become consul in 145 BC. His participation in the campaign, and the military distinctions he must have won for being first over the wall (though Pliny makes no mention of a crown or other decoration), would have played their part in his success. It is therefore striking that Pliny singles out not *uirtus* but *comitas* for comment, and part of the reason for this must be that Mancinus himself already tells the story of his military achievement in which *uirtus* is assumed to play a part. In a similar way, Fabius need only refer in the briefest terms to the defeats at Trasimene and Cannae in order to make his point, namely that circumstances require the election of a particular kind of consul. Thus, the military narratives, and the success or failure they imply, are taken as already read, known to both internal and external audiences and recalled by direct reference to them through trophies, spoils, old wounds, or literary or painted narratives. In this sense, elections, like triumphal debates, are a medium in which older narratives find recirculation within the text, and in this they function themselves as narrative topoi.[11] The assumption that these narratives are already established in the audience's awareness allows the episode to move its focus to other qualities. Pliny foregrounds *comitas* as the characteristic that mediates Mancinus' military success to the voters, while Fabius foregrounds the criteria he believes the electorate should prioritize. In other words, assuming that the military narrative is already known allows the author or speaker to use it as a rhetorical stepping stone for his own purposes.

But the Mancinus example is also an imprecise analogy for the Fabius example, since Fabius is exhorting the people to elect someone for a specific task under specific circumstances, while Mancinus is not. A closer parallel is Marius' electoral campaign during the Jugurthine War in 108 BC, a

[10] Pliny's primary purpose is to talk about the painting of Carthage, but within the logic of the Mancinus anecdote the emphasis on *comitas* nevertheless requires explanation. Further, Mancinus is here taking credit for an accomplishment more properly due to the general himself. In this, Mancinus' example comes closer to Marius' campaign, discussed below. On the offense to Aemilianus: Astin 1967: 71; Gruen 1992: 118.

[11] On visual proofs for exemplary deeds: Roller 2004: 10–23. On triumphal debates as recycling older narratives: Pittenger 2008: 181–6, 257–8.

campaign unusual for its cosmopolitan scope.[12] Marius, eager to secure the command against Jugurtha, canvassed not only in Rome but also in Africa, from where he had scores of letters sent complaining of Metellus' conduct of the war (*Iug.* 65.4). This move made the drawn-out war the focal point of the election, and Marius campaigned on the promise that he would bring it to a swift end. But even though both accounts of the campaign, one in Cicero's *de Officiis* and the other in Sallust's *Bellum Jugurthinum*, agree on this point, they diverge markedly in how they develop their respective versions.[13]

(1) at enim cum permagna praemia sunt, est causa peccandi. C. Marius, cum a spe consulatus longe abesset et iam septimum annum post praeturam iaceret neque petiturus umquam consulatum uideretur, Q. Metellum, cuius legatus erat, summum uirum et ciuem cum ab eo, imperatore suo, Romam missus esset, apud populum Romanum criminatus est, bellum illum ducere, si se consulem fecissent, breui tempore aut uiuum aut mortuum Iugurtham se in potestatem populi Romani redacturum. itaque factus est ille quidem consul, sed a fide iustitiaque discessit, qui optimum et grauissimum ciuem, cuius legatus et a quo missus esset, in inuidiam falso crimine adduxerit. (Cic. *Off.* 3.79)

But when the rewards are especially great, there is opportunity for offense. Gaius Marius had only a distant hope of the consulship and was already six years past his praetorship, nor did it appear likely that he would ever be a candidate for the consulship. Then, when he was sent to Rome by Q. Metellus, his general, an outstanding man and citizen, Marius accused him before the people of drawing out the war and said that if they made him consul, he would bring Jugurtha, dead or alive, under Roman power in a short time. And so Marius indeed became consul, but he abandoned loyalty and justice, for he brought an excellent and most dignified citizen, his own commander and the person who had sent him to Rome, into ill repute by a false charge.

(2) et Romae plebes litteris, quae de Metello ac Mario missae erant, cognitis uolenti animo de ambobus acceperant. imperatori nobilitas, quae antea decori fuit, inuidiae esse; at illi alteri generis humilitas fauorem addiderat. ceterum in utroque magis studia partium quam bona aut mala sua moderata. praeterea seditiosi magistratus uolgum exagitare, Metellum omnibus contionibus capitis arcessere, Mari uirtutem in maius celebrare. denique plebes sic accensa, uti opifices agrestesque omnes, quorum res fidesque in manibus sitae erant, relictis operibus

[12] For analysis of the campaign: Yakobson 1999: 13–19.

[13] On the episodes see Dyck 1996: 595–8 for Cicero, and Paul 1984: 190–209 for Sallust. Cf. Plut. *Mar.* 8.9.

frequentarent Marium et sua necessaria post illius honorem ducerent. ita perculsa nobilitate post multas tempestates nouo homini consulatus mandatur. (Sall. *Iug.* 73.3–7)

And at Rome, when the plebs had heard the content of the letters that were sent about both Marius and Metellus, they willingly believed what was said about both men. The nobility of the general, which earlier had been an ornament to him, became a cause for jealousy; but Marius' humble stock added to his popularity. For both men, however, partisanship was more influential than their own good or bad qualities. Besides, seditious magistrates whipped up the people, summoning Metellus on capital charges in every assembly, and celebrating Marius' valor even more. Finally the plebs were so fired up that the artisans and all the rustics, whose livelihood and credit rested in their labor, left their work and gathered around Marius, considering their own necessities less important than his election. And so, with the nobility thus shaken after many clashes, the consulship was given to a new man.

Both Cicero and Sallust make use of moral language. Cicero describes Marius with *peccandi, a fide iustitiaque discessit* and *falso crimine*, while Metellus is consistently *summum, optimum, grauissimum ciuem.* Sallust, for his part, brings up the issue of good and bad qualities (*bona aut mala sua*) but is quick to emphasize that both were eclipsed by the spirit of partisanship (*studia partium*). And although Marius retains his *uirtus* (*Mari uirtutem in maius celebrare*), Sallust effectively overshadows it by the language he uses for the company Marius keeps: *seditiosi magistratus*, and the *uulgus* whom they fire up (*accensa*). Thus, despite the consistent interest in morality, each author focuses his evaluative language in different areas: Cicero assesses Marius himself, while Sallust is more broadly concerned with the effects of partisanship.

For both authors, however, the moral issues arise directly from military contexts. Cicero is focused on Marius' abandonment of the military bonds (*fides et iustitia*) between the general and his subordinates. This rupture of bonds between a commander and his staff was a broader concern: Cicero usefully employed it in the *Diuinatio in Caecilium* of 70 BC, in which he secured his position as the prosecutor in the subsequent trial of Verres. Caecilius, who sought the same position, was Verres' *quaestor* in Sicily, and argued that this was reason enough to prefer him to Cicero (*Diu. Caec.* 59). Cicero in answer points out that the quaestor–governor connection makes Caecilius rather more friendly than inimical to Verres (59), and, he continues, even had Caecilius been wronged, he would do better to bear his misfortune with equanimity, rather than turn on his former superior

(60 *etenim si plurimas a tuo praetore iniurias accepisses, tamen eas ferendo maiorem laudem quam ulciscendo mererere*). Since this rhetorical gambit is played before an audience and jurors, it must have seemed to have at least a chance of being effective. The values explicitly aired in Cicero's rhetoric in the *Diuinatio* also underlie his narrative of Marius' election in the *de Officiis*: having betrayed the bonds of *officium* owed to a commander by his staff, Marius is condemned for moral bankruptcy and cast as a usurper to Metellus' rightful command.[14]

Sallust fills in what Cicero leaves out – the excitement of an electoral campaign conducted vigorously. Sallust chooses to focus on this topic for a particular purpose, since the *Bellum Jugurthinum*, besides commemorating a long and difficult war, marks the moment when aristocratic control was first shattered, leading to further and far-reaching consequences for the Roman state.[15] A few items are worth noting. First, from Sallust's brief description, one might mistakenly infer that Metellus himself was also a candidate for the consulship, an ambiguity which might have been clear to Sallust's contemporaries, but not necessarily to future readers. The actual candidates are passed over in silence. This rhetorical manipulation exposes the main issue at stake: to elect Marius is to indict Metellus, but the fact remains that the question of military command in Numidia is left implicit until *after* (*Iug.* 73.7 *postea*) the election. What remains instead is a description of a hotly contested topic, revolving around the personal attributes and class affiliations of the contestants – but competence as a general, the actual issue at hand, is discussed very little. In fact, any mention of battlefield prowess is reserved for Marius' speech after the elections (*Iug.* 85). However, even with the lack of explicit interest, there is no mistaking the relevance of military action for this particular election.[16]

As a piece of political analysis, therefore, Sallust's account engages two overlapping questions. The first is internal to the narrative and belongs properly to Marius, who asks, as Fabius does, if the consul ought not to be

[14] On Cicero's rhetorical techniques in the *diuinatio*: Craig 1985, Tempest 2007: 22–7. On the quasi-parental bonds between the *quaestor* and his commander: Thompson 1962.

[15] *Iug.* 5.1–2 *bellum scripturus sum, quod populus Romanus cum Iugurtha rege Numidarum gessit, primum quia magnum et atrox uariaque uictoria fuit, dein quia tunc primum superbiae nobilitatis obuiam itum est; quae contentio diuina et humana cuncta permiscuit eoque uecordiae processit, ut studiis ciuilibus bellum atque uastitas Italiae finem faceret* ("I shall write the war which the Roman people waged with Jugurtha, king of the Numidians, first because it was great and fierce, and victory was changeable, but also because then for the first time there was resistance to the arrogance of the nobility; this struggle confused everything human and divine and reached such a pitch of madness that only war and the devastation of Italy made an end to partisan strife").

[16] As in Cicero, Metellus is specifically designated as a general (*imperatori* 73.4), but emphasis is placed not on his success but on his nobility and Marius' humble birth.

a match for the enemy. The second question is Sallust's own, which focuses on the tension between the senate and the plebs, thus turning the campaign into an issue of class, just as Cicero had interpreted the same behavior as an issue of morality. Neither reading, it should be noted, challenges Marius' basic assertion, that he would bring the war to a swift end. Sallust, in fact, does not even include the slogan in his account of the campaign but has it instead six chapters earlier, where he echoes Cicero's *criminatus* with his own *criminose*: *Iug.* 64.5 *criminose simul et magnifice de bello loqui: dimidia pars exercitus si sibi permitteretur, paucis diebus Iugurtham in catenis habiturum* ("he spoke of the war both slanderously and boastfully: if he was given but half the army, he would have Jugurtha in chains in a matter of days"). The omission of the slogan is itself telling, because it directs the reader's attention from Marius' agenda to Sallust's interpretative framework – class struggle and the decline of the nobility – the same effect which Cicero achieved by provoking the reader's moral outrage.

Thus, both accounts use this particular campaign to develop two different dialectics on the values at issue in the election. Cicero's particular inflection of the story is moral and ethical – he wishes to determine if Marius is a good man or bad (*Off.* 3.81 *possumusne aut illum Marium uirum bonum iudicare aut hunc?*), as an illustration of the distinction between *utilitas* and *honestas*, for which Marius' conduct serves as an example.[17] Sallust, meanwhile, is interested in the shattering of the nobility by plebeian efforts, and the pressing tension between birth and merit. These different interpretations make for different exemplary products: Marius might be seen as a military hero, as a moral failure, or as a new man, that is, an *exemplum* of *uirtus*, *perfidia*, or *nouitas*. The inflections, however, are meaningful, and they are determined in large part by the individual commitments of either work. Cicero, for whom *nouitas* cut close to the bone, was writing a moral and didactic treatise; Sallust, on the other hand, took for his subject not only the war against Jugurtha, but also the complex process by which war abroad impacted on politics at home. What is common to both Sallust and Cicero, as well as Pliny's Mancinus and Livy's Fabius, is that military action and reputation are used rhetorically to

[17] Cicero moves from his previous discussion to the *exemplum* of Marius by concluding: *ut enim, quod turpe est, id, quamuis occultetur, tamen honestum fieri nullo modo potest, sic, quod honestum non est, id utile ut sit effici non potest aduersante et repugnante natura* (*Off.* 3.78 "for just as what is shameful, however much it is concealed, cannot in any way become honorable, so too what is not honorable cannot be made useful, since nature resists and opposes it"). For the aristocratic aversion to campaigning, especially the abandonment or manipulation of *honestas* it entailed, see Tatum 2007. For Cicero's complex relationship with Marius' memory, which included a composition of a poem entitled *Marius*: Carney 1960, Lavery 1971.

turn the candidate into a stereotype which fits the purposes of the text and author. In so doing, electoral narratives generate not only magistrates but also *exempla* – of valor, depravity, or status – and thereby also discursively construct components of the magisterial *persona*.

The magistrate as heroic *exemplum*

In this section, I want to return to the episode with which the chapter opened – Fabius' speech in Livy's twenty-fourth book – and analyze the ways in which it constructs the consul as a particular type of *exemplum*. After the initial demand for electing a commander on a par with Hannibal, and before the invective against Otacilius, Fabius provides three *exempla*, which illustrate the kind of qualities he has in mind for the consul:

> ... sed cum in hoc bello, in hoc hoste nunquam ab ullo duce sine ingenti nostra clade erratum sit, eadem uos cura qua in aciem armati descenditis inire suffragium ad creandos consules decet et sibi quemque dicere: "Hannibali imperatori parem consulem nomino." hoc anno ad Capuam Vibellio Taureae, Campano summo equiti, prouocanti summus Romanus eques Asellus Claudius est oppositus. aduersus Gallum quondam prouocantem in ponte Anienis T. Manlium fidentem et animo et uiribus misere maiores nostri. eandem causam haud multis annis post fuisse non negauerim cur M. Valerio non diffideretur aduersus similiter prouocantem ad certamen arma capienti Gallum. quemadmodum pedites equitesque optamus ut ualidiores, si minus, ut pares hosti habeamus, ita duci hostium parem imperatorem quaeramus. (Livy 24.8.2–6)

> but since in this war, against this enemy, under not one leader has there been an error which did not result in an immense defeat for us, it behooves you to apply the same care in electing the consuls as you do when you form the battle line under arms, and for each to say to himself: "I name a consul who is a match for the commander Hannibal." In this year near Capua, Asellus Claudius, an outstanding Roman knight, faced the challenge of Vibellius Taurea, an outstanding Campanian knight. Our ancestors once sent Titus Manlius, a man who trusted in his spirit and strength, against the challenge of the Gaul on the bridge over the Anio. Nor would I deny that for the same reason, not many years later, there was confidence in Marcus Valerius when he took up arms against a Gaul who similarly challenged him to a contest. Inasmuch as we hope that we have infantry and cavalry who are stronger than the enemy, or at least its match, so too let us seek a general who is equal to the leader of the enemy.

Fabius' choice of these particular *exempla* is not hard to fathom, though each *exemplum* appeals on slightly different grounds. The first, Asellus and Taurea, was very recent, and the audience, both internal and external, could reliably be expected to recall it.[18] The latter two *exempla*, Manlius and Valerius, celebrated Roman success against overwhelming odds, a situation which had obvious resonances in 215 BC, when Rome's prospects against Hannibal seemed uncertain. Manlius' *exemplum*, in particular, would have had added rhetorical potency in the specific context of these elections. Manlius' deed took place *in ponte Anienis* and the *centuria praerogatiua* that day was the *Aniensis iuniorum*, the junior century of the *Aniensis* tribe, some of whom might further identify with Fabius' young heroes (Torquatus is *iuuenem* in 7.10.5; Valerius is *adulescens* in 7.26.2).[19] The word *pons*, moreover, while referring to the bridge on which Manlius fought, could also designate the wooden planks on which the voters approached the voting urns (*OLD* s.v. 2c).[20] The rhetorical ploy of using topography, visible or imagined, gives Fabius' argument a moral thrust:[21] the memory of the Roman success at the Anio, won by courage and correct leadership, should not be overshadowed by the ill-considered choice of the *iuniores Anienses*; it also suggests that what applies in the field of battle applies equally in an election.

The type of scene Fabius chooses to focus on, however – that is, the formal duel – is not entirely apt as a magisterial *exemplum*, despite the neat correlation of consul and duelist set up by the topical relevance of the *exempla*. Stephen Oakley has analyzed the republican practice of formal single combat, that is to say, in response to a challenge, as opposed to spontaneous monomachy in the course of battle – an exclusion that has interesting and relevant consequences, as we shall see. In comparison with other cultures, Oakley argues, the Romans were unique in not allowing combat by champions to determine the outcome of a war, but it is more interesting in this context to note the relatively low political ranking of the combatants.[22] Of the republican duels collected by Oakley, not a single one

[18] On the rhetorical efficacy of recent *exempla* in Livy and Roman rhetorical practice: Chaplin 2000: 106–36. Morstein-Marx 2004: 72–6 argues, based on references in Cicero, *Leg. Agr. II*, that even examples like Taurea and Asellus were recognizable to the commons in Cicero's day.

[19] 24.7.12 *eo die cum sors praerogatiuae Aniensi iuniorum exisset eaque T. Otacilium M. Aemilium Regillum consules diceret* ("on that day, the young men of the Aniensis tribe drew the lot to vote first, and they pronounced T. Otacilius and M. Aemilius Regillus consuls . . . ").

[20] The presiding magistrate in an election also sat on a *pons*: Taylor 1966: 39.

[21] The use of topography in rhetoric has been explored in detail by Vasaly 1993 and Morstein-Marx 2004: 92–107, focusing particularly on Cicero, but with more general applicability. On Livy's use of topography, see Horsfall 1982 and 1985, and Jaeger 1997, which explores Livy's use of topographical monuments for narrative purposes.

[22] Oakley 1985, cf. also Fries 1985, with Oakley's 1987 review. The obvious exception, the battle of the Horatii and the Curiatii, is traditionally assigned to the reign of Tullius Hostilius and therefore

was fought by a magistrate in office, though some former combatants, such as Torquatus and Corvus, later obtained political office.[23] Andrew Feldherr has refined Oakley's analysis, suggesting that the procedures of the formal duel both enacted the hierarchies of command in the Roman state and demonstrated success through the cooperation of the state, embodied in the magistrate, and the individual citizen-soldier.[24] Both of these views flesh out the task of the magistrate on the occasion of a duel: he has the right to allow or prohibit the engagement, and he is also the first to award praise or blame to the duelist.[25] He does not himself fight, however. The magistrate's responsibility is therefore reduced: he can determine whether to commit the combatant but has very little control over, and gains very little credit for, anything else that happens in the course of the duel.[26]

This exemplary misfit becomes more pronounced when we consider the other *exempla* that were available to Fabius to make the same point. Most conspicuous in its absence is any mention of the *spolia opima*, the trophies won by a Roman commander in single combat with the enemy leader. The topic seems an obvious and natural fit for Fabius' purposes if his intention was to highlight heroic leadership where the magistrate does indeed fight, and it would have allowed him the same pattern of ancient examples (e.g. Romulus) along with more recent ones (e.g. Marcellus).[27] His *exempla* are all of single combat, and his demand that the people elect a consul to match Hannibal is highly suggestive of an outcome in which the Roman consul and Carthaginian general meet face to face, as indeed Scipio Africanus and Hannibal do at the battle of Zama, even if only for

predates the scope covered by Oakley. The duel does, however, offer an interesting *exemplum* for the reception of the conquering hero: see Solodow 1979 and Feldherr 1998: 123–44.

23 Oakley 1985: 395 lists the one exception, the fictional duel of the father of Africanus, Publius Cornelius Scipio *cos.* 218, with a Gaul during the battle of the Ticinus (Sil. 4.264–310). Plutarch tells us that Marius fought a duel in his youth (*Mar.* 3.2), but in Frontin. *Str.* 4.7.5 we hear that as a consul he declined a challenge from a Teuton.

24 Feldherr 1998: 92–105.

25 The formulaic procedure is traceable in most duels, though most noticeable in those reported by Livy. Oakley 1985: 406 holds the procedure to be part and parcel of republican dueling practice, but note the suggestion in Feldherr 1998: 96 n. 47 that in most cases the request for permission was in fact a Livian insertion.

26 On the tension between the competing needs for individual heroics and military discipline and their effect on combat, see Levithan 2013. Chaplin 2000: 78–85 discusses how *exempla* do not always work in the way they were intended.

27 For Marcellus and the *spolia opima* see *MRR* 1.233. Flower 2000 explores Marcellus' place in the *spolia opima* tradition, while Flower 2003 and McDonnell 2006: 206–35 discuss Marcellus' fortunes after the dedication. Livy discusses the *spolia opima* at some length in 4.20, and they were clearly a sensitive issue under the Augustan regime; the issue has garnered substantial scholarly attention, most famously Syme 1959, and most recently (with full bibliography) Sailor 2006. On military *spolia* more generally: Lendon 2005: 172–8.

a contest of words (Livy 30.30–1). Appian (*Pun.* 188–9), indeed, has them engage in a duel to determine the outcome of the war. The choices Fabius does make, however, suit him perfectly, since, unlike the *spolia opima*, the strand of dueling tradition he chooses focuses on the avoidance of legionary battle, in keeping with Fabius' characteristic tactics of delay.[28] Fabius' *exempla*, therefore, are the product of deliberate choice between two available exemplary strands, and the misfit between the content of the *exempla* and the context in which they are invoked must form an important part of the impact of the speech.

Fabius' decision to use duels as his *exempla* appropriates a rhetorical model already used by Hannibal early in the third decade. Just before the battle of the Ticinus, both Hannibal and Publius Scipio address their troops.[29] Scipio opens his speech by establishing that he is as new to the soldiers as they are to him (21.40.4 *nouo imperatori apud nouos milites*), a device that emphasizes the narrative pause on the verge of this new war's first battle. He explains that he has left his old army behind so that they, the soldiers, might have a consul lead them against the enemy (21.40.4 *ut consulem ducem . . . haberetis*), and he goes on to assure them that the enemy is in fact one they had previously defeated: 21.40.5 *ne genus belli neue hostem ignoretis . . . quos . . . priore bello uicistis* ("do not be ignorant of the kind of war this is or of the enemy . . . whom you have defeated in the previous war").[30] Fabius' recurrence to *hoc bello, in hoc hoste nunquam ab ullo duce* (24.8.2), however, negatively interprets Scipio's opening gambit. Consuls have proven as inadequate as anyone in this war, against this enemy.

Hannibal's parallel exhortation makes use of not only speech but also symbolic performance. Before the assembled Carthaginian troops, Hannibal stages an exhibition of paired captives (21.43.1 *paribus*), each given the

[28] I am grateful to Matthew Roller for this point. I would add, however, that, while the *exempla* Fabius does choose avoid legionary battle through the duel of champions, Fabius could not actually have intended them as practical models for the voters, unless his view of the upcoming campaign was more romantic than his usual characterization admits.

[29] Livy is here reworking the sequence of events in Polybius, who has Hannibal's exhibition and speech (3.62–3) preceding that of Scipio (3.64): Levene 2010: 272–3. Significantly, when Scipio addresses his removal from his own army in Spain, Polybius has none of Livy's emphasis on the importance of having a consul at the head of the army but focuses instead on the strategic importance of holding Hannibal back from Italy. On these paired speeches as precursors to the meeting at Zama between Hannibal and Scipio Africanus: Levene 2010: 16–17.

[30] On battle exhortations in ancient historiography: Hansen 1993 and 1998; on Livy's practice Walsh [1954] 2009: 217, who points out that "[i]n this type of speech the elaboration made by Livy lies chiefly in examples – apposite references to previous battles or hardships overcome." The Roman insistence on defining the identity of the enemy and the type of war will be seen again not only in Fabius' speech but in the two other elections that reprise Fabius' recall of the *praerogatiua*, to which I return in the next section.

opportunity to duel to the death in exchange for freedom. Livy dwells on the detail of their weapons, which he classifies as Gallic (21.42.1 *armisque Gallicis*), which in a dueling context must recall the Romans' typical opponent, the gigantic Gaul.[31] After dismissing the pairs, Hannibal addresses the soldiers and explicitly assimilates the upcoming battle to the duels they have just seen: they must show the same spirit in fighting as they have in watching, and they, like the prisoners, are enchained by their geographical position and therefore must win or die (21.43.1–3). If Fabius' speech verbally alludes to Scipio's speech, his *exempla* allude to Hannibal's Gallic duels, and their relevance as a symbol of the kind of fortitude that would win the war. Fabius' *exempla*, then, point to duels not as an expression of youthful vigor, but as a tried-and-true means of victory. The allusion, too, is composite: on the one hand the duels are a motivating image, as they are for the Carthaginian army; on the other hand, they are suggestive of Roman victories against earlier enemies. In answering Scipio's rhetoric, Fabius rejects the assumption that any consul is sufficient against the enemy, because this enemy has defied expectations while the consuls have failed to meet them; a new paradigm is therefore necessary to re-establish parity between Rome and Carthage. Fabius' appropriation of Hannibal's model, however, also makes him, rather than the consular candidates, a match for the Carthaginian general, a parallelism that the Fabian tradition supports and upholds.[32] That in turn explains the importance of the duelist's subordination to a higher authority; as Otacilius suspected, Fabius aims to promote himself, if not as a consul proper, then as a paradigm for emulation, just as he attempted to do with Aemilius Paulus before the defeat at Cannae (22.39.9 *una ratio belli gerendi aduersus Hannibalem est qua ego gessi*, "the only way to wage war with Hannibal is the way I have waged it").

31 On the tradition of Romano-Gallic duels: Oakley 1998: 124–5, though he sees them as a "side-show, usually of little relevance to the outcome of the main fight." Their symbolic importance, however, is considerable, as Hannibal's and Fabius' respective uses of single combat show.

32 On the Fabian tradition: Elliot 2009a: 535–6 (with Sallustian parallels in 540–1), and Roller 2011. Hannibal himself recognizes Fabius as his equal in 22.16.5 *nec Hannibalem fefellit suis se artibus peti* ("nor did Hannibal miss that he was being fed his own medicine") and acknowledges it explicitly in 27.16.10 *"et Romani suum Hannibalem" inquit "habent; eadem qua ceperamus arte Tarentum amisimus"* ("The Romans, too, have their own Hannibal," he said. "We lost Tarentum by the same means as we won it"). Also relevant here is Scipio's reference to Hannibal as *aemulus itinerum Herculis* (21.41.7), a comparison which would have been especially topical in the context of Fabius' speech. The Fabii derived their descent, in one version, from Hercules himself: Wiseman 1974: 154, with further references. Note also that Scipio's standard exhortation to the troops to fight as if they were at the gates of Rome itself (21.41.15 *uelut si ante Romana moenia pugnemus*) is answered in the second of the three *praerogatiua* episodes (on which see pp. 115–18 below): 26.22.8 *uixdum requiesse aures a strepitu et tumultu hostili, quo paucos ante menses cesserint prope moenia Romana.*

Fabius' duelists, however, do not exemplify the paradigm in the same way: Torquatus and Corvus, both of whom engage Gallic opponents, are a more obvious model than Taurea and Asellus.[33] Moreover, Corvus consciously imitates Torquatus, which Torquatus himself recognizes.[34] Both go on to win consulships and lead Roman armies, Corvus in particular as a direct result of his dueling victory. As such, they are more appropriate as examples of young men on their way up, consular candidates rather than veteran commanders. Again, this interpretation both accords with the structural context – an election – and jars with the specifics: Fabius wishes for a veteran commander and goes on to be elected himself. But this fits with a different interpretation of youthful merits: duelists have, to some extent, already furnished proof of their success in war. Torquatus and Corvus indeed become linked in an exemplary chain emblematic of Roman superiority over the Gauls and as such make a good rhetorical parallel to Fabius himself, who has likewise already enjoyed proved success against Hannibal in the field during his dictatorship of 217 BC and was trying, with some success, to associate his own tactics with survival and victory over Hannibal.[35] The same issue recurs more explicitly on the next occasion when a *praerogatiua*'s vote is contested. In the consular election for 210 BC the *praerogatiua*, the *Voturia iuniores*, returned the name of T. Otacilius and Manlius Torquatus, descendant of the duelist. Manlius immediately asked the presiding consul to repeat the vote, since an eye ailment precluded him from effective generalship (26.22.6 *oculorum ualetudinem excusauit*),

33 Two further differences are worth noting: (1) Taurea and Asellus never actually come to blows. The elimination of physical violence, however, need not suggest that the duel was irrelevant: Asellus wins glory by showing his opponent to be a lesser man. (2) Taurea and Asellus are both mounted cavalry, unlike Torquatus and Corvus, who fight on foot. On aristocratic cavalry: McDonnell 2006: 185–95. McDonnell further points out (p. 192) that Corvus' is the last reported duel fought on foot; Fabius' speech thus responds to changes within aristocratic honor-culture as well as mapping out a change in exemplary discourse.

34 Corvus imitating Torquatus: 7.26.2 *M. erat Valerius tribunus militum adulescens, qui haud indigniorem eo decore se quam T. Manlium ratus*... ("M. Valerius was a young tribune of the soldiers, who thought himself no less worthy of this glory than T. Manlius . . . "); Torquatus' recognition: 7.26.12 *dictator*... *aemulumque decoris sui absentem M. Valerium Coruum – id enim illi deinde cognominis fuit – summo fauore populi, tres et uiginti natum annos, consulem renuntiauit* ("and the dictator, with the highest approval of the people, declared the imitator of his own glory, M. Valerius Corvus – for such was his nickname from now on – consul in his absence at the age of twenty-three").

35 Perhaps the clearest statement comes in Fabius' advice to Paulus on the eve of Cannae: 22.39.9 *sed ita res se habet: una ratio belli gerendi aduersus Hannibalem est qua ego gessi* ("but this is the way things are: the only way to wage war against Hannibal is the way I waged it"). By book 28 and the debate over Scipio's African plan, he unbends enough to say *uincere ego prohibui Hannibalem ut a uobis quorum uigent nunc uires etiam uinci posset* (28.40. 14 "I kept Hannibal from winning so that he can now be defeated by you whose strength still flourishes").

and the *iuniores* accordingly ask to consult their senior counterparts.[36] The *seniores* of tribe Voturia offer three new candidates: Quintus Fabius and Marcus Marcellus, who already had honors to their names (26.22.12 *duobus plenis iam honorum*), or, if they truly wished for someone new (26.22.12 *si utique nouum aliquem . . . uellent*), Marcus Valerius Laevinus, who fought *egregie* ("exceptionally") against Philip. Marcellus and Laevinus are elected. Thus the *seniores* associate *nouitas* not with the *temeritas* associated with *noui homines*, like Varro and Flaminius, nor with Otacilius' lackluster record, but rather with the transformation of early exceptionalism in one theater to a more mature exceptionalism in another.

If the two Gallic duels showcase experience, they emphatically do not address the issue of parity, so prominent at the opening of Fabius' speech. In fact, in both duels, the emphasis is on a seeming lack of parity: the Romans are small and nimble, while the Gauls are huge and lumbering. The Taurea and Asellus example, however, treats the question of parity directly.[37] Taurea and Asellus are well matched in excellence: 23.46.12–13 *unus eum Romanus Claudius Asellus gloria equestri aequaret* ("only Claudius Asellus among the Romans matched him in equestrian fame").[38] Their duel, moreover, means to ape the very consular duels Fabius deliberately overlooks, the *spolia opima*: 23.46.14 *cur non ferro decerneret daretque opima spolia uictus aut uictor caperet* ("why should [Asellus] not decide the matter by the sword, and either surrender the *spolia opima* in defeat, or bear them away in victory"). Thus, Taurea imagines the duel to be one between two leaders, which necessarily casts Asellus in the role of the consul. Whether as consul or cavalryman, however, the duel never materializes. As the maneuvers move from parade to rough ground, Taurea withdraws, coining the odd phrase *minime, sis, cantherium in fossam* (23.47.6 "geldings do

36 Those who think Livy is without a sense of humor might note that Torquatus' *oculorum ualetudinem* actually makes him a very suitable opponent for Hannibal, who loses his own eye at 22.2.11, during the crossing of the Apennines.

37 The names of both Taurea and Asellus reference animals (bull and ass, respectively). Both of the other duels likewise have animal references: Torquatus refers to his Gallic opponent as *belua* (7.10.3), while Corvus gains his animal *cognomen* because of the raven which alighted on his helmet (7.26.3; Gell. *NA* 9.11 and Dion. Hal. *Ant. Rom.* 15.1.4 attest that Corvus' statue in the Forum Augustum depicted him with a raven on his helmet, though Livy predates the statue by some years: Luce 1990). Cf. Oakley 1985: 394, who doubts "whether the annalists told the story correctly. For Gallic helmets regularly had animals or birds on top and the capture of one of these might easily have led to the *cognomen Coruus.* The story of the raven will then be a facile secondary tradition of a kind not uncommon in the works of the annalists."

38 Their parity is signaled from their very introduction, which is chiastic in structure: Livy 24.8.3 *Vibellio Taureae*, ***Campano summo equiti***, *prouocanti* ***summus Romanus eques*** *Asellus Claudius est oppositus.* The verb *est oppositus* draws explicit attention to the chiasmus.

not belong in a ditch"). As a parting shot, this falls rather flat, despite its proverbial status, and Taurea's meaning continues to baffle.[39]

The consular model Taurea offers for their equestrian duel, however, suggests one context in which horses and ditches mix well, and that is the *deuotio*, especially as figured by the legendary leap of Marcus Curtius in 7.6.5 (*in specum immisisse*). Like Taurea and Asellus, Curtius is an equestrian figure, and he is explicitly said to have devoted himself (7.6.4 *se deuouisse*) by his forum-bound leap. In the case of Asellus, too, the leap into the gulch precedes victory, but in less dramatic and fatal fashion: like Curtius, Asellus descends, but his journey then returns him to level ground (23.47.7 *perequitasset* – a pun on *equus* and *aequare*, perhaps?) and he returns to the camp in glory. The better known *deuotio*, in which the consul dedicated himself to the spirits of the underworld and then charged into the enemy forces was performed only by consuls, the two Decii Mures, in battle.[40] Indeed, the act was another possible alternative for exemplifying consular activity on the battlefield and, as Andrew Feldherr has shown, formed a narrative parallel to the formal duel.[41] This correspondence is most emphatically demonstrated in book 7 of the *AUC*, when both consuls perform exemplary deeds. In one case the Manlius Torquatus cited by Fabius executes his son for breaking ranks in imitation of his father's *exemplum*.[42] The other consul, Decius Mus, devotes himself to the nether gods to ensure a Roman victory. Thus, the example of Taurea and Asellus expands Fabius' range of reference beyond the duel proper, but nevertheless within the broader realm of individual martial heroism.

As an equestrian *deuotus*, Curtius is a revealing example to consider in this context, not least because, while he is not a consul in Livy's version, Varro (*Ling.* 5.150) preserves another version of the story, in which the *lacus Curtius* derived its name "from Curtius the consul" (*a Curtio consule . . . Curtium appellatum*), who ordered the area monumentalized in

39 Livy tells us that the phrase *minime sis cantherium in fossam* became a *rusticum prouerbium* (23.47.6), but the phrase does not occur again in extant Latin.

40 The *deuotio Deciana*: Livy 8.9.8 and 10.28.13. A thorough discussion of the issues can be found in Oakley 1998: 477–86, and Rüpke 1990: 156–62. Curtius' leap, naturally, echoes the *deuotio Deciana* only in part, since Curtius cannot dedicate an enemy to the gods, a central element in the tradition. However, even this partial overlap is rhetorically significant. Cf. Dyck 2004b on Cicero's use of the *deuotio* as a paradigm in the *post Reditum* speeches. Vergil was likewise sensitive to the resonances of the verb and has Turnus declare in 11.440–2 *animam hanc . . . deuoui* (although Pascal 1990 rejects the interpretation of *deuoui* as a Decian-style *deuotio*). Regardless of the precise nature of Curtius' leap, however, he presents himself as a symbol of Roman martial valor, and as such he is as symbolic of the Roman state as the consuls themselves.

41 Feldherr 1998: 82–92.

42 On the implications of the execution for the construction of the magisterial image, see my discussion in Chapter 1, above.

honor of a lightning strike. Whether or not Livy was aware of the variant, the relevance of the Curtius *exemplum* is underscored not only by his *deuotio*, but also by the fact that the episode, like Fabius' duelists, highlights youth and success in war. Curtius himself is depicted as a "young man excellent in war" (7.6.3 *iuuenem bello egregium*), a position he shares with all of Fabius' duelists. His youth, excellence, and weaponry together form the sacrifice which finally closes up the chasm in the heart of the city. The validity of the sacrifice is immediately put to the test by the consul Genucius, who must straightaway leave the city to deal with the menacing Hernici. Genucius is also the first plebeian consul to wage war under his own auspices, and the city is on tenterhooks waiting to see the outcome (7.6.8 *in exspectatione ciuitas erat, quod primus ille de plebe consul bellum suis auspiciis gesturus esset*). From a structural point of view, there can be no doubt that Genucius is a negative foil for Curtius. As a representative of his class, he stands in for their untried military record, in contrast to the well-caparisoned Curtius;[43] and while the Curtius episode builds a momentum that culminates in his leap into the very center of the *ciuitas*, Genucius also leaps – 7.6.9 *praecipitaret* – but away from the city and into enemy hands. Curtius becomes an *exemplum* in his own right, despite the aetiological confusion over the *lacus*; Genucius, by contrast, is unrecognized even by his enemies, who kill him unaware (7.6.9 *ab insciis*) that they have captured a Roman consul. Nevertheless, when the defeat is announced in Rome, Genucius does become a *documentum*, albeit of plebeian incompetence and impiety, tainting the auspices and with them Roman military prowess (7.6.11 *deletum cum duce exercitum documento fuisse*). Thus, Genucius immediately and emphatically appears to invalidate Curtius' sacrifice. And yet the simplicity of the opposition is precisely what makes both it and other related *exempla* an unsuitable choice for Fabius' speech. The cases of consular *deuotiones* and the *spolia opima* represent a straightforward *exemplum* of martial heroism that fails to convey the particular quality Fabius wishes to see in a magistrate and leaves too little room for redefinition. The martial heroism of the duelist, however, despite being *prima facie* an imprecise fit for a consular election, turns out to be an immediate success, at least from Fabius' point of view: he is elected consul,

43 Thus Lipovsky 1981: 50: "They (i.e. plebeians) stand, as it were, at the beginning of a long road; they shall prove their worth only when they have established a similar record of excellent service. Only thus will they be able to refute accusations, based on individual cases, that they are unfit for office." Oakley 1998: 102 n. 1 adds that in fact plebeian military tribunes must have already commanded armies. The episode, therefore, is more about patrician attitudes than the plebeian record.

Rome gains a respite before the disaster at Cannae, and the lessons of the past are learned, even if for a short time.

Variations on the *centuria praerogatiua*

Fabius' speech shares its basic structure with two other episodes, to which I now turn in order to situate the Fabius episode within the broader context of the third decade, as well as illustrating how the three episodes function together as variations on a unified theme. The three instances appear fairly close together in the text (24.7.10–9.3; 26.22; 27.6), and all three address the same basic issue of the suitability of the candidates for the task at hand. In Roman elections, a century, known as the *praerogatiua*, was selected by lot to cast the first vote, and this century plays a part in all three episodes. Its vote was entered and announced before the other centuries proceeded to vote, and it was thus thought to be highly influential, if not determinative of the final result.[44] In these three cases, after the *praerogatiua*'s vote is announced, someone (the presiding magistrate, the candidate himself, and a tribune of the plebs, respectively) intervenes to argue that the choice of the *praerogatiua* is unsuitable and sends the voters back to retake the vote. Thus, all three episodes, in addition to their structural similarity, also focus on the competing questions of whom to elect and according to which criteria.

The *praerogatiua* in our first example (the second of the three) is *Aniensis iuniorum*, the junior century of the *Aniensis* tribe. It returns the names of Titus Otacilius and Marcus Aemilius Regillus. Upon the announcement of these names, Fabius Maximus orders silence and makes the speech in which he urges the people to elect an altogether different consul, who would be a match for Hannibal. The century obeys, and Otacilius complains that Fabius only wishes to remain in office (24.9.1 *continuare consulatum uelle*). Thus, our episode already establishes two strands of interpretation: the first focusing on expediency, and the second on procedure. Strikingly, the two later episodes depict exactly the same bifurcation. In 26.22, the consular election in 211 BC, the *iuniores* of tribe Voturia return Titus Otacilius (at long last) and Titus Manlius Torquatus. The latter, however, asks the consul to recall the *praerogatiua* and requests exemption from service on account of an eye ailment (26.22.3–5). Like Fabius, he recurs to the ship-of-state metaphor to claim that he is unfit as either *gubernator* or *imperator* (26.22.6), and the voters must therefore elect someone else, being mindful

[44] On the *centuria praerogatiua*: Taylor 1966: 91–6, esp. 93–4.

of both the war in Italy and the plight of the state (26.22.7 *meminisse in consulibus creandis belli quod in Italia sit temporumque rei publicae*), especially after the recent siege of Rome. When the voters pronounce their minds unchanged, Manlius finally exclaims:

> "neque ego uestros" inquit "mores consul ferre potero neque uos imperium meum. redite in suffragium et cogitate bellum Punicum in Italia et hostium ducem Hannibalem esse." (Livy 26.22.9)
>
> "As consul," he said, "I will not be able to bear your customs, nor will you be able to bear my command. Go back to the ballot and consider that there is a Punic war in Italy, and that the leader of the enemy is Hannibal."

The reciprocal intolerance of consul and voters is itself typical of contional banter at Rome and is especially appropriate to a descendant of a man nicknamed *Imperiosus*.[45] It is to Hannibal, however, that the speech draws attention as the only clear index for suitability for office. The message is identical to Fabius' – that the new consuls must be a match for Hannibal – though here Hannibal is the trump card in Manlius' argument, rather than the initial premise as he is in Fabius' speech. The episode thus offers a precedent for Fabius' more fleshed-out rhetoric and illustrates thereby the escalating urgency of Rome's situation, which militates heavily for electoral expediency at the expense of both principle and procedure.

In counterpoint to Manlius' focus on Hannibal, the third iteration of the *praerogatiua* scene concentrates entirely on procedure and process. The *praerogatiua* – this time the *iuniores* of tribe Galeria – votes for Q. Fulvius and Q. Fabius, whereupon the tribunes of the plebs threaten to veto: 27.6.4 *qui neque magistratum continuari satis ciuile esse aiebant et multo foedioris exempli eum ipsum creari qui comitia haberet* ("they said that to hold magistracies back-to-back was hardly constitutional, and for the person presiding over the vote to be elected was a worse precedent by far"). This attention to procedure, and especially the technical term *magistratum continuare*, directly recalls Otacilius' complaints in 24.9.1 (*continuare consulatum*). The dictator, Q. Fulvius, in turn invokes a sequence of *exempla* to justify the election's results. He begins with Trasimene and ends with the recent example of Fabius himself, in which he repeats the now thematic

[45] He is introduced in Livy 22.60.5 as a man of *priscae ac nimis durae . . . seueritatis* ("of an old and too harsh sternness"). On his adherence to family traditions: Feeney 2010: 212. See Oakley 1998: 86 for the ascription of the statement in Dio fr. 35.9 and the *de uiris illustribus* 28.5 to the first Torquatus. For this kind of contional banter compare, e.g., Scipio Nasica in Val. Max. 3.7.3 *"tacete, quaeso, Quirites," inquit "plus ego enim quam uos quid rei publicae expediat intellego"* ("Silence, please, Citizens," he said, "for I know better than you what is useful for the republic").

phrase *consulatum continuare*: 27.6.8 *recens* [*sc. exemplum*] *Q. Fabi, qui sibi continuari consulatum nisi id bono publico fieret profecto nunquam sisset* ("and recently Q. Fabius, who would never have stood for back-to-back consulships unless it was ultimately in the public good . . . ").[46] The tension is finally resolved through senatorial mediation, which determines that the state, at this time, ought to be led by "veteran commanders, who had experience and skill in war" (27.6.10 *ueteres et expertos belliquae peritos imperatores*). So, unlike the two previous episodes, the vote of the *praerogatiua* is upheld, bringing the sequence to a close.

These three episodes, which together offer structural and verbal variations on the same theme, interrogate the tension between the people's electoral decisions and the overarching concern for the pressing military task. Both Otacilius and the tribunes object to the continuations in office of seasoned generals, which the tribunes explicitly declare "unconstitutional" (27.6.4 *neque . . . satis ciuile esse*).[47] The consular and senatorial opposition, in the persons of Fabius, Manlius, and Fulvius, however, see the central issue as something wholly different: the military needs of the moment, they argue, override any concern for proper procedure and legitimize whatever course of action best serves Rome's survival. All three episodes justify the blatant disregard for normal constitutional niceties because of the pressure exerted by Hannibal's presence in Italy, and Rome's continued failure to contain him. Indeed, the first and second *praerogatiua* episodes bracket the siege of Rome in 26.7–11, an event which graphically illustrates the peril faced by the city. Under such harrowing circumstances, the episodes reiterate, priorities must be realigned, and the task of the voters must be narrowed down to the needs of the hour. As such, these episodes situate themselves further along a continuum which charts an increasing mismatch between the legitimacy of procedures and the peril of circumstances. Increasingly dangerous situations generate greater interest in the question of whether

46 Livy's persistent attention to *magistratum continuare* here is paralleled by Fabius' designation of Hannibal in 24.8.7 as *ueterem ac perpetuum imperatorem* ("an old and consistent general"), in counterpoint to Rome's annually changing magistrates (*in annum creatus . . . comparabitur*). This paradigm can also be inverted, as in the Alexander digression (esp. 9.17.9–10), in which Livy contrasts the youthful Alexander with Rome's gallery of experienced commanders (but see also 9.18.12–15, where Livy identifies annuity and collegiality as one of the problems plaguing Roman commanders).

47 I follow Yardley 2006: 385 in translating *nec satis ciuile* as "unconstitutional," which should not be taken in its modern sense of "irreconcilable with a written charter" but rather as an act or a quality unbecoming in a citizen (cf. *OLD* s.v. *ciuilis*). We might compare Livy on Africanus 38.56.9 *magis pie quam ciuiliter*, when, during the trials of the Scipios, Africanus resorted to *uis* in order to defend his brother from his accusers.

and how "proper procedure" ought to be maintained. The pressured circumstances of the Hannibalic war, in which all three *praerogatiua* episodes take place, explain in part both their recurring interest in procedure and Fabius' effort to generate a magisterial *exemplum* – the obedient duelist – which is emblematic of subordination to proper procedure.[48]

The magistrate manqué

If wartime elections stand on one end of a continuum charting the incursion of war into domestic politics, further along we find situations in which the city and the army grow increasingly separate, and in which the army itself apes civic procedures independently of the city. These situations, usually falling within the army-as-city topos, intensify the persistent concern with procedural legitimacy.[49] That preoccupation is also fueled by the idea that the shift from city to army entailed a decrease in the people's ability to exercise their voting rights freely. Livy explores this idea in an episode from the end of his narrative for 357 BC. It is narrated almost in passing as the sole notable action taken by one of the consuls:

> ab altero consule nihil memorabile gestum, nisi quod legem nouo exemplo ad Sutrium in castris tributim de uicensima eorum qui manumitterentur tulit. patres, quia ea lege haud paruum uectigal inopi aerario additum esset, auctores fuerunt; ceterum tribuni plebis non tam lege quam exemplo moti, ne quis postea populum seuocaret, capite sanxerunt: nihil enim non per milites iuratos in consulis uerba, quamuis perniciosum populo, si id liceret, ferri posse. (Livy 7.16.7–8)
>
> Nothing worth remembering was done by the other consul, except that in his camp near Sutrium he passed a law of a new type through the tribes, about a one-twentieth tax on those who were manumitted. The fathers approved this, because through this law a not inconsiderable income would be added to the impoverished treasury; but the tribunes of the plebs, moved not so much by the law but rather by the example it set, made it a capital offense if anyone should summon away the people. For if this was permitted, there was nothing, however detrimental to the people, which could not be passed by soldiers bound by oath to follow the consul.

48 For a similar triadic structure, where Livy offers variations on the same theme (an "episodic polyptoton" of sorts) see my discussion of the "Rullianus cycle" on pp. 159–69. In both cases the situation is rife with irony, since a common insistence on proper procedure disguises Fabius' and Rullianus' willingness to push proper procedure to its limits.

49 On the army-as-city topos: Hornblower 2004; for another instantiation of the trope, see my discussion of the army at Caudium on pp. 72–3.

We might reconstruct any number of scenarios to account for a law being passed in such circumstances, but Livy himself does not provide much context for this unusual procedure.[50] The opening sentence compacts all the relevant issues: the new precedent (*nouo exemplo*), the location near Sutrium – emphatically not Rome – and then the collocation *in castris tributim*, which encapsulates the impossible coexistence of civic and military structures.[51] The tribunes likewise slide between the two frames of reference as they develop the principle of separation between army and people. The reason why any withdrawal of the people is potentially dangerous (*perniciosum*) is that any reconstitution of the city in a military guise entails an important shift in the identities of the voters. They move from being regular citizens to soldiers sworn to follow the commands of the consul (*milites iuratos in consulis uerba*). As *milites*, they are therefore bound to pass anything, even if dangerous to their own interest as members of the *populus*.

The tribunes attempt to nip the new *exemplum* in the bud by offering their own counter-measure, which itself has some exemplary pedigree: a prohibition on removal of parts of the voting populace (*ne quis postea populum seuocare*). In this context, and with the tribunes speaking, the phrase *populum seuocare* alludes to the synonyms *secedere* and *auocare*, and through them to the secessions of the plebs.[52] The plebeian secessions are both a perplexing allusion and an especially evocative one, the former because the secessions were one of the tools employed by the plebeian leaders to obtain concessions from the patricians (the opposite of the scenario at Sutrium), the latter because the secessions are themselves an instance of the army-as-city topos. The secessions are successful because of a pressing military need, and because the plebs, who comprised the majority of the citizen-army, constituted themselves also as an alternative city. The first secession is a particularly telling parallel: the army fortifies itself in a camp on the Aventine, in which setting it elects magistrates and administers an oath.[53] Thus, the tribunes' action here is self-referential,

[50] For the law see Oakley 1998: 181–3; Elster 2003: 18–19. Attention is usually drawn either to the tax itself or to the identity of the assembly as the *comitia tributa populi*. Livy mentions it again in 27.10.11–12, when the consuls decide to use the gold for the war effort.

[51] On the *comitia tributa*, Lintott 1999: 50–5 summarizes the problem of identifying a tribal assembly encompassing the whole people, which was therefore separate from the exclusively plebeian *concilium plebis*. Crucially, the tribal assembly was held within the *pomerium*, unlike the *comitia centuriata*, which constituted the people in its military guise and convened in the campus Martius outside the city.

[52] E.g. Cic. *Mur.* 15 *ut rursus plebes in Auentinum seuocanda esse uideatur.*

[53] Army camp on the Mons Sacer: 2.32.4 *uallo fossaque communitis castris*. Election of magistrates: 2.33.1–3; cf. Ogilvie 1965: 309–14. Livy further tells us that they were without any leader (2.32.4 *sine*

evoking and inverting the historical actions of the tribunes of the plebs in order to block what they see as another potential injustice.

The senate, at least, seems to have taken the lesson to heart. In the narrative of 212 BC they had occasion to apply the same logic to a slightly different instantiation of the same topos. The brothers Publius and Gnaeus Cornelius Scipio, father and uncle to the future Africanus, had perished in Spain within a few weeks of each other, leaving Roman forces in Spain without a leader and facing a direct threat from the Carthaginian armies in their vicinity. The situation is salvaged by the initiative of L. Marcius, himself an instantiation of another favorite Livian topos, the *unus uir* who swoops in to save the day.[54] With a daring plan, Marcius leads the army back into relative safety. He then promptly writes to the senate in Rome with news of events. In his missive, he also espouses the title *propraetor*. The senate's response is mixed:

> principio eius anni cum de litteris L. Marci referretur, res gestae magnificae senatui uisae: titulus honoris, quod imperio non populi iussu, non ex auctoritate patrum dato "propraetor senatui" scripserat, magnam partem hominum offendebat: rem mali exempli esse imperatores legi ab exercitibus et solemne auspicandorum comitiorum in castra et prouincias procul ab legibus magistratibusque ad militarem temeritatem transferri. (Livy 26.2.1–2)

> In the beginning of this year, when the letter of Lucius Marcius was discussed, the senate judged his achievements laudable; the label of office, however, offended a great number of people, since he wrote "the propraetor to the senate," though his command had not been authorized by the people, nor given through the authority of the senate. [They felt that] it set a bad example for commanders to be chosen by armies and for the solemn rite of elections, which must be held under auspices, to be undertaken, with all the rashness of the military, in camps and provinces, away from laws and the magistrates.

ullo duce), another recurring feature in the episodes analyzed here: the army's lack of leadership spurs them into varying types of electoral scenarios. The tribune's move from *plebs* to *populus* may also be significant, since the noun *populus* and its cognate verb *populari* have strong military connotations (*OLD* s.v. *populor*), underscoring further the collapsed distinction between army and city. For the idea of *populus* as *exercitus*: Rüpke 1990: 58–94. Note in comparison, however, that in Caudium, Livy designates the tribunes as *militum* while in the gorge, and *plebis* while in the city – though he admittedly conflates two types of tribunes.

54 25.37.2 *uir unus res perditas restituit* ("one man brought back the situation from the brink of ruin"). For the Livian use of the topos: Santoro L'Hoir 1990: 230–3. Other notable instances of the topos include Horatius Cocles (2.10.2), Camillus (5.47.8–9), and especially Fabius Maximus (30.26.9, following Ennius). On the Marcius episode more generally: Jaeger 1997: 107–24, focusing on Marcius' ability to manipulate historical memory, especially as it pertains to the Scipios; and Walter 2001: 275–6.

The senatorial sentiments expressed in this short passage recognize two main faults with Marcius' assumption of the title *propraetor*, as well as defining four necessary criteria for the proper election of generals. The two main faults are familiar: Marcius was not elected by the people (*non populi iussu*), nor was he appointed by the senate (*non ex auctoritate patrum*). Marcius himself, it might be noted, clearly sees his position as justified *de facto* if not *de iure* – the person in charge of the army behaved like a Roman magistrate and was therefore entitled to be addressed as such. His justifications for this view are themselves revealing, and I will return to them shortly. Nevertheless, the senate is far more interested in procedural definitions than in functional ones, an emphasis which is reflected in the legalistic attention to boundaries and demarcation. The fathers proceed to explain what they feel is a bad *exemplum* of electoral process: the voters are soldiers rather than citizens (*ab exercitibus*), the location is in a military camp and a province rather than in Rome (*in castra et prouincias*), the appointment is made with military haste rather than solemnly and with the auspices (*solemne auspicandorum comitiorum . . . ad militarem temeritatem transferri*), and finally, it is made far from the laws and the magistrates (*procul ab legibus magistratibusque*).[55] This rhetoric echoes, thematically if not verbally, the concerns voiced by the tribunes at Sutrium, with the added element that the army was not following orders but rather arrogating to its present circumstances the same rights as it would be entitled to in its citizen guise.

This is the same concern that animates the elaborate legalism of Camillus' election during the siege of Rome in book 5, where the Romans go to great lengths in order to maintain correct procedure in an extreme situation. The army in Veii decides to recall Camillus, exiled in Ardea, as their leader in liberating Rome from the Gauls. Despite the physical distance and the Gallic siege, however, they insist on consulting the senate in Rome and obtaining its legal permission. Livy then editorializes: 5.46.7 *adeo regebat omnia pudor discriminaque rerum prope perditis rebus seruabant* ("so much did a sense of propriety direct everything and so carefully did they preserve the distinction of things even when their affairs were near ruin"). This acute sense of propriety leads to an almost comical procedure, where the army and senate elect Camillus by correspondence and despite great danger (5.46.8 *ingenti periculo*):

[55] The preposition *procul* again emphasizes the importance of location and implicitly associates laws and the magistrates with Rome, or at least dissociates them from *castra* and *prouinciae*.

> [*sc.* nuntius] . . . in capitolium euadit, et ad magistratus ductus mandata exercitus edit. accepto inde senatus consulto uti comitiis curiatis reuocatus de exsilio iussu populi Camillus dictator extemplo diceretur militesque haberent imperatorem quem uellent, eadem degressus nuntius Veios contendit. (Livy 5.46.9–10)
>
> [*sc.* the messenger] . . . sneaked into the Capitol and, after being taken to the magistrates, issued the missives of the army. He received the senate's decree, namely, that Camillus was summoned from exile by the assembly of the curiae, and by the order of the people he was immediately to be called dictator, and that the soldiers should have the general they want. Bearing that response, the messenger rushed back to Veii.

Throughout the preceding narrative of the sack of Veii, the physical city, as Christina Kraus has argued, is doubled and tripled, with Rome and Veii both offering competing paradigms for the legacy of Troy.[56] The Gallic sack prevents the unification of the city, and the distribution of senate and army literally creates an *altera Roma*. The fact that Veii is a second Rome, however, is not sufficient to make the appointment of Camillus a constitutionally straightforward procedure. Legalism here works to bridge the geographical gap, and it is striking to note how reciprocal it is. The army at Veii recognizes the legitimacy of the city, and through the messenger answers exactly the kinds of complaints that will be made by the senate in the Marcius example above, namely, that elections be held near the magistrates and the law (note *magistratus* in 5.46.9), and away from the camps and the military, a physical separation emphasized by the obstacles faced by the messenger: river, buoy, and rock-climbing – three activities which at least partially prefigure the Gauls' subsequent attempt at taking the Capitol (5.47.1–6, esp. 2 *seu uestigio notato humano qua nuntius a Veiis peruenerat*). The senate, for its part, recognizes its own limitations: the senators are, effectively, exiled in their own state, without the people to give legitimacy to any electoral act. They therefore correctly convene a *comitia curiata* to ratify, but not promulgate or decide on, Camillus' recall and his new position as dictator and *imperator*.[57] They can thus maintain procedural propriety, while also recognizing the civic identity of the soldiery as an elective body and affirming the expression of their will, as if in a normal election.[58]

[56] Kraus 1994b, esp. 278–83. [57] Ogilvie 1965: 732–3; Lintott 1999: 49.

[58] The phrase they use, *militesque haberent imperatorem quem uellent*, is a variant of a sentiment the senators often express in electoral contexts, e.g. in 32.7.11, the example with which this book opened: *populo creandi quem uelit potestatem fieri aequum esse* ("it is fair that the people should have power to elect whom they will"). See my discussion in Chapter 4.

In fact, when Marcius applies to the senate as *propraetor*, he does so based on an election held by the soldiers, which apes in procedures and vocabulary a proper election in the city:

> sed tantum praestitit eques Romanus auctoritate inter milites atque honore, ut castris citra Hiberum communitis cum ducem exercitus comitiis militaribus creari placuisset, subeuntes alii aliis in custodiam ualli stationesque, donec per omnes suffragium iret, ad L. Marcium cuncti summam imperii detulerint. (Livy 27.25.5–6)
>
> But the Roman knight so excelled among the soldiers in authority and respect, that it was decided, when a camp was established on this side of the Ebro, that the commander of the army should be elected in a military election. And they all stood in for each other on guard duty on the ramparts and at the sentry posts, until everyone voted, and they unanimously elevated L. Marcius to the highest office.

These elections have a strong military tint: Livy carefully qualifies them as *militaribus*, as held *in castris*, by an *exercitus* and in order to elect a *dux* – all stock military vocabulary. The tension between civic and military in this environment is vividly drawn by the detail of the men taking turns at the guard post and the ballot. But these elections have parallels to normal elections as well: Marcius has a competitor, Titus Fonteius, P. Scipio's legate, and Livy's emphasis on Marcius' good qualities, as well as his rank and excellence (*praestitit eques Romanus*) evokes the kind of canvassing candidates normally engage in. Each of the men has *suffragium*, and they produce (*creari*, an electoral term)[59] *summam imperii*, a circumlocution for the simpler *imperium*, which they were not technically allowed to endow. The superlative *summam* is suggestive also of Marcius' movement up the *cursus honorum*, since the elections improve on the *honor* ("respect," but also a synonym for the magistracies) Marcius already has. In fact, when Marcius addresses the troops to lay out his battle plans, he both refers to his office as his *imperium* (25.38.2) and adverts to its civic resonances: 25.38.3 *cogor uestram omnium uicem . . . unus consulere* ("I am forced, alone, to take counsel on all your behalf").[60] However, even this elaborate election is insufficient to bridge the gap between Rome and the army camp. What was possible for Camillus because of the short distance between Rome, Veii, and Ardea, is rendered impossible for a Roman army in Spain. This considerable difference in circumstances, however, does not lead the senate

[59] *OLD* s.v. 5 a–b. Synonyms in Livy include, e.g., *dictator diceretur* (Camillus, 5.46.10, and again at 5.46.11 *dictatorque . . . dictus*), or of Marcius himself, *legi* (26.2.2), but *consul creari* is regular enough in contemporary Latin that the use of the verb must be pointed.

[60] On counseling as the consular activity par excellence, see my discussion in Chapter 2: 64–74.

to reconsider the validity of the legalistic procedure, nor its value as an *exemplum*. On the contrary, it insists on emphasizing the distance (*procul*) between Rome and the army, and it overlooks entirely the considerable efforts to which the army goes to legitimize the election, thereby rejecting Marcius as a magisterial *exemplum*.

The Marcius episode raises another relevant consideration. Like Camillus and Fabius, Marcius is an instantiation of Livy's *unus uir* topos, in which one man single-handedly saves the state.[61] Marcius is immediately distinguished from Camillus and Fabius in his class and rank – an *eques* to their senatorial aristocracy – but his circumstances are also considerably more urgent than theirs: Camillus manages to obtain senatorial approval for his appointment; Fabius presses the *praerogatiua* beyond normative bounds because of wartime demands; and Marcius pushes his army even further beyond the norm because their situation is more critical still. Positioned in this way, one might wonder how well Marcius himself would fit the exemplary paradigm Fabius sets up in his speech. Marcius is certainly no duelist, although he is both heroic and more than up to the task at hand, extricating his army from the clutches of not one but three Carthaginian armies. His situation is an extreme microcosm of the Roman position in Italy: they are pressed by Hannibal and must find someone who can rescue them from the snare. Further, despite the senate's rejection of his self-assumed title "pro-praetor," his adherence to procedure is as scrupulous as circumstances allow. He seems to be hindered by the distance from Rome and the hazardous conditions, not by any desire to avoid a proper electoral process. In any case, as the third *praerogatiua* episode shows, the circumstances are sufficiently dire to permit moving beyond standard protocols. Thus Marcius seems, in some important ways, to fit Fabius' paradigm, with suitable adjustments for the more prosaic conditions of war over the poetics of heroic duels. The senate's rejection of his *exemplum*, however, militates otherwise: Marcius' procedural omission suffices to mark him as the wrong kind of *exemplum*, whereas the duelist paradigm emphasizes correct procedure over results or, more precisely, accepts as legitimate only those results obtained through the proper channels.[62]

If Marcius cannot be a magisterial *exemplum*, what kind of *exemplum* is he? I have already mentioned the *unus uir* topos, though it is telling

[61] See n. 54 above.

[62] The senatorial rejection of Marcius as a consular *exemplum* is all the more striking since, as Santoro L'Hoir 1990: 231 suggests, the "*unus uir* constantly exercises the wisdom and *imperium* of a consul . . . " In one case, that of Appius Claudius in 495 BC, Livy even defines *unus uir* as *id enim plus esse quam consulem* (2.28.4 "for that was more than a consul").

that Marcius himself alludes to much humbler exemplary stock than the likes of Manlius and Corvus. When he exhorts his troops before battle, Marcius tells them that the coming battle will be a *documentum* (25.38.9 "proof") that the Roman name was not yet extinct, just as the Roman *uis atque uirtus* (25.38.10 "might and bravery") was not routed at Cannae. As a point of comparison, Cannae is apt: if the Romans were able to recover from that defeat, they should *a fortiori* be able to overcome their current predicament.[63] But Cannae is also apt because the situations are very similar in structure, and indeed both form cases of a Roman army stranded behind the line by a catastrophic defeat. In the aftermath of the battle of Cannae, several groups of Romans were left behind, including, most prominently, those Romans and Italians who fell captive to the Carthaginians.[64] Besides these, however, another group consisted of soldiers left in the Roman camp after nightfall, who banded together to break through the Carthaginian lines at the instigation of Sempronius Tuditanus, the *tribunus militum* (22.50.6). There is, of course, no election or semblance of one, and Livy qualifies the escape as fortuitous (*cuique aut fors dabat)*, unplanned (*ex consilio ipsorum*), and under no single command (*imperio cuiusquam*).[65] Tuditanus nevertheless gives exhortations, which culminate, in 22.50.9, with *ferro atque audacia uia fit quamuis per confertos hostes* ("with sword and daring there will be a path even through the thick of the enemy"). Although the parallel between Tuditanus' *ferro atque audacia* and Marcius' *uis atque uirtus* is verbally inexact, the context and especially the explicit connection Marcius makes with Cannae suggest that the two phrases form a pattern of allusion, which connects the ideas of valor (*audacia, uirtus*) with the means to demonstrate them (*ferro, uis*). In both cases the formula

63 On Cannae as *exemplum*, Chaplin 2000: 62–5. Chaplin sees Marcius' reference as "more a passing characterization than an exhortation to action" (62 n. 38) and so does not include him in her reading of the Cannae *exemplum* as "a measuring stick for Roman and Carthaginian progress through the course of the war" (62).

64 Their request for ransom and repatriation was firmly rejected by the senate, finally and effectively severing the bonds between army and city, with Torquatus explicitly citing the behavior of Sempronius Tuditanus as the *exemplum* they should have emulated (22.60.8–14). Likewise those legions which had fought at Cannae were kept under arms but far from Rome throughout the war (23.25.7–8; they eventually fight in Africa with Scipio Africanus: 29.24.11–12), effecting a less severe kind of separation. These two groups have in common a failure to return to the fold under their own steam, or in other words, to constitute themselves as a body able to exist independently of its circumstances. On Torquatus' speech as a reiteration of the Cannae narrative: Chaplin 2000: 57–62; note especially 59–60, on Torquatus' elaboration of the Tuditanus episode over and above Livy's own primary narrative.

65 22.50.12 *haec apud uictos magis impetu animorum, quos ingenium suum cuique aut fors dabat, quam ex consilio ipsorum aut imperio cuiusquam agebatur* ("This was done by the defeated more by impulse, as much as each man's talent or luck allowed him, rather than by any counsel or under anyone's command").

also serves to isolate and identify the cultural characteristics which will extricate either army from its current predicament.

The Cannae *exemplum* unifies Marcius and Fabius in yet another way. For Fabius, it is a model for avoidance. The Roman voters must not return yet another incompetent general, like Varro or Flaminius, but must instead choose someone with experience or proper respect for the channels of command and procedure. Fabian tactics, whether on the field of battle or in the electoral campaign, are the only means of survival. Marcius, however, selects his *exemplum* with greater specificity, which allows him to treat Cannae as a positive example. It is, for him, a model for imitation, since the two groups can save themselves by the same means: force and daring. Marcian tactics, in Spain, will win safety for the Romans, just as they did earlier, in the aftermath of Cannae. Thus, Fabius and Marcius each develop their different Cannae *exempla* in mutually exclusive ways: the Fabian tactic of delay cannot coexist with the Marcian tactic of daring. This dialectic, as Matthew Roller has shown, is fundamental to the exemplary tradition which grew around Fabius Maximus, but in the context of magisterial *exempla* it has a particular potency.[66] The rejection of Marcius as a suitable *exemplum* for magistracy validates the prioritization of Fabius' exemplary model and thus obfuscates Fabius' own transgressions against proper procedure, namely his disruption of the vote, which he himself acknowledges as, under normal circumstances, dismissive of the people's *libertas*.[67] The army *in extremis*, therefore, offers a useful device for political exemplarity: in removing the constraints of the city, it develops an alternative strand of *exempla*, which are not negative in and of themselves, but *are* negative in the narrower context of the city. This makes better sense also of Fabius' choice of the duelist, which is, after a fashion, the most tractable form of heroism available in Rome: a performer of glorious deeds in the service of the state, but only once proper procedure has been satisfied.

Just as Fabius thoughtfully deploys his examples, Marcius, too, explores the contours and gradations of the consular *persona*, highlighting by contrast both the desirable elements in it as well as the conditions in which success can be achieved. In this complicated matrix, *exempla* operate as both precedent and stereotype and guide Livy's reader as the narrative itself develops a composite image of the consul-general. The army-as-city topos serves as a literary background to this question, adding a layer of contextual

66 Roller 2011, with further references.

67 24.28.1 *is mihi parum meminisse uideretur uestrae libertatis* ("he would appear to me too little mindful of your liberty" quoted in text on p. 97 above).

complexity in which all the *exempla* participate, and which helps to organize the problem by highlighting two mutually exclusive concerns: that the army and city be at the same time alike and different. This delicate negotiation translates into the exemplary realm as well: the consul should be similar to, but not exactly like, a duelist; he must be experienced, but not worn down; he must represent the Roman people as their champion but not arrogate glory to himself. These are all, in their own ways, literary manifestations of political problems, and the texts analyzed in this chapter – Livy, Cicero, Sallust, and Pliny – leave most of these problems without explicit answers. What is more important than any simplistic solution is rather the process by which magisterial *exempla* are constructed. Both Cicero and Sallust use Marius' electoral campaign to generate a stereotypical image of the protagonist, which can change based on the author and the genre. Genucius, too, undergoes the same process: he swiftly becomes a negative *exemplum* of plebeian impiety and defeat, just as Marius became an *exemplum* of *nouitas* and perfidy. Fabius' speech offers a more fully elaborated view of the image of the magistrate. None of these examples offers a decisive or satisfactory conclusion. They do not determine whether consuls in wartime ought to be young or old, patrician or plebeian. They do, however, draw lines in the sand, shifting constructions that highlight what a consul *could* be: a duelist, a paragon of virtue, a symbol of social or national superiority, and above all, a constantly changing *exemplum* of its own values and conduct.

CHAPTER 4

Elections as narratives of magistracy

Early in 184 BC the *praetor urbanus*, C. Decimius, died. In due course a by-election was held to fill the vacancy, and four candidates presented themselves to the voters. Of these, Livy's attention was held by Q. Fulvius Flaccus, the *aedilis curulis designatus* (39.39.2), who contested the praetorian vacancy despite having already won himself a magistracy for the year.[1] Because such a candidacy was legally and practically disallowed, Flaccus' announcement and subsequent refusals to back down caused a stir in the political community. The tribunes of the plebs, normally those most likely to obstruct such displays of ambition, were, unusually, divided in their opinion.[2]

> et postquam primo aequare mox superare etiam est uisus, pars tribunorum plebis negare rationem eius habendam esse, quod duos simul unus magistratus, praesertim curules, neque capere posset neque gerere; pars legibus eum solui aequum censere, ut quem uellet praetorem creandi populo potestas fieret. (Livy 39.39.3–4)
>
> And after he appeared first to equal and then even to draw ahead, part of the tribunician college asserted that his candidacy should not be considered valid, because one man could not win or exercise two magistracies at once,

[1] For a brief sketch of the episode: Feig Vishnia 1996a: 120–2; Merola 2001: 109–10; Briscoe 2008: 347–50; and Lundgreen 2011: 81–2. Walsh 1994: 154 calls it "an *exemplum* of the golden days of Roman *libertas* controlled by the rule of law, in which the senate demonstrated practical wisdom in solving the impasse." Briscoe 2008: 347 finds this description "misleading" and sees instead a simple senatorial override of the law governing the number of praetors. Tatum 2013: 136 finds Livy "especially disappointing" on electoral topics in general and sees this episode as a "technical matter misunderstood by Livy" (n. 17). This concern with constitutional details has tended, in general, to obscure what value there is to be gained from the literary representation.

[2] Russell 2013: 109 cautions against monolithic views of the college of tribunes and argues that while the tribunes "all appealed to the same basic ideological repertoire, they differed on how it should be defined and interpreted, and, of course, who was best qualified to represent it." What is perhaps most striking about Livy's tribunes here is the willingness of at least some of the college first to espouse, and then hold on to, an opinion that not only was unpopular but also aligned them explicitly against the people's desires and interest. In their neat division, the tribunes also enact the historiographical *sermones*, the topos standardly used to convey opposing opinions.

> especially of the curule variety; the other part thought it was fair that he be exempt from the laws, so that the people would have the power to elect as praetor whomever they wished.

With the tribunician college thus divided, the consul, L. Porcius, announced that he would not accept Flaccus' candidacy and then referred the matter to the senate. The fathers batted the issue back to the consul, while the candidate himself loudly proclaimed his good faith to any who would listen. The matter was eventually resolved by a senatorial decision to make do with the existing number of praetors (39.39.14 *senatum censere satis praetorum esse*); no votes were ever cast.

In its detailed political squabbling, this relatively minor episode is a classic instance of the annalistic genre. Tacitus, lamenting his lot, envies earlier historians for being able to narrate exactly such domestic affairs: *Ann.* 4.32 *discordias consulum adversum tribunos, agrarias frumentariasque leges, plebis et optimatium certamina libero egressu memorabant* ("they recalled with free rein the quarrels of consuls ranged against the tribunes, agrarian and grain laws, and the struggles of the plebs and the elites").[3] While this canvass does not feature agrarian or grain laws, it certainly fits Tacitus' bill in all other ways. Livy makes much of the *certamen* both between Flaccus and his rival candidates, especially the *flamen Dialis* (39.39.2), as well as within the tribuncian college, divided as they are in their opinions and alliances (39.39.13 *ingens certamen tribunis et inter se ipsos et cum consule fuit*), and he refers to the entire episode as a *maxima contentio* (39.39.2). The image of tribunes ranged against senate and consul is itself iconic of the class struggles of the early and late republic, and here it finds expression in the opposition Livy sets up between the wishes of the people on the one hand, and the customary law, championed by the senators and the consul, on the other. Thus, while this particular election is unusual both for being a by-election as well as for Flaccus' double-dipping, it nevertheless participates in a broader pattern of domestic political reportage in the *AUC*.

More specifically, however, the episode explicitly engages a set of questions about electoral eligibility: who can stand, who determines the validity of any candidacy, and what sort of arguments are more or less compelling in each of those cases.[4] Such questions are, in a very concrete sense,

[3] On the entertainment value of such fare for the reader: Woodman 1988: 180–5; Martin and Woodman 1989: 169–71.

[4] In formulating this set of questions, I am focusing deliberately on process rather than identity-politics, a choice which excludes, most prominently, the various claims made for opening the magistracies, beginning with the consulship, to the plebeians (a topic which occupies the latter half of Livy's book 6 in particular: Lipovsky 1981: 29–86; Kraus 1994a: 305–27; and C. J. Smith 2006: 258–80 with

constitutive of republican magistracy and of the ways in which modern historians have thought about it, since a magistrate was by default a successful candidate, not only in the sense of having achieved a majority of the voting centuries, but also in having cleared the various obstacles involved in having one's candidacy accepted. Eligibility criteria, therefore, serve an important function as an institutional gatekeeper to executive power, both in narrowing the eligible field to specific groups – patricians, men of a certain age and of certain achievements, and so forth – and in removing undesirable elements within those groups, whether, like Flaccus, for an indecorous display of excessive ambition, or as part of political maneuvering, as in the case of Catiline in 66 BC, or of Caesar in 58 BC.[5]

But the Flaccus episode is especially striking not in its interest in eligibility *per se*, but rather in the rhetorical presentation of the arguments. The divided tribunician college, as often in Livy, expresses two positions that are in dialogue with one another: first, that the canvass ought to be rejected, because it ran against law and custom, and conversely, that it should be allowed to stand, because the people's freedom of electoral choice ought to prevail over the laws. Both of these positions appeal to abstract principles of Roman constitutionality, and both importantly relate to Roman ideas of *libertas*.[6] Neither, however, expresses a concrete rule, and in fact even the tribunes who support Flaccus, and indeed Flaccus himself, do not deny the existence of the laws precluding his candidacy, even as all parties engage in a lengthy debate on how those laws ought to be interpreted and applied. Both the rule of law and the people's *uoluntas* are fundamentally important for expressing ideas about magistracy. The elected offices of the republic were within the people's *beneficium* and therefore relied *a fortiori* on the people's willingness to vote for a particular candidate.[7] Equality before the

further references). Although these claims offer a trenchant illustration of the centrality of magistracy for Roman identity, they neverthless offer a limited view on the experience of magistracy itself. An important exception to that is the story of Flavius the scribe (Livy 9.46.9–10; Gell. *NA* 7.9.5–6), which I discuss in the Epilogue. A different sort of view is offered by the story of Fabia Minor (Livy 6.34.5–35.1), who, like Hispala Faecenia, finds the consul's entourage terrifying: Kraus 1991.

5 Catiline: Sall. *Cat.* 18.3; Asc. *In Toga Candida* 89.7–17, with Marshall 1985: 302–5. Caesar: App. *BCiu.* 2.8; Suet. *Jul.* 18; Dio 37.45.

6 On *libertas* as a political idea: Wirszubski 1968. Roller 2001: 229–32 expands the meaning of *libertas* to include social, as well as political, implications. See also Hellegouarc'h 1972: 542–65; Bruno 1966; and the recent and extensive treatement in Arena 2012, esp. 45–72.

7 Cicero, *Comment. pet.* 16 *et petitio magistratuum diuisa est in duarum rationum diligentiam, quarum altera in amicorum studiis, altera in populari uoluntate ponenda est* ("running for office is made up of two areas of diligent effort: the first must be invested in arousing the enthusiasm of your friends, the other in arousing the willingness of the people"). *Voluntas*, of course, is not restricted to the people, and the *commentariolum* is keen to impress upon Cicero the importance of cultivating the *uoluntas* of noble men, particularly of former consuls (e.g. 4 *hominum nobilium uoluntas et*

laws, meanwhile, was a cornerstone of republican ideology, especially as it pertained to the integrity of the Roman citizen's freedom from oppression. The tension between these two principles, which finds a very blunt articulation in Flaccus' case, forms a background to many of Livy's electoral campaigns, which in turn explore various views on the role and place of the magistrates within the state. In Flaccus' case, magistrates function as partisan representatives of an interest group (here the people as well as Flaccus himself), as an executive branch of the government, or, as in most other cases, both at once.[8]

This chapter explores a set of episodes broadly focused on some of the various forms of electoral narratives. These are, more specifically, unusual elections, in which normal procedure is disrupted for a variety of reasons: bribery, the reluctance or excessive eagerness of the candidate, or the dismissal of a legal or normative obstacle.[9] These disruptions are all civic in nature, and in that regard this chapter forms a mirror image to the previous chapter, which treats elections in a military context and under the pressures of military campaigns. In both cases I treat elections as a locus and mechanism for generating images of magistracy but, whereas the previous chapter focused on the exemplary nature of military leadership, in this chapter I examine the broader context of those images, which is to say the electoral campaign itself. These episodes and the campaigns they describe are instructive not only in restating the old adage that rules are better seen in the breach than in the observation, but also because they all construct a narrative about magistracy: who is eligible for it, under what conditions, and for what reasons. Beyond such technical and constitutional questions, which form the institutional background to all Roman electoral activity, the episodes are especially interested in the candidate's ability to shape the

maxime consularium), and specifically of Pompey (51 *ut sciant omnes Cn. Pompei summam esse erga te uoluntatem*). On *uoluntas* in relation to "written" material: Dugan 2012.

8 I use this modern phraseology in the full knowledge that it has no exact parallel in the ancient political vocabulary. Rather, these modern terms function as a convenient shorthand for political phenomena for which we have a more robust and precise terminology than did the Romans, even if that shorthand also connotes more complex political structures than existed in republican or imperial Rome. For Roman terminology for political interactions: Hellegouarc'h 1972, which should now be read alongside newer work on the Roman vocabulary of interpersonal relations (e.g. Krostenko 2001, Roller 2001, and Stroup 2010), as well as on individual aspects of Roman political terminology (e.g. Robb 2010, Richardson 2008, Arena 2012). For discussion of reception and politics: Vlassopolous 2009 and Hölkeskamp 2010.

9 Lundgreen 2011: 62–73 lists chronologically elections in which rules and norms are negotiated, which he treats under the rubrics of iteration, continuation, and premature candidacy (*altersvorschriften*). Although the following sections deal with examples of each of Lundgreen's types, my treatment is generally narrower, partially because I focus on magistracy rather than elections in and of themselves, and partially because not every instance offers the rich narratives in which this book is interested.

election and its participants – that is, the senate, presiding magistrate, and voters – according to his own will. This expression of assertive agency, besides being of primary importance for any leader, is also a distinctively textual phenomenon, as characters vie with each other and with the author to assert control over their own narratives. As such, electoral narratives are uniquely self-referential, pointing both to the annual recurrence of elections, as well as to the creative process whereby characters rise to exert authorship and *auctoritas* over the yearly narratives of the Roman state.[10] The value of these episodes lies also in their formal features: in the verbal and narrative articulation of political principle, and in the intricate connections which dramatize political behavior as a process of call-and-response among the various participants. Finally, these episodes illustrate the role that exemplary thinking plays in the deeper structures of Roman political thought, not only explicitly and on the surface of the text, as in the previous three chapters, but also as an underlying guiding principle, much as it was in Roman political life.[11] As such, magistracy emerges not as a positivist collection of rights and duties but as a subject of a larger political and historiographical conversation, which concerns itself with defining, within broad boundaries, the forces that ought to bear on the election of magistrates.

Cicero's *pro Murena*: consul knows best

In November of his consulship Cicero, having presided over the consular elections for the following year, defended the victorious candidate, Lucius Murena, against allegations of electoral bribery brought by one of his rivals, Servius Sulpicius Rufus.[12] The trial must have been an awkward affair, since during the election Cicero supported not his client, Murena, but rather Sulpicius, a jurist whose forum-bound pursuits made for a greater natural affinity with the equally wordy Cicero. Further, the law under which Murena was brought to trial, the *lex Tullia de ambitu*, was authored by Cicero himself, who was thus maneuvered into the impossible position of arguing against his own former allegiance as well as his own

[10] Caesar's *commentarii* are the *locus classicus* for the general/historian, but for Livy see Feldherr 1998: 51–81 and Haimson Lushkov 2014.

[11] For exemplarity "on the ground" in Roman political life see my discussion in the Introduction and Hölkeskamp 2003 and 2010.

[12] Cicero deploys many of the same strategies in the later *pro Plancio*, where he defends Plancius, a newly elected aedile, from charges of bribery brought by one of Plancius' competitors. On the two speeches: Adamietz 1986; May 1988: 58–69, 116–27; and Riggsby 1999: 21–49.

law.[13] The problem was no doubt exacerbated by the fact that Cicero now had to argue that Murena's gifts, which lay in generalship and logistics, were naturally superior to those of Sulpicius, and by implication to his own as well. What Cicero and Murena had in common, however, was the simple fact of having triumphed in a consular election, and the elevated status such a victory conferred. Cicero and Murena were consuls, present and future, while Sulpicius was not, despite his birth, talent, and industry. Cicero's task in the trial was therefore to justify this result, and in the course of doing so he necessarily discusses a host of relevant issues, chiefly what forces bear on the election of magistrates and what qualities successful candidates exhibit. Cicero therefore discusses two campaigns: Sulpicius', parts of which he narrates in the body of the speech and in which he participates, and Murena's, the campaign Cicero both recounts and means to re-validate with his court appearance. On a secondary level, however, the speech is also about Cicero himself, his participation in the campaign, his role in shaping the candidate and the message, and his role as validator of the eventual results. The *pro Murena*, in other words, offers a kaleidoscopic image of an electoral campaign, projecting multiple images and aspects of the same events and mediating them through a singular point of view – that of Cicero himself. In this sense, the speech performs in much the same way as the historiographical narratives we have seen, especially Livy's, and, like them, the speech attempts to establish a paradigm of candidacy and of magistracy against which to find Sulpicius and Murena a success or failure.

Throughout the speech, one of Cicero's main strategies in deflecting the bribery charge is simply to ignore it, concentrating attention instead on Sulpicius' flaws as a jurist, aristocrat, and candidate, as well as on the many details of the campaign itself. This achieves a rhetorical re-enactment of the original campaign, a ploy evident from as early as the speech's *exordium*.[14]

> quae precatus a dis immortalibus sum, iudices, more institutoque maiorum illo die quo auspicato comitiis centuriatis L. Murenam consulem renuntiaui, ut ea res mihi fidei magistratuique meo, populo plebique Romanae bene atque feliciter eueniret, eadem precor ab isdem dis immortalibus ob eiusdem hominis consulatum una cum salute obtinendum, et ut uestrae mentes atque sententiae cum populi Romani uoluntatibus suffragiisque consentiant,

[13] On the *lex Tullia*: Rotondi 1912: 379; Berger, *RE* s.v. "lex Tullia de ambitu."

[14] On the relationship of the trial to the campaign: Adamietz 1986, with the critique of Riggsby 1999: 47–9, and Tatum 2013: 139–40.

eaque res uobis populoque Romano pacem, tranquillitatem, otium concordiamque adferat. (Cic. *Mur.* 1)

On that day when I took the auspices and pronounced L. Murena consul in the *comitia centuriata*, I prayed to the immortal gods, judges, in accordance with ancestral habit and custom, that this matter should turn out well and prosperously, for me, my good faith, my magistracy, the people and the Roman plebs. That same prayer I offer to the same immortal gods, that the consulship should be retained by this man, along with his well-being, that your minds and feelings should agree with the wishes and votes of the Roman people, and that this matter should bring to you and to the Roman people calm, tranquility, peace, and harmony.

The two halves of this periodic sentence match each other in content and structure. Cicero offers the same prayer (*quae precatus* ~ *eadem precor*), to the same gods (*ab isdem dis immortalibus*), for the same purpose, that the matter – Murena's election – should turn out well for the Roman people. Cicero then rounds out his opening by offering a slight variation of the same theme: . . . *idem consulem uestrae fidei commendat qui antea dis immortalibus commendauit, ut eiusdem hominis uoce et declaratus consul et defensus beneficium populi Romani cum uestra atque omnium ciuium salute tueatur* (2 "the same man now commends a consul to your trust, who commended him before to the immortal gods, so that he, being declared consul and defended by the voice of the same man, may keep the gift of the Roman people along with your well-being and that of all citizens").[15] With the emphasis on sameness bolstered by polyptotonic *isdem* and *consul*, Cicero and Murena are equal, ceremonially and verbally.

This dense repetition sets up a sequence of parallels between the events of the trial and the consular elections, as well as between the jurors, the gods, the voting people, Murena, and finally Cicero himself. The jurors are asked to perform the same task – acquitting Murena – in two different guises: as voters themselves, and as divine guardians of the people's *beneficium*. This rhetorical move, which plays on the unspoken identity between the jurors *qua* jurors and the jurors *qua* citizen voters, allows Cicero to request explicitly a repetition of the electoral result. The jurors are meant to have the same feelings as the voting people, not only in their sentiments about the candidates, but also in their actual votes (*uoluntatibus suffragiisque consentiant*). In case those feelings should differ, however, Cicero also provides the jurors with a god's-eye perspective, where the moral authority of the immortal gods, a phrase repeated emphatically (note *isdem*) throughout

[15] On the rhetoric of the *exordium*, Fantham 2013: 83–6.

the passage, ensures the holding of both trial and election according to all proprieties (*more institutoque maiorum, auspicato*). Thus, apart from suggesting to the jury that the acquittal of Murena is the only correct conclusion, the opening has the further effect of setting the speech up as a re-enactment of the electoral campaign, with the jurors playing the part of the voters. Cicero himself, moreover, plays a double role as advocate and as electoral consultant, re-narrativizing the elections for the jurors' benefit and in his client's interest.

The charge of *ambitus* also introduces a level of complexity familiar from Livy's account of Flaccus quoted above, since bribery, as imagined by the law, threatened to decouple the electoral results from the expression of the people's *uoluntas*: a bought vote represented not its owner's *uoluntas*, but rather the candidate's.[16] The trial, therefore, replicates the problem Flaccus faces (as does Fabius Maximus in the previous chapter): a procedural or legal obstacle stands in the way of the people's exercise of their *uoluntas*. The law, in both cases, provides the opposition with the vocabulary and the rhetoric to argue otherwise. What Livy describes in the pages of history, Cicero encounters in his own political life: the incongruity between what the people want and what the law allows them to have. I will return to Flaccus' case below, as well as to the rhetorical strategies which Livy deploys to explore this issue; in the *pro Murena*, however, one of Cicero's tasks is to reject the prosecution's claims that this *uoluntas* was manufactured rather than genuine. Conversely, he must also show that the people's affection for Murena was in fact both true and demonstrable. Cicero's main strategy in dismissing the opposition's case, although he indulges also in *ad hominem* attacks and open criticism of Sulpicius the candidate, is simply to deflect attention from it, offering images of Murena as consul instead of an actual refutation of the charges. These images advance the broader strategy of twinning campaign and trial, while offering a glimpse, whether historically accurate or not, into electoral propaganda and electioneering.

Through these images Cicero purports to offer the jurors a privileged view of both campaigns. One of the two – Sulpicius' canvass – may be authentic, as Cicero was genuinely involved; in the case of Murena's campaign, however, Cicero has no genuine insider knowledge. He relies instead

[16] On the economics behind *ambitus* charges: Riggsby 1999: 21–49 with direct reference to the *pro Murena*, and Rosillo López 2010: 49–86, who sees corruption as an endemic trend saturating all levels of Roman society, including the political. Indeed, recent trends have seen bribery as less a problem of electoral corruption (for which see Linderksi 1985, Deniaux 1987) and more as a democratizing procedure: Lintott 1990; Gruen 1991: 255–7; Yakobson 1992. The most recent treatment is Feig-Vishnia 2012: 134–48, who situates bribery within the practices of electioneering and the culture of ambition.

on generic impressions, which both he and the jurors had shared during the actual canvass, and which thereby increase the sympathy between them. Thus, in response to Cato's allegation that the crowd that went out to welcome Murena on his return to Rome from his province was paid, Cicero nonchalantly shrugs his shoulders:

> "multi obuiam prodierunt de prouincia decedenti." consulatum petenti solet fieri; eccui autem non proditur revertenti? "quae fuit ista multitudo?" primum, si tibi istam rationem non possim reddere, quid habet admirationis tali uiro aduenienti, candidato consulari, obuiam prodisse multos? quod nisi esset factum, magis mirandum uideretur. (*Mur.* 68)

> "Many people came out to meet him when he came back from his province." This is what normally happens when someone seeks the consulship; and anyway doesn't this happen whenever someone comes home? "What was this crowd?" First, even if I were not able to answer you on this score, why should it be odd that many came out to meet such an admirable man and a consular candidate on his return? It would have been odder still if it hadn't happened.

Here too, we find some assimilation of speech and electoral campaign: when Cicero replies directly to the prosecution, he does so using vocabulary (*rationem reddere*) which suggests – though it does not substantiate – that Cicero has access to such privileged knowledge as the identities of the men in the crowd.[17] The important point, however, is that the picture Cicero paints is both consular and highly generic. The admiration is reserved entirely for Murena, his qualities (*admirationis tali uiro*), and his campaign (*candidato consulari*), rather than the actions of the crowd, though the very presence of such a crowd speaks volumes about Murena's popularity and prospects. Murena's motion, further, is steady, linear, and purposeful. He approaches Rome, meets with the adoring crowd, and thus fulfills exactly what was expected of him. The standard image of a returning general (Murena is returning from his province) is impactful precisely because it fits the bill of consular behavior so well.

Murena, of course, has other factors working in his favor too, of which Cicero identifies as especially powerful his military career, and in particular the favor of his men towards him. He presents their opinion in direct speech: *Mur.* 38 *me saucium recreauit, me praeda donauit; hoc duce castra cepimus, signa contulimus; numquam iste plus militi laboris imposuit quam sibi sumpsit, ipse cum fortis tum etiam felix* ("he took care of me when I was

[17] *Rationem reddere* may also allude to the electoral technical term *rationem habere* ("to take official account of [a candidacy])" (*OLD* s.v. *ratio* 8c), for which see n. 33 below.

wounded and gave me spoils; we captured the camp under his leadership and fought a pitched battle; he never assigned more labor to a soldier than he took on himself, and he is not only brave, but also lucky"). It is in this moment of *sermo castrensis*, albeit stylized, that we can also recognize one of the fissures in Cicero's presentation. After all, Cicero himself could lay little claim to military experience, a fact which he managed to turn into a rhetorical advantage by casting himself as of the same sort as Sulpicius – but an orator rather than jurist, a choice which makes all the difference. Indeed, the *sermo castrensis*, in its appearance of honesty and paratactic simplicity, stands in marked opposition to the elaborate and obscurantist language of the jurists, which serves only to confound.[18] Instead, it functions as a clear *documentum* of Murena's abilities, advertising achievements of the past in the service of the present moment.[19] Even here, Cicero actively shapes an idea of consularity, first by naturalizing Murena as an obvious and logical choice, and second by using Sulpicius as a foil for his construction of Murena. From the speech as a whole, however, emerge three distinct images of what a consul might be, each represented by one of the parties: a legal authority (Sulpicius), a military leader (Murena), and an orator (Cicero).[20]

Where Cicero associated Murena with direct action and military support, Sulpicius fails as candidate twice over, once in failing to obtain victory, and another by failing to fulfill even the role of the candidate. A jurist to the last, Sulpicius looks to the trial even in the midst of the campaign and shows himself to fall squarely outside the expected image and behavior required of a candidate:

> itaque sic statuo fieri nullo modo posse ut idem accusationem et petitionem consulatus diligenter adornet atque instruat. unum sustinere pauci possunt, utrumque nemo. tu cum te de curriculo petitionis deflexisses animumque ad accusandum transtulisses, existimasti te utrique negotio satis facere posse. uehementer errasti. (*Mur.* 46)

> And so I declare that it simply isn't possible that the same person should diligently draw up and prepare both a legal charge and a campaign for the consulship. Few can sustain even the one, and nobody can do both. When

18 Obscurantist juridical speech: *Mur.* 25–8. On *sermo castrensis*: Castro 2005. On the introjection of sub-literary orality into a text: Oesterreicher 1997.

19 On careers furnishing electoral *documenta* cf. Fabius' rhetoric, in 24.8.14 (*haud sane cur ad maiora tibi fidamus documenti quicquam dedisti*, "you have given no proof to trust you with larger affairs") and Flamininus below. On Cicero's use of exemplarity in the speeches: Bücher 2006: 228–55 and van der Blom 2010: 129–36 and 2011.

20 On the creative power of Cicero's rhetoric: Gildenhard 2010: 146–59, and especially 156–9 on the importance of consuls having a consular attitude.

> you turned yourself away from the business of canvassing and transferred your attention to legal charges, you thought you would be able to do enough for both. How grievously off course you were.

Sulpicius, as Cicero argued earlier (15–19), not only made too much of the entitlement of his birth and juristic expertise but also committed the cardinal error of not devoting his every resource to the campaign.[21] Cicero's language makes Sulpicius out to be radically off course in his calculations (*errasti*), turning away from the canvass towards the trial. Cicero's choice of verbs, however, especially *deflexisses* and *transtulisses*, paints Sulpicius as not only distracted from the campaign but also deliberate in his attempt to obstruct and pre-empt the vote; Murena, meanwhile, moves deliberately through the landscape towards victory (note, e.g., *aduenienti* in 68).[22] Thus, in his tactical miscalculation, Sulpicius shows himself not only as a generally incompetent candidate (and therefore consul), but also, more specifically, as one who is unable to recognize and pursue the correct course. Since Cicero claims to have advised Sulpicius to keep his focus on the election, a rather more personal lesson can also be drawn: to ignore Cicero is to be a failed candidate; to listen to him is to choose the right path to high office. This sleight of hand, in turn, encourages the jurors to ignore Cicero's earlier support of Sulpicius, which might be interpreted as continued electoral support, and transfer it instead to Murena, the candidate for whom Cicero is now advocating.

Despite Cicero's assurances that the elections were won or lost for identifiable reasons, he also admits openly that the people bestow their *beneficium* erratically and unpredictably. One of the justifications the prosecution offered for their *ambitus* charges was that Sulpicius had come top of the polls when he and Murena both ran for the praetorship together. What then could have induced the same voters to change their minds now, other than the purchase of their vote?

> nihil est incertius uolgo, nihil obscurius uoluntate hominum, nihil fallacius ratione tota comitiorum . . . nam, ut tempestates saepe certo aliquo caeli signo commouentur, saepe improuiso nulla ex certa ratione obscura aliqua ex causa concitantur, sic in hac comitiorum tempestate populari saepe intellegas quo signo commota sit, saepe ita obscura causa est ut casu excitata esse uideatur. (*Mur.* 36)
>
> For nothing is more uncertain than a crowd, nothing more impenetrable than the wishes of men, nothing more deceptive than the whole business of

[21] For the expectation that candidates devote every resource to the campaign: Tatum 2013: 150, and e.g. Cicero, *Comment. pet.* 4 (*omni ratione efficiendo*), 20 (*omnino . . . fac*).

[22] For the dangers in consular deviation from a marked path, see my discussion in Chapter 2: 66–7.

elections ... For, just as storms often rise at some sure sign of the heavens, and often they stir for no obvious reason or discernible cause, so in this kind of electoral storm of the people you might sometimes know what caused it, but often the cause would be so obscure that the storm would almost seem to have risen by chance.

This criticism of the people's *uoluntas* as fickle and unpredictable is striking, especially in a speech which aims to replicate that will in the jurors. Rhetorically, Cicero is attempting to smooth Sulpicius' ruffled feathers, pinning the reason for his defeat on the ineluctable mysteries of the people's *uoluntas.* The difference between the two *tempestates*, further, is keyed exactly to the two types of candidates: Sulpicius' origins, though noble, are obscure and academic, while Murena's career furnishes a sure sign of his suitability for office. Indeed, very shortly after this metaphor of stormy seas, Cicero will specify Murena's good reputation among the soldiery as the reason for his electoral success. Murena's conduct brings out the *uoluntas militum*, and the soldiers' good report induces in turn the favor of the people: *hoc quanti putas esse ad famam hominum ac uoluntatem?* (*Mur.* 38 "how much impact do you think it has on reputation and inclination?"). If the contional atmosphere can be likened to a rising storm, the proof of a military career is by analogy the "sure sign" in the heavens, not the cause of the storm but the indication that provides foreknowledge for those who can read it. Further, despite Cicero's coyness, there can be no doubt that he knows how to master such electoral storms and what might be their cause or effect. The theme of unexpected *tempestates* brackets the speech in 4 and 81 and constructs a continuity between Cicero's year in office and the incoming consul's task: *quo tandem me esse animo oportet prope iam ex magna iactatione terram uidentem in hunc cui uideo maximas rei publicae tempestates esse subeundas?* (4 "how, then, am I to feel towards this man, whom I see must undergo these great storms of the state, when I am just within sight of land after being cast about myself?"). In this, too, Cicero and Murena share an important consular quality: they possess a measure of agency over the unpredictable events of popular assemblies, while Sulpicius, lacking such consular qualities, is left to wonder at the seemingly inscrutable result.

In context, the storm metaphor evokes for the modern reader Vergil's famous simile of the orator soothing an angry crowd (*Aen.* 1.148–53):[23]

ac ueluti magno in populo cum saepe coorta est
seditio, saeuitque animis ignobile uolgus,

[23] On the simile see, e.g., Pöschl 1962: 20–3; Otis 1964: 229–30; Harrison 1988; Adler 2003: 92–3; Hardie 1998: 92.

iamque faces et saxa uolant – furor arma ministrat;
tum, pietate grauem ac meritis si forte uirum quem
conspexere, silent, arrectisque auribus adstant;
ille regit dictis animos, et pectora mulcet, . . .

As if when, in a great crowd, often sedition rises, and the lowly mob rages in its spirits, and already torches and stones go flying – rage supplies arms; then, if by chance they see some man dignified with piety and merit, they fall silent, and they stand with pricked ears; he directs their spirit with words and soothes their anger . . .

Despite some obvious differences, not least the exchange of *ratio comitiorum* with violent *seditio*, some similarities are immediately apparent, especially the temporal designator *saepe* (148), which Cicero repeats four times in *Mur.* 36, and the emphasis on chance (*forte* [*Aen.* 1.151] ~ *improuiso, casu* [Cic. *Mur.* 36]). Vergil's simile, however, clearly communicates the almost god-like power of the public speaker to smooth over an enraged crowd, just as Neptune soothes the seas which toss about Aeneas' ships. Leaving aside the problem of the *Aeneid*'s politics and Aeneas' nation-building task, Vergil's simile paints an extreme version of the scenario Cicero imagines, though the solution Vergil offers – a single pious man – has more than a touch of autocracy about it. *Mutatis mutandis*, this is also a representation of any political leader, and indeed of the task facing any electoral candidate: make the crowd, which is preoccupied with its own frenzies, direct its energies to the leader's own end, whether peacefully or violently.

Of course, Murena's and Sulpicius' two campaigns are actually a single event, the electoral competition in the year 63 BC, as well as the single topic of Cicero's particular speech. Murena's successful strategy balances out Sulpicius' failure, while Cicero is certainly keen to present Sulpicius, at least, as lacking some crucial qualities that Murena possesses, chiefly military ability and a good reputation among the voters. That quality is in direct contrast to Murena's display of consular behavior. Sulpicius therefore lacks precisely Murena's visible "consularity," rhetorically constructed though the idea must be.[24] Further, within the speech, both "campaigns" are naturally the product of Cicero's rhetoric, and part of a unified strategy aimed at convincing the jury to reproduce the electoral

[24] Although the abstract noun *consularitas* is unattested before the *codex Theodosianus*, the adverb *consulariter* ("in a consular manner") appears once in Livy 4.10.9 *uitaque omnis consulariter acta* ("his whole life was conducted in a consular manner"), to emphasize that the consul, Titus Quinctius Capitolinus, was the equal of his colleague Geganius, even though he was not as warlike as his colleague.

vote. This is especially apparent when Cicero eventually reaches the refutation of the bribery charge, an opportunity he takes to advertise to the jurors Murena's popularity and to draw a picture of an energetic canvass. By contrast, Sulpicius emerges as a stereotypical jurist, looking to the trial, as a lawyer might, even in the midst of the campaign, and therefore not only demonstrating his unsuitability but even actively rejecting the candidate's primary task of securing an electoral win. The result, nevertheless, is that Cicero's speech presents to the jurors two strategies of reproducing the elections: one explicit, describing both campaigns, and the other through a more sustained comparison between the two candidates, focusing on their suitability and *ethos*.[25] It offers also three different images of the consul – orator, jurist, general – producing an image of a successful candidate that is multi-faceted and composite in nature.

Fulvius Flaccus: magistracy in context

At this point, we can return to the candidacy of Fulvius Flaccus, which, at two full Teubner pages, makes for an unusually rich account. Its density of description allows us to see both Livy's artistry as well as the full gamut of political actors and discourses at play. One of the episode's prominent features is the predominance of speech and speech verbs, which accounts, in one form or another, for roughly half of the episode's narrative.[26] Livy thus devotes considerable scope to reporting the words of the various actors. His choice is all the more striking considering how much repetitive speech occurs in this episode. The consul, perhaps most conspicuously, spends most of his time repeating the instructions of the senators, who themselves repeat, with steady elaboration, their own earlier pronouncements.[27] Those, in turn, refer back to the consul's initial opinion. Nor do any of the

[25] On *ethos* as a form of argument in Cicero's speeches: May 1988, Gildenhard 2010: 50–68.

[26] On speeches in the context of political turmoil, especially on their use to reflect a multiplicity of voices and idiosyncratic histories, C. J. Smith 2010.

[27] 39.39.5–8 *L. Porcius consul primo in ea sententia esse, ne nomen eius acciperet; deinde, ut ex auctoritate senatus idem faceret, conuocatis patribus referre se ad eos dixit, quod nec iure ullo nec exemplo tolerabili liberae ciuitati aedilis curulis designatus praeturam peteret; sibi, nisi quid aliud iis uideretur, in animo esse e lege comitia habere. patres censuerunt, uti L. Porcius consul cum Q. Fuluio ageret, ne impedimento esset, quo minus comitia praetoris in locum C. Decimii subrogandi e lege haberentur. agenti consuli ex senatus consulto respondit Flaccus* ("L. Porcius, the consul, was against accepting his candidacy from the start; later, so that he could act on the authority of the senate, he convened a meeting of the senate and told them he was referring the matter to them, because there was no sanction or precedent acceptable in a free state by which a curule aedile designate could seek the praetorship; for himself, he intended to hold the elections in accordance with the law, unless they had other sentiments on the issue. The senators decided that L. Porcius the consul should speak with Q. Fulvius, so that he would not be a hindrance to the holding of the by-election for C. Decimius'

other participants undergo real change: the tribunes remain consistently at odds from beginning to end, while the contional audience remains steadfast in its support of Flaccus' ambition (39.39.10 *fauorem populi magis magisque in eum inclinari*). The contional audience is the only element that does not speak for itself. The tribunes, who would normally be the mouthpiece for popular sentiments, are too divided to offer a representative opinion. Instead, the audience is ventriloquized by Livy himself, once, and in response to Flaccus' speech: 39.39.12 *haec uero tam obstinata uox tantum ei fauorem accendit, ut haud dubius praetor esset, si consul accipere nomen uellet* ("but this insistent speech kindled such great favor for him, that there was no doubt he would be made praetor, if only the consul was willing to accept his candidacy"). Two problems emerge at once: first, although this is the most extended description of popular opinion in the episode, it is uncertain to what extent it represents the people's own opinion or Flaccus' ventriloquism of it; second, even if we took it as articulating popular opinion, it nevertheless directly responds to what Flaccus has just told them: 39.39.11 *quotienscumque declarandae uoluntatis potestas facta esset, praetorem se uoluisset facere* ("whenever they were given the opportunity to declare their inclination, they wanted to make him praetor").[28] The people thus assert their support most clearly at the point where they have been primed to do so. The only one to vary his speech to any degree is Flaccus himself, and even he does so within the very constrained limits of defending his position.[29]

There is thus little by way of plot development, and what there is is driven largely by deferral and repetition. The main culprit is of course Flaccus himself, who resists every attempt to disallow his canvass, and whose speeches in fact grow in length and sophistication each time an attempt is made to stop him. In this, Flaccus comes to mirror his antagonist, the consul, who serves as the main force attempting to restore order and hold the elections according to the laws.[30] Both the consul and

replacement, in accordance with the law. When the consul spoke with Flaccus, on the senate's authority, Flaccus answered . . . ").

28 On contional ventriloquism, see Morstein-Marx 2004: 136–43, and n. 68 below.

29 Even this is striking and unusual, since, as Tatum 2013 points out, candidates had limited opportunities to give full oratorical speeches during the campaign. The consul's attempts to get Flaccus to back down thus give him a unique stage from which to advertise his message (e.g. 39.39.11 *contione aduocata*, where Flaccus makes his longest and most ingratiating speech to the people). For the *contio*, the "crucial moment of political performance at Rome" (Tatum 2013: 135), see also Pina Polo 1996, Morstein-Marx 2004, and Hölkeskamp 2010.

30 On the role of the presiding magistrate in accepting or rejecting the *professio* of candidates: Rilinger 1976: 63–91. On the rejection of *professio* as a declarative rather than legally binding act, Levick 1981: 381.

Flaccus have three appearances each, the only two actors to do so. Flaccus' speeches, however, are all substantive, and they increase both in length and in inflammatory content as the episode progresses. His first speech is a six-word assurance that he would do nothing beneath his dignity (39.39.8 *nihil, quod se indignum esse, facturum*). His second and third speeches, of twenty-five and twenty-seven words respectively, allege the injustice done to him by consul and senate, assert his good faith, and align him closely with the people and their wishes.

The consul, by contrast, follows the opposite trajectory. In his first appearance, he speaks to the senate at some length (twenty-seven words, the same as Flaccus' last appearance), and his stance to a large degree determines the senatorial position. Afterwards, however, his two appearances are almost entirely procedural, and while his speech is implied, it is also elided by the verb *agere*, a presentation which emphasizes his parroting of the senate's advice (39.8 *agenti consuli*; 39.11 *cum egisset consul*; cf. 39.7 *patres censuerunt uti L. Porcius consul cum Q. Fuluio ageret*; 39.10 *censuerunt frequentes . . . ad populum cum Flacco agendum*). The use of *agere* for both Flaccus and the consul, while an unexceptional use of the verb, also underscores the tension between the two men at the center of the episode, and their contest to each assert his own agency over proceedings.[31] Their mirroring is so complete that Flaccus himself ends up echoing the consul's limited language: he begins his final speech by thanking the people, 39.11 *gratias populo Romano egit*, repeating more definitely the consul's *egisset*, and echoing perhaps also the traditional speech of thanks given by a consul at the beginning of his year. It is at this point, where his victory is almost assured and he begins to sound like a magistrate, that the senate steps in to block the elections altogether.

This tension can be seen more schematically in the way Livy formally arranges the various elements in the episode. In addition to a framing device announcing the elections (A, 39.1–2 ~ 39.14), there are four main components: the tribunes (B, 39.3–4 ~ 39.13), the consul (C, 39.5–6 ~ 39.8 ~ 39.11), the senate (D, 39.7 ~ 39.10), and the candidate himself (E, 39.8 ~ 39.9 ~ 39.11). Following the order of their appearance,

[31] On plain words in artistic speech: Easterling 1999. Focusing on Sophocles' *Philoctetes*, Easterling offers three models to account for what she calls "plain dealing" (96): (1) tension between opposites; (2) oscillation or shading between literal and metaphorical meaning; (3) "charging" of themes through concentration and varied repetition. Although Livy's language is not quite so dense as Sophoclean drama, it does show a version of all three categories: *ageret* captures the tension between magisterial and private actions, it has a real as well as metaphorical sense of "acting" and "doing," and it is repeated in a variety of forms within a reasonably dense clustering of other relevant electoral words and themes.

the episode is structured ABCD^{C}E ~ ED^{C}EBA, with the superscript ^{C} indicating those places where the consul's appearance consists only of the verb *agere*, as in 39.8 *agenti consuli*, rather than by fully articulated speech. The structure is chiastic, or ring-compositional, with one flaw: the consul's slot in the front half of the ring composition, C, is taken over in the second half by Flaccus' E, so that instead of a symmetrical ABC ~ CBA the symmetry collapses to produce ABC ~ EBA. The resulting asymmetry, however, is itself revealing: while the consul is technically in a position of authority over the proceedings, it is very much Flaccus who drives the plot. In fact, it is his increasing control of this short narrative that prompts the senate to cancel the election outright, reverting to the original situation of a decreased praetorian college. The flawed ring structure thus helps to clarify the dramatic irony of the scene, instantiating at the level of form what Flaccus attempts to achieve at the level of content. It also highlights the legal problem around which the episode revolves: Flaccus behaves like an elected official because he is one, and his attempt to skip one office disrupts both the electoral proceedings and the symmetries of the text.

On a more minuscule level, such transpositions characterize the episode from start to finish. For example, the word *certamen* appears twice, once early and once late in the episode (39.3 ~ 39.13). In both cases, it describes a political rivalry, first between Flaccus and his opponent (39.3 *certamenque ei cum flamine erat*), and then referring to the tensions within the tribunician college and between them and the consul (39.13 *ingens certamen tribunis et inter se ipsos et cum consule fuit*). The appearances of the programmatic word *certamen* match also the appearances of the tribunician college. They are the first to comment on Flaccus' candidacy, and they do so a mere nine words after the candidacy has been labeled a *certamen*, albeit so far only with the other prominent candidate, the *flamen Dialis*.[32] The division of the college into two neatly articulated opinions for and against the

[32] I take *certamen* here to mean simply that the two men were the front-runners, and were closely drawn, rather than that specifically personal animosities existed (though of course that cannot be ruled out). However, a further detail is worth noting in this context. Livy specifies that Flaccus was *sine toga candida* (39.2), the chalked garment worn by candidates seeking office. The detail is problematic for a number of reasons, chiefly the disputed chronology and the possibility that the *toga candida* was illegal by 184 BC. Broughton, therefore, argues that Flaccus was already *aedilis curulis* in 184 and was *sine toga candida* "presumably because he was in office, and could not take off the *praetexta*" (*MRR* 1.377 n. 1; Broughton is here following Mommsen 1887, vol. 1: 513 n. 3. See also Briscoe 2008: 348). The *praetexta* would have been a clear sign of his ineligibility, but if Flaccus did wear the *praetexta*, he was not alone. The *toga praetexta* was also part of the paraphernalia of the *flamen Dialis*, Flaccus' electoral rival, who was himself barred by a long list of *caerimonia* from full participation in political life (on the regalia: Livy 27.8.8; on the *caerimonia*: Gell. *NA* 10.15; Plut. *Quaest. Rom.* 44 = *Mor.* 275C–D, and discussion in Vanggaard 1988: 88–104). Thus, the dress of the two candidates manifests the irregularity of their petitioning for office and makes them doublets

canvass (39. 3–4 *pars... pars*) mimics the *certamen* between Flaccus and his rivals and performs the more important role of transposing it from an individual struggle to a systemic constitutional argument. Indeed, by the time *certamen* appears again, it has become a matter of principle, and it has been attracted from the group of rival candidates to the realm of elected office-holders, as the tribunes become participants rather than critics. In microcosm, then, we have the pattern *certamen* : tribunes :: *certamen* : tribunes, a parallel structure that nevertheless repeats a similar dynamic to that enacted between Flaccus and the consul – a quality that belonged with one side has contaminated the other. Flaccus acquires some of the trappings of a magistrate, while the magistrates themselves – tribunes and consul – have taken on Flaccus' quarrel for their own.

Despite Flaccus' success in affecting the formal features of the narrative, it is rather the tribunes who programmatically articulate the opposing positions in the quotation with which this chapter opened. Those positions are seemingly simple: either (A) Flaccus' candidacy is illegal and should be denied (39.4 *negare rationem eius habendam esse*), or (B) an exception should be made, so that the people might freely exercise their electoral function.[33] Eventually it is the consul's insistence on holding the election according to the law (*e lege*) that determines which of these arguments wins out. The senate affirms the consul's position by repeating the same phraseology, *e lege*, in 39.7, and again in slightly modified form at the final pronouncement which calls off the election in 39.14, *ne legibus*. This triple repetition thus anchors one side of the argument and lends it a consistent and unified appearance. The tribunician college, however, complicates matters, since the consul and senate pick up the verbal cues from the

of each other. It seems too much to assume that Livy meant to draw our attention to this sartorial undercurrent, and indeed he has nothing to say about the accouterments of the *flamen Dialis* here, but it stands as testament to the alternative accounts that authors could draw out of the annalistic tradition; for Livy's use of the notes for such parallel histories: Scafuro 1987: 252, and Haimson Lushkov 2014.

[33] For the political sense of *rationem habere*: *OLD* s.v. *ratio* 8c, esp. Cic. *Att.* 7.1.4 and 7.9.4, where *ratio* simply means "candidacy," and Hellegouarc'h 1972: 421–4. Briscoe 2008: 349 formulates the principle somewhat differently: "[t]he principle involved, as stated here, was that a law passed by the people could not prevent the people from electing whomever they chose . . . or, put another way, that no meeting of the assembly could bind its successors . . . " Feig Vishnia 1996a: 51 argues that such exemptions were, strictly speaking, *priuilegia* and prohibited by Twelve Tables 9.1. The text does not survive, and the *testimonia* to it are chiefly from Cicero. The clearest formulation is in Cic. *Dom.* 43 *uetant xii tabulae leges priuatis hominibus inrogari. Id est enim priuilegium*. However, this suggests only that the Twelve Tables prevented *rogationes* against *priuati*, which Cicero interpreted as *priuilegia* so as to assist his case against Clodius. In our case, Flaccus was not a *priuatus*, nor was the provision directed *against* him. For the sources and a skeptical view of the issue of *priuilegia*: *RS* 2.696–701.

pro-Flaccan half of the college, who first introduce the word *lex* into the episode (39.4 *legibus . . . solui*). The anti-Flaccus opinion, by contrast, appears in ostensibly more gnomic and abstract languge (39.4 *duos simul unus magistratus, praesertim curules, neque capere posset nec gerere*) and says nothing on so topical an issue as the law.

As both Walsh and Briscoe have noted, the law in question can reasonably be taken to refer to a plebiscite passed in 342 BC, which appears in a reported packet of legislation at the end of the seventh book of Livy's *AUC*, generally referred to as the Genucian plebiscites:[34]

> praeter haec inuenio apud quosdam L. Genucium tribunum plebis tulisse ad plebem ne fenerare liceret; item aliis plebi scitis cautum ne quis eundem magistratum intra decem annos caperet neu duos magistratus uno anno gereret utique liceret consules ambos plebeios creari. (Livy 7.42.1–2)
>
> I have also found among certain sources that Lucius Genucius as tribune of the plebs made a motion to the people to prohibit lending at high interest; it was also provided in other decrees that no one should hold the same magistracy again within ten years nor exercise two magistracies in one year, and that it should be permissible to elect two plebeian consuls.

While we can be certain of neither the historical reliability of the legislation, nor of its specific application in Flaccus' case, the existence of the passage on its own suggests an intratextual dimension to the legal argument made by the tribunes. Such a reading, however, comes up against some obstacles, since the tribunes not only fail to specify the *lex Genucia* as their reference but also depart quite considerably from the language of the original.[35] Where the plebiscite of 342 specified only *duos magistratus gereret* (7.42.2), the tribunes in 184 expand on the original language: *duos . . . magistratus, praesertim curules, neque capere posset neque gerere* (39.39.4). This departure is grounded in part in the exigencies of the moment. Flaccus was threatening both to gain two offices (*capere*) and to act in those capacities (*gerere*), so that the tribunes' language can be taken as legalistic precision.[36] Nor are

34 Walsh 1994: 154, who suggests also that "some doubt has been cast on the historicity of this edict, since the first prohibition [i.e. repeating a consulship within ten years] never obtained." Briscoe 2008: 350: "Flaccus is exploiting a loophole in the *lex Genucia*, which has clearly not envisaged the possibility of the current situation." This set of plebiscites is also mentioned in Zonaras 7; references, commentary, and previous scholarship are collected in Elster 2003: 40–3. Scholarly interest has centered on the last clause allowing the election of two plebeian consuls.

35 On such intratextual failures in Livy, especially by tribunes of the plebs: Haimson Lushkov 2010.

36 As an intratextual moment, the tribunes' embroidery suggests (perhaps punningly) a slip of textual memory, since they essentially attract the verb *caperet*, which in 7.42.2 belongs in the first colon (*ne quis eundem magistratum intra decem annos caperet*), into the second colon, which adjudicates against the holding of a double magistracy (*neu duos magistratus uno anno gereret*).

the tribunes alone in their awareness of the scope of the legal issue. When canvassing, Flaccus asserts that his enemies are fostering envy against him because of his double office (39.39.9 *geminati honoris*), as if it were not clear that he was going to abdicate the one as soon as he was elected to the other (39.39.9 *tamquam non appareret, ubi designatus praetor esset, extemplo aedilitate se abdicaturum*). Despite the absence of any explicit verbal echo to either version of the Genucian plebiscite, Flaccus here is clearly offering a correction of the tribunes' position; his defense, while conceding that he might win two magistracies (*capere*), insists that he should not exercise them (*gerere*) at the same time. In other words, Flaccus adheres narrowly to the language of the law – *ne quis duos magistratus uno anno gereret* – as a basis for allowing his canvass. The tribunes, by expanding on the language of the law, argue for maintaining its spirit.

If the tribunes speak in legal terms, it is nevertheless the consul who connects the language of the law to custom and usage, offering a more nuanced process of determining political action. His speech to the senate, while brief, focuses on precedent, or rather the lack thereof: 39.6 *nec iure ullo nec exemplo tolerabili liberae ciuitati* ("by no law nor any example tolerable in a free state").[37] The two categories the consul singles out are well balanced: *ius* has the flavor of both justice and propriety, and it alludes as well to the primary function of the *praetor urbanus*, to dispense the law.[38] In counterpoint to the broad strokes of *iure ullo*, the consul's use of *exemplum* is highly particularized, since he refers not just to any precedent or model, but more specifically to the kind of *exemplum* appropriate to a free state. The accumulation of *honores* was in itself a problematic feature of republican elite culture, and here it is certainly meant to suggest that Flaccus' ambition was not only misguided but also dangerous. Especially within the confines of Livy's *AUC*, a work predominantly concerned with the lessons of the past and their mediation by *exempla*, this absence of precedent makes for a highly effective gambit. It is telling, therefore, that the phrase *exemplo tolerabili* has a very recent precedent in the *AUC*, in a context explicitly concerned with the creation of suitable *exempla*:

> haec enim ipsa Ti. Gracchus queritur dissolutam esse a priuato tribuniciam potestatem, et ad postremum, cum auxilium L. Scipioni pollicetur, adicit tolerabilioris exempli esse a tribuno plebis potius quam a priuato uictam uideri et tribuniciam potestatem et rem publicam esse. (Livy 38.56.10)

[37] On *exemplum* as precedent, with specific reference to this episode: Chaplin 2000: 137–8.
[38] On the legal duties of the *praetor urbanus*: Brennan 2000: 125–35.

> For this was what Ti. Gracchus complained about: that tribunician power was violated by a private citizen. Later, when he promised help to L. Scipio, he added that it would have been a more acceptable precedent if the tribunician power and the state were seen to be undermined by a tribune of the plebs than by a private citizen.

The context of this passage is the trial of L. Scipio, the second of the trials of the Scipios, which take up the latter half of book 38. *Haec enim ipsa*, more specifically, refers to Africanus' clash with the tribunes of the plebs upon discovering his brother's imprisonment, behavior which Livy famously termed *magis pie quam ciuiliter* (38.56.9 "more family-minded than with civic feeling"). In its opposition between tribunician power and individual ambition, assisted by fractures within the tribunician college, the situation bears some resemblance to Flaccus' campaign. Gracchus' use of *tolerabilior* here is further suggestive of both a graduated hierarchy of situations and precedents, as well as a keen awareness of how political events transform into *exempla*. The undermining of the tribunician college will create an *exemplum*, Gracchus suggests, but it would be better if that *exemplum* were of a fractured tribunician college than of a private citizen undermining the state. *Mutatis mutandis*, the logic applies to Flaccus' situation as well: if the integrity of magisterial election must be undermined, it is best done by a fellow magistrate. Further, if Gracchus' view is forward-looking – the establishment of less-than-ideal precedent – the consul's is very much in the historiographical mode – he has looked for, and has not found, such examples as would be tolerable in a free state. The consul therefore argues the opposite to Gracchus' view: such undermining must not take place, because the undermining of magistracy by a magistrate constitutes a contradiction in terms, a *ciuitas* that is not free.

What the consul's formulation back in book 39 ignores, and what the pro-Flaccus tribunes argue for, is the introduction of the people's *uoluntas* as an authorizing principle for Flaccus' canvass. Indeed, Flaccus does not trade mainly on personal authority but rather on the vocabulary of *uoluntas*, which brackets the speeches in the episodes, opening with the tribunes' initial *quem uellet* (39.4) and ending with Flaccus' *uoluntatis... uoluisset* (39.11), which doubles and intensifies the idea of popular desire. Throughout, Flaccus' main rhetorical technique is arousing the indignation of the crowd. Heralded by the strident *criminando* and *extorqueri* (39.9), Flaccus' rhetoric plays up the grave injustice he wants the audience to believe they and he have suffered together: they by the consistent denial of their expressed will, their *beneficium* (39.9, and emphasized by the expansive outline of the Roman political institutions immediately preceding: *a consule et senatu populi Romani beneficium*), and he by being forced to disappoint their hopes (39.12 *studia . . . destituere*).

The rhetoric is underlined once again by Livy's use of symmetrical language for the protagonists: Flaccus is disinclined to disappoint the people's hope (39.12 *non esse in animo*), while the consul causes the whole debate by being inclined equally as forcefully to hold the election by the letter of the law (39.6 *in animo esse e lege comitia habere*). Nor is *uoluntas* characteristic of only the people. Flaccus' reasoned first response raises the hopes of those who interpret it to fit their own ideas (39.8 *ad uoluntatem*), while the only will that really matters turns out to be that of the consul, no matter how inflamed popular support for Flaccus is: 39.12 *ut haud dubius praetor esset, si consul accipere nomen uellet* ("and there was no doubt he would be made praetor, if only the consul was willing to accept his candidacy"). The cycle is completed by another symmetrical arrangement: the senate's final pronouncement, which identifies the main impediments (39.14 *impedirent*, cf. 39.7 *impedimento*, used of Flaccus alone) as the mule-headedness (*pertinacia*) of Flaccus and the people's *praua studia*, echoes, with an important change, Livy's indirect report of the consul's perception of Flaccus' popularity (39.10 *pertinaciam petentis crescere et fauorem populi . . . cerneret*). While *pertinacia* here remains a constant, the transition from *fauor* to *studia* is mediated by Flaccus himself, who in 39.11 speaks of the *studium* of the people, and in 39.12 of their *studia*, which he hopes not to let down.[39] This stubborn utterance (39.12 *obstinata uox*) inflames the people's *fauor* towards him, such that his election, if it had been allowed to continue, was all but guaranteed. As we have seen, however, the people's putative *uoluntas*, though enthusiastically expressed in contional presence, never finds an official expression through election, and the episode ends practically as it began.

Here form and content meet. The episode opens with a standard connective device, laconically connecting this episode with another immediately preceding, and explaining the circumstances, namely the death of Decimius: 39.1 *hac sedata contentione alia subinde C. Decimii praetoris morte exorta est.* The reader is reminded of the purpose of the by-election throughout, chiefly through the formalistic language of the senate (39.7 *praetoris in*

[39] Livy reserves for himself the word *fauor*, using it once as the full phrase *fauorem populi* (39.10) and another in the shorter form *fauorem* (39.12). Nevertheless, both occurrences are focalized through the consul's perspective, once explicitly, as the consul observes (39.10 *cerneret*) Flaccus' increasing popularity, and again more indirectly, as Livy qualifies the report of his imminent success by the begrudging *obstinata uox* (39.12).

locum C. Decimii subrogandi; 39.14 *praetoris subrogandi*). At the very end the senate decides to call the election off, and P. Cornelius is charged with the double *prouincia* of *praetor urbanus et peregrinus*, and with the holding of the Apolline games.[40] Quite apart from being an anticlimactic ending both for Flaccus' hopes and for the repeatedly stated purpose of filling Decimius' vacant seat, the senate's final decision reads very much like an annalistic notation. In fact, a putative alternative scenario might have omitted the detailed political altercation and informed the reader simply that one praetor had died and another was charged with his duties. The narrative Livy chooses to give instead thus fills out what would have been a much more embryonic notation and does so in an elaborate and mannered fashion, which eventually calls attention to its own lack of resolution.

As David Quint has noted for the epic tradition, this kind of cyclical ring-composition is characteristic of narratives of the defeated, doomed to repeat their actions in search of redemptive resolution.[41] In epic poetry, as in Livy's text, this cycle of repetition is a marker of a rupture of exemplarity, as various people fail to comprehend the true lesson of previous exemplary acts. Flaccus' case is a somewhat pedestrian instantiation of the trope, but it is nevertheless instructive for how the political vagaries of republican politics meshed with the conventions of the text. Thus, for example, Flaccus can be read as the inarguable loser of this particular incident, since he fails to accomplish what he sets out to do. This failure, like all electoral failures, opens the way to repetition of the canvass in the next electoral cycle. Indeed, Flaccus is, in that regard, entirely typical of a host of Roman "also-rans," who presented themselves to the voters with varying degrees of success. From a textual point of view, however, repetition has limited value: not only are elections eminently interchangeable, but Flaccus has already achieved entry into the text and commemoration within it as well as obtained a virtual victory, supported by the people only to be foiled at the last turn – all this on top of the perfectly good office he won in the last round.[42] The consul's intervention prevents Flaccus from becoming a precedent, an *exemplum*, of any kind, except as part of the episode as a

[40] On the different functions of the *praetor urbanus* and *peregrinus*: Brennan 2000: 98–100; on the holding of the *ludi Apollinares* as praetorian *prouincia*: Brennan 2000: 103–4. Brennan uses our episode to deduce that "no other praetor (i.e. than the *praetor urbanus*) could fulfill the religious duties of the *ludi Apollinares* without a special *extra ordinem* grant, to judge from Livy's notice of the arrangement for *provinciae* for 184."

[41] Quint 1993.

[42] Flaccus went on to be elected to the praetorship in 182, in which capacity he served succesfully in Spain. He was elected consul for 179 while awaiting his triumph outside Rome (Livy 40.43.5), but there is no report of his electoral campaign, which must have been driven by his military laurels (cf. the summary in Briscoe 2008: 348). He is most famous for the desecration of the temple of Juno Lacinia in 174–3 BC while he was censor (Livy 42.3, for which most recently see Jaeger 2006

whole, which stands as a single instance of the ability of rhetorical language to reflect the pressures of political process and principle.

Africanus and Flamininus: credentials and exemplarity

Electoral failure, of course, was only one of two options, and the annals of the republic are riddled with examples of men who won over both crowds and elites to secure office before their time. In this section I want to look at two of those cases, the aedilician election of Scipio Africanus in 212 BC (Livy 25.2.6–7), and the consular election of Titus Quinctius Flamininus in 198 BC (Livy 32.7.8–12), as *comparanda* to the more extended treatment of Flaccus in the previous section. A few changes immediately stand out, in addition to the smaller scope Livy assigns to Africanus and Flamininus: in the case of Flaccus, as we have seen, the tribunician college is too internally fraught to play an important part other than as catalyst, and Livy certainly gives no indication that the tribunes attempted to thwart the election. For both Africanus and Flamininus, however, we see explicit tribunician obstruction. Second, and more obvious, is the change in outcome: Flaccus fails to force his candidacy through, while Africanus and Flamininus both win and go on to distinguished careers. All three episodes, however, are united by their structural and political content, since all three are abnormal in much the same way. None of Flaccus, Africanus, or Flamininus is eligible for the office he seeks, and, crucially, the tension between legal eligibility and the fulfillment of the people's wishes is a key element in each case.

In 212 BC the young Scipio Africanus stood for the curule aedileship and was duly obstructed by the tribunes of the plebs:

> aedilis curulis fuit eo anno cum M. Cornelio Cethego P. Cornelius Scipio, cui post Africano fuit cognomen. huic petenti aedilitatem cum obsisterent tribuni plebis, negantes rationem eius habendam esse quod nondum ad petendum legitima aetas esset, "si me," inquit "omnes Quirites aedilem facere uolunt, satis annorum habeo." tanto inde fauore ad suffragium ferendum in tribus discursum est, ut tribuni repente incepto desisterint. (Livy 25.2.6–7)

> P. Cornelius Scipio, later known as Africanus, was curule aedile in that year, along with M. Cornelius Cethegus. When the tribunes of the plebs obstructed him in his campaign for the aedileship, saying that his candidacy should not be accepted, because he was not yet of the right age for seeking office, he said: "If all Roman citizens wish to make me aedile, I am old enough." There was a rush to carry the vote in the tribes with such enthusiasm that the tribunes quickly stopped what they began.

and Briscoe 2012: 158–63), and for his suicide by hanging, which popular opinion took as divine retribution for the desecration (42.28.10–12).

Unlike more extended narratives elsewhere, this scene consists of a single exchange, and the focus is very much on Africanus' assertion and the consequent popular approval it generates.[43] It is, therefore, a basic unit of the larger template used to describe such events and structurally consists of three elements: the obstruction, the candidate's quip, and the intensification of popular fervor in the wake of the candidate's speech. This is, in fact, exactly what we have observed in Flaccus' case, though there each of the elements is more expansive, and the obstruction and response are each repeated multiple times and from multiple angles. This linear construction is further bolstered by the bracketing of the episode with tribunician action, marked specifically with *–sistere* cognate verbs: ***obsisterent tribuni plebis*** ~ ***tribuni repente incepto desisterint.*** The ring composition is also emphasized by the inverted word order and the marked used of *repente incepto*, which points back to the initial action of obstruction.

At the level of content, the tribunes here also dramatize the tension between legality and popular will, though unlike the Flaccus episode, there is no higher authority, such as the presiding consul, to mediate the dispute. The limited cast of characters in this vignette not only focuses attention on the interplay between Africanus and the tribunes but also requires the tribunes to perform a larger set of their typical roles. They start out by launching an objection to Africanus' electoral eligibility – an act which Livy regularly shows tribunes performing in all contexts of political disturbance. The verb Livy uses to describe them, *obsisterent*, recalls also their traditional role as protectors of the *plebs* against patrician abuses, and in particular elite demagoguery, as well their penchant for obstruction.[44] Thus, the tribunes are seemingly operating here according to their historical role as both representative and protective of the people and its assumed will. The argument they make, however, is not grounded in any consideration towards the people, but rather in the validity of Africanus' candidacy. Although neither side here alludes to a specific law, the phrase *legitima aetas* assumes for the tribunes the authority of institutionalized custom,

[43] The episode has a parallel in the election of Scipio Aemilianus to the consulship of 147 BC (App. *Pun.* 112), where the tribunes threaten to veto the elections, and the senate suspends the law on elections for the year. However, according to Oakley 2005b: 180, the episode is a middle ground between Africanus here and Flamininus below. Chaplin 2013 suggests that it was Aemilianus who generated such stories about Africanus in order to enhance his own image and appear more like his ancestor.

[44] Compare Rullianus' exchange with the tribunes, discussed below, where the tribunes step in to offer an exemption against Rullianus' wishes: he remains steadfast (10.13.10 *perstabat*), while they offer release (10.13.9 *solueretur*). On the *intercessio* of the tribunes of the plebs as a form of political obstruction: De Libero 1992: 29–49. On movement and *imperium*, see my discussion in Chapter 1 above.

with all its rules and regulations.[45] For Livy's contemporary reader, as well as for Livy's annalistic sources, of course, *legitima aetas* could have been more straightforwardly an allusion to the *lex Villia annalis*, passed in 180 BC, which regulated minimum ages for the magistracies. The legal anachronism notwithstanding, the important point is that the tribunes rely on an institutionalized regulatory force, which they, at least, assume derives either from their own constitutional powers of obstruction, or from a commonly held sense of political decorum.

Scipio's answer, however, for all its flippancy effectively reframes the terms of discussion: the people, he claims, have the power to determine the legitimacy of his candidacy, over and above any other regulatory claims. Scipio's phrasing (*si . . . omnes Quirites . . . uolunt*) here even alludes to legal language, in counterpoint to the tribunes' insistence on *legitima aetas* as a validating criterion.[46] As with Flaccus, this answer clinches the favor of the people, and the tribes rush to vote with such enthusiasm that the tribunes give up their enterprise. Both the result-clause *ut . . . desisterint* and the adjective *repente* emphasize that the tribunes' change of mind was the result of the exigencies of the moment rather than any genuine change of heart, caught out by the volume and vigor of Scipio's popular support. Thus, although minimalist in expression, this episode tracks a range of tribunician expressions of the tension between regulatory pressures in the form of law and custom on the one hand, and the people's desires on the other. The figure of Scipio himself, finally, should not be downplayed, since it is his speech which inclines the people his way. Such effective speech acts, characteristic of the great personages of the republic in general and

45 Compare Ostwald 1986: 93–108 on the equivalent *nomos* and *nomimos* in Athens. While norms for office-holding surely existed in the third century BC, the upheavals of the Punic Wars caused the occasional oversight of constitutional proprieties. Minimum ages for office were probably not set down before the *lex Villia annalis* of 180 BC, and *legitima aetas* may thus be an anachronism, drawn from later practice: Astin 1958: 31–46. On the concretization of the *cursus honorum* and political careers, see also Develin 1979, 1985, and now Beck 2005. It may also be that by *legitima aetas* the tribunes do not refer to biological age but to an inappropriate sequence of office. Scipio served as military tribune under his father but had not been *quaestor* (Val. Max. 5.4.2 refers to the campaign as his *tirocinium*, but without reference to his exact rank). Similarly, Hoyos suggests in the notes to Yardley's *Oxford's World Classics* translation (2006: 660), that *legitima aetas* refers to the convention by which "a man did not seek office until he had served 10 campaigns, starting at the age of 16 or 17."

46 The legal formula of a *rogatio*, *uelitis iubeatis*, is most fully recorded in Gell. *NA* 5.19.9, with the particular example of an adoption formula: *eius rogationis uerba haec sunt: "uelitis iubeatis, uti L. Valerius L. Titio tam iure legeque filius siet?"* ("the words of this proposed measure were as follows: 'Is it your wish and command that L. Valerius should become the son of L. Titius, in law and in right?'"). The formula is also attested in, e.g., Cic. *Dom.* 80: *si tribuno plebis rogante "Velitis iubeatisne"* ("if, when the tribune of the plebs asks 'Is it your wish and command . . . '"). For a brief survey of its appearance in epigraphically preserved legislation, *RS* 1.10.

of Africanus in particular, reveal the two faces of the republican political *ethos*: popular desires were liable to be articulated and manipulated by the speaking classes who comprised the political elite, while the rule of law, at least in the sense of an equally applicable set of rules, was likewise a pliable discourse.

The same elements, but differently deployed, appear in the consular elections of T. Quinctius Flamininus in 199 BC, which I briefly mentioned at the opening of this book, and in which the future Liberator of Greece attempted to skip a stage (the praetorship) of the *cursus honorum*.[47] The episode occurs too early to apply the strictures of the *lex Villia Annalis*, and indeed legality here plays the opposite role – it is invoked to allow the canvass, rather than circumscribe it.[48] Beyond this reversal of so-far familiar roles, this episode is remarkable also for the elaborate speech the tribunes make against the candidacy of Flamininus, in which they think explicitly not only about the parameters of eligibility, but also the reasons behind these public expectations of political decorum.

> neque ipse consul memorabile quicquam gessit, comitiorum causa Romam reuocatus; quae ipsa [i.e. comitia] per M. Fuluium et M'. Curium tribunos plebis impediebantur, quod T. Quinctium Flamininum consulatum ex quaestura petere non patiebantur: iam aedilitatem praeturamque fastidiri nec per honorum gradus, documentum sui dantes, nobiles homines tendere ad consulatum, sed transcendendo media summa imis continuare. res ex campestri certamine in senatum peruenit. patres censuerunt qui honorem quem sibi capere per leges liceret peteret, in eo populo creandi quem uelit potestatem fieri aequum esse. in auctoritate patrum tribuni fuere. creati consules Sex. Aelius Paetus et T. Quinctius Flamininus. (Livy 32.7.8–12)

> However, the consul achieved nothing worth remembering, because he was summoned back to Rome to hold the elections. These were held up by M. Fulvius and M' Curius, tribunes of the plebs, because they would not allow T. Quinctius Flamininus to seek the consulship after the quaestorship: they said that noblemen now spurned the aedileship and the praetorship and did not strive for the consulship through the steps of office, thus giving proof of themselves; instead, through skipping the middle offices, they joined the lowest to the highest. The matter was debated in the Campus

47 On Africanus and Flamininus as "two young patricians who made it to the top at an early age": Develin 1985: 231–51, quotation at 231. On Flamininus' early career, see also the account in Plut. *Flam.* 1–2. Badian 1971: 109–10 and Carawan 1988: 211–12 reconstruct Flamininus' career before this election. On the episode: Briscoe 1973: 180–1. Flamininus was not yet thirty in 199 BC (Polyb. 18.12.5; Plut. *Flam.* 2.2).

48 On the *lex Villia annalis*: see n. 45. On premature candidacy as a conflict of rules: Lundgreen 2011: 74–84.

Martius and then reached the senate. The senators determined that, so long as a person sought an office which the laws allowed him to hold, it was fair that the people should have the power to elect whomever they wish. The tribunes accepted the authority of the senate, and Sex. Aelius Paetus and T. Quinctius Flamininus were elected consuls.

Unlike Africanus' case, here the candidate himself does not speak, nor is the issue one of legality or eligibility. When the senate concludes the matter by allowing the candidacy on the grounds that it was allowed by law (*per leges liceret*), the tribunes follow the senatorial decision without requiring an overt demonstration of popular support for Flamininus. In this sense, at least, the insertion of the tribunician rationale for obstruction, together with the fuller pronouncement of the senate, complements exactly Africanus' case, where only the candidate speaks, and the tension is resolved by a seemingly spontaneous action of the people. Further, despite the fact that the episodes are otherwise identically arranged, both following the obstruction–speech–intensification structure, here the intensification, that is, the senatorial discussion, is a secondary step, rather than, as with Africanus, a direct result of the candidate's speech, and this despite the fact that the tribunician speech here is of greater length and complexity than Africanus' pithy sound-bite.

This speech is particularly interesting, however, because the tribunes take issue with Flamininus not in his own right, but rather as a representative of a larger tendency by young noblemen (witness Africanus) to shun (*fastidiri*) the aedileship and praetorship, and to move directly from the quaestorship to the consulship (*consulatum ex quaestura petere*). The tribunes clearly mean to invoke aristocratic excess and ambition, and they make their meaning abundantly clear at the end of their speech, especially with the phrase *summa imis continuare*, a verbal turn which marks Flamininus' behavior as "immoral and excessive."[49] Still, the choice of *fastidiri* is striking, both because it is a rare usage in Livy, and because it connotes a snobbery of which the tribunes clearly disapprove.[50] As Robert Kaster

49 Briscoe 1973: 180 for the phrase, and Edwards 1993: 137–72 for Roman ideas of moral and luxurious excess. Nisbet and Hubbard 1970: 384–5, commenting on Hor. *Carm.* 1.34.12 (*ima summis*) note that "Horace's description of Fortune's actions suggests the conventional complaint of Roman constitutionalists against radical innovators." They list, e.g., Cic. *Leg.* 3.19 *omnia infima summis paria fecit*... and Vell. Pat. 2.2.3 (Tiberius Gracchus) *summa imis miscuit.*

50 The passive infinitive *fastidiri* occurs here only, though *fastiditur* occurs in 4.3.13 and *fastidieris* in 10.8.6. Otherwise, *fastidium* and its cognates are relatively rare in Livy, occurring only fifteen times in the extant books, mostly as verb forms (in addition to the above: 2.41.4, 3.1.7, 4.3.13, 6.40.8, 6.41.2, 28.40.9, 32.21.30, 32.21.35, 34.5.13, 34.54.7, 38.50.12, 42.62.13).

has shown, Roman *fastidium* came in two main forms: first, a more or less reflexive disgust, for instance as aroused by rotten flesh or a foul stench, and usually leading to a physical and visceral reaction; and second, a more calculated version of the emotion, wherein disgust emerges not automatically, but as a conscious aversion to those things one perceives as beneath him. Kaster refers to this type of *fastidium* as "deliberative ranking" or "aversive connoisseurship,"[51] and Flamininus' *fastidium* comfortably belongs in the latter rubric, since his imagined *fastidium* recoils from the middle offices as mere delay en route to bigger and better things.

More broadly, however, deliberative ranking, along with the fastidious ambition it generates, describes an attitude fostered by the republican political system, where election functioned as an entrée to higher offices and an increasingly exclusive political club. The tribunes' ascription of *fastidium*, therefore, not only criticizes Flamininus for displaying the emotion but also imagines him criticizing the *cursus honorum* as placing a restriction on political careerism. This sense of *fastidium* likewise answers to one of the tribunes' primary concerns, that in going through the middle offices the candidates give proof of themselves (*documentum sui dantes*). The tribunes, we might reasonably presume, offer their claim in the spirit of political empiricism: an able quaestor makes for an able aedile, who makes for an able praetor, and so on. Flamininus' refusal to tread the path thus robs the voters of a detailed account of his past doings and therefore advertises the candidate's disdain for both office and voters. Such public display, however, also furnishes a *documentum*, albeit of a negative sort, and shows Flamininus as the sort of haughty aristocrat, like Africanus before him, who dispenses with convention out of some self-assurance of the visibility of his merits.

Flamininus and his potential *exemplum* become more concretized in Plutarch's version of the same events, and we might at this point usefully compare the two accounts:[52]

> τοῦτο δ' αὐτὸν ἐπῆρε μάλιστα τὰς διὰ μέσου καὶ συνήθεις τοῖς νέοις ἀρχὰς ὑπερβάντα, δημαρχίαν καὶ στρατηγίαν καὶ ἀγορανομίαν, εὐθὺς αὐτὸν ὑπατείας ἀξιοῦν, καὶ κατῄει, τοὺς ἀπὸ τῶν κληρουχιῶν ἔχων προθύμους.

[51] Kaster 2005: 113. For *fastidium* in general, see Kaster 2005: 104–33. Kaster defines this kind of *fastidium* as applying both to one's idea of oneself as superior, and to one's idea of the object of *fastidium* as inferior and therefore repulsive.

[52] The substance of Plutarch's account was probably drawn not from Livy himself, but from an annalistic source: R. E. Smith 1944, Carawan 1988: 209–12. Regardless of how much, if at all, Plutarch worked with Livy's text, his account represents a further step in the development of a tradition that both authors shared. For Plutarch's adaptation of sources more generally: Pelling 1980.

τῶν δὲ περὶ Φούλβιον καὶ Μάνιον δημάρχων ἐνισταμένων, καὶ δεινὸν εἶναι λεγόντων ἄνδρα νέον εἰς τὴν μεγίστην ἀρχὴν εἰσβιάζεσθαι παρὰ τοὺς νόμους, οἷον ἀτέλεστον ἔτι τῶν πρώτων ἱερῶν καὶ μυστηρίων τῆς πολιτείας, ἡ μὲν σύγκλητος ἀπέδωκε τῷ δήμῳ τὴν ψῆφον, ὁ δὲ δῆμος ἀπέδειξεν αὐτὸν ὕπατον μετὰ Σέξτου Αἰλίου, καίπερ οὔπω τριάκοντ' ἔτη γεγονότα. (Plut. *Flam.* 2)

And this raised him very greatly so that he ignored the middle offices, which young men usually stand for, the tribunate, praetorship, and aedileship, and considered himself worthy of the consulship straight away. He stood for the office, having his colonists as supporters. The tribunes Fulvius and Manius obstructed him and said that it was an unnatural thing for a young man to force his way to the consulship against the laws, and, as it were, uninitiated into the first rites and mysteries of the state. The senate, however, referred the matter to the people, and the people voted him consul along with Sextus Aelius, even though he was not yet thirty.

Plutarch's version follows in outline the same plot as Livy's, with Flamininus' candidacy obstructed by the tribunes and the impasse later resolved by the senate, but the differences are perhaps more revealing. First, the tribunician speech, although following the same verbal structure of imposition-verb followed by indirect statement, is considerably different in content. The very Roman concern with exemplarity and display, emphatically evinced by *documentum sui dantes*, is replaced by a Hellenic stress on force (εἰσβιάζεσθαι), legality (παρὰ τοὺς νόμους), and the metaphor of government as an initiation cult (οἷον ἀτέλεστον ἔτι τῶν πρώτων ἱερῶν καὶ μυστηρίων τῆς πολιτείας), with the elections of the early *cursus* serving, presumably, as the initiation rites. This change is important, not only because it highlights Livy's distinctive interest in exemplarity and its functions as well as Plutarch's in religion, but also because in Livy's version, unlike in Plutarch's, we learn of Flamininus' sentiments through the speech and perspective of the tribunes of the plebs. In Plutarch, this Livian voice has been appropriated by the narrator, whose account of Flamininus' arrogance and ambition reproduces the tribunes' opinions thematically, if not verbally.[53] In a very concrete sense, then, the exemplary process that was initiated by Livy's tribunes – Flamininus' behavior furnishing a *documentum* out of his *fastidium* – is completed in Plutarch's account of the same event, where his arrogance is already assumed.

53 The technique whereby the original authorial voice is reproduced in the voice of one of the characters in later intertexts (i.e. Livy's voice is reproduced in the mouth of Plutarch's tribunes) is itself Livian, which may add another layer to the intertextual relationship here. For the technique in Livy: Levene 2010: 149–54.

The ending of the episode is another place where Livy and Plutarch differ markedly from each other. The basic outline is again roughly identical: the matter arrived at the senate house, but where Livy has the senate actually pronounce, Plutarch has them refer the matter back to the voters, who vote Flamininus in as consul. This dynamic, wherein the tribunes object to the election of the people's favorite, is familiar already from Livy's account of Africanus' attempt at the aedileship, and it once again emphasizes the potential for disjunction between the tribunes as representatives of the people and the people's actual expression of their political inclinations. Livy's ending is somewhat more complex. The senate invokes the people's right to free election (32.7.11 *quem uelit potestatem fieri*) as a justification for allowing Flamininus' candidacy, but it is a carefully circumscribed concession. The people may choose whomever they wish, so long as that man sought such office as he was legally allowed (*per leges liceret*) to seek. Here too Plutarch makes revealing changes. His tribunes obstruct Flamininus because they find his candidacy anomalous (δεινόν) and against the law (παρὰ τοὺς νόμους). In articulating their argument in this way, they move away from the Livian version, with its emphasis on *fastidium*. Certainly describing something as δεινόν can also entail feeling *fastidium* towards it, in which case Plutarch's tribunes neatly feel towards Flamininus what he, in Livy's version, allegedly feels for the middle offices, and in consequence for them. However, in articulating their aversion as grounded in a legal argument rather than emotion, the tribunes ironically arrogate for themselves the language of Livy's senate, which pronounces exactly the opposite opinion: that the candidacy is legal (*per leges*) and fair (*aequum*). The two episodes therefore create an intertextual chiasmus, with Livy's version of events used as a naturalized template for Plutarch's account.

The pronouncement of Livy's senate is an inverted form of the hierarchy advocated by the senate in Africanus' case. Whereas there the senate proclaimed that the people's will supersedes any current law or custom, in Flamininus' case it defines the arena in which the people's will is supreme as precisely the scope left to it by the laws. So long as a candidacy is not illegal, the people may exercise their will. This pronouncement has further ramifications, of course: it allows the people significant scope in which to operate, as well as the *de facto* right to adjudicate in cases where there was no law already enacted. In this regard, at least, the senate shows the same spirit it had in Africanus' election: a willingness to allow popular inclination to prevail over magisterial action. Where the Flamininus episode diverges, however, is with the creation of more nuanced conditions for applying the principle of popular sovereignty, and subordinating that sovereignty to the rule of law (itself one of the ways in which the people exercised its symbolic powers).[54]

Between them, the episodes surveyed so far reflect a unified, if highly flexible, discourse critiquing certain consequences of the protean operation of Roman politics. In one case (Flaccus) the tribunes argue for exemption from an existing law to allow a candidate to stand, while in another (Flamininus) the senate argues against the tribunes that where no law exists, the people's free election ought to be upheld. In the *pro Murena*, likewise, Cicero uses his position as mentor and patron to both sides to show two views of the same event, even if, in the service of his advocacy, he falls short of arguing *in utramque partem*. It is here, therefore, that one of the great virtues of political narratives is visible, though historiography naturally offers a broader and more flexible scope for nuanced expression: the ability to sustain a remarkably broad vision of the permutations and consequences of constitutional scenarios, at each point illustrating the fundamental role of rhetoric in the outcomes, political and textual, of those scenarios.

Spontaneous election and the reluctant magistrate

The previous three episodes have been characterized and unified, above all, by the willful agency of the candidate himself. Whether successful or not, Flaccus, Africanus, and Flamininus actively sought public office, even in the face of institutional sanction and the risk of opprobrium. The following set of episodes, which I will call the "Rullianus Cycle" (10.9.10–13; 10.13.5–13; 10.15.7–12), by contrast feature a very reluctant candidate, whose notable characteristic, in fact, is his adamant refusal even to campaign, much less obtain the office.[55] This reluctance, which Rullianus shows under three quite different sets of circumstances, inverts some of the dynamics we have seen operate in the previous sections of this chapter. Rather than piling up obstacles, the senate, people, and tribunes fall over themselves to induce Rullianus to canvass. Rullianus' coyness, therefore, is rhetorically calculated and in fact allows him to assume a great deal of agency in directing the results of the elections to his liking. Rullianus' conduct is, in other words, a subtler form of political manipulation, and the various arguments he brings

54 A similar phenomenon can be observed in the use of the term *popularis*, which was broadly applied across the political gamut, and to wildly differing and often contradictory purposes: Brunt 1988: 443–502 and Mackie 1992; Morstein-Marx 2004: 204–40; Robb 2010.

55 The historicity of this cycle is dubious, as all three of its episodes share structural similarities, and all feature Q. Fabius Rullianus exerting personal authority to influence the proper channels of election to office. For the relationship of the episodes to one another, and their reliance on "annalistic fiction": Oakley 2005b: 139–44.

up, as well as the form in which Livy presents them, show another aspect of magisterial behavior. We have seen already that part of what makes Flaccus' campaign successful with the people and threatening to the senate was his arrogation in practice of consular authority, a technique Cicero employs as well in his presentation of Murena's canvass. Africanus and Flamininus both show the same kind of assurance, expecting and receiving popular support in their claims to office. Rullianus, on the other hand, manages, with his studied humility, to have the same dispensations offered to him only to refuse in two cases out of the three. Moreover, Rullianus' direction of events, while reminiscent of Flaccus', demonstrates again that the same types of arguments – the people's wishes, the power of the law, and the rightness of special dispensations – can be deployed towards seemingly opposite rhetorical ends: to have a magistrate elected against the norms and customs, or to admonish the people against it.

Rullianus' refusal to seek or accept office is the verbal glue that holds this triad together.[56] He is described as *non petentem* ("not canvassing" or, more forcefully, "not running for office")[57] twice in the first episode (10.9.10 and 10.9.11), and in the following two episodes his non-campaigning is further extended. In the second episode *non petentem* (10.13.5) is bolstered by *recusantem* ("refusing"[58]) twice (10.13.5, and 10.13.10 *recusando*), as well as by means of an elaborate speech. In the third episode he once again refuses office (10.15.9 *abnuere*) with a speech, although in shorter form than his previous *recusatio*. The language of refusal is bolstered by internal cross-referencing between the three episodes. The central event, in 10.13.5–13, receives the most extended treatment, and the other two, each in its own way, refer backwards or forwards to it, and they both probably offer annalistic elaborations on it. However, the episodes also escalate, as Rullianus moves from uncertain or deferred election, to reluctant election, to outright refusal of election. Further, since Livy openly acknowledges that the first

56 Chaplin 2000: 112–15 connects Rullianus' refusal to his personal story in book 8.

57 On the difference between actively seeking office and having one's name put forward as candidate: Oakley 2005b: 144, with further references. Oakley compares this episode to Africanus' aedilician election, which Livy narrates in Livy 25.2.6–7 (discussed above), where Africanus is elected without technically canvassing. The comparison is apt, because it captures the difference in attitudes between the two candidates. Africanus is *seeking* office, even if he is not allowed to put his name forward (25.2.7 *quod nondum ad petendum legitima aetas esset*, "because he was not yet of the right age for canvassing"). Rullianus, by contrast, wishes to do neither.

58 The *recusatio* is also a standard poetic topos, where the poet affiliated himself with a particular generic tradition by shunning another, usually history or epic. In so doing, the poet typically also shows off his ability to perform the poetry he shuns (as in, e.g., Verg. *Ecl.* 6; Ovid, *Amores* 1.1). Read in literary-critical terms, therefore, *recusantem* highlights Rullianus' coyness, and it is therefore fitting, perhaps, that two of his *recusationes* actually end up in his holding office, and only his third is a proper refusal. On coyness as a political tactic under the late republic and early empire, see n. 69 below.

and second iterations may be a doublet, this tripartite cross-referencing links the three episodes into a single narrative unit.

Despite their internal connections, however, only the later two instances are fully integrated into their surrounding narrative: fear of an Etruscan-Samnite arming turns all eyes to Rullianus in 10.13.2–5, while his refusal of candidacy a year later in 10.15.8 is interwoven with the parallel campaign of Appius Claudius and the effort to edge out plebeian candidates.[59] The first instance, however, is more loosely connected to the narrative preceding it, so much so that it is properly speaking a short digression in which Livy reports a variant on the information he has just conveyed, in this case the identity of the new consuls for 299 BC:

> in eum annum cum Q. Fabium consulem non petentem omnes dicerent centuriae, ipsum auctorem fuisse Macer Licinius ac Tubero tradunt differendi sibi consulatus in bellicosiorem annum: eo anno maiori se usui rei publicae fore urbano gesto magistratu; ita nec dissimulantem quid mallet nec petentem tamen, aedilem curulem cum L. Papirio Cursore factum. id ne pro certo ponerem uetustior annalium auctor Piso effecit, qui eo anno aediles curules fuisse tradit Cn. Domitium Cn. filium Caluinum et Sp. Caruilium Q. filium Maximum. id credo cognomen errorem in aedilibus fecisse secutamque fabulam mixtam ex aediliciis et consularibus comitiis, conuenientem errori. (Livy 10.9.10–13)
>
> In that year all the centuries voted in Q. Fabius as consul, even though he had not formally stood for the office, at least according to Licinius Macer and Tubero. They say also that he was responsible for deferring his consulship for a more warlike year: in the present year, he said, he would be of more use to the republic in an urban magistracy. Thus, without hiding his preferences, and still not formally seeking office, he was made curule aedile with L. Papirius Cursor. Piso, an older writer of annals, causes me to doubt this, since he writes that in that year the curule aediles were Cn. Domitius Calvinus, the son of Gnaeus, and Spurius Carvilius Maximus, son of Quintus. I think that the nickname caused confusion about the aediles, and consequently a story was made up befitting the mistake, conflating the aedilician and consular elections.

[59] Fear of Italian mobilization: 10.13.2–5 *fama exorta Etruscos Samnitesque ingentes conscribere exercitus . . . hic terror, cum illustres uiri consulatum peterent, omnes in Q. Fabium Maximum primo non petentem, deinde . . . etiam recusantem conuertit* ("a rumor arose that the Etruscans and the Samnites were drafting a huge army . . . this fear turned everyone towards Q. Fabius Maximus, although famous men were seeking the consulship, and although he at first did not stand . . . and afterward refused outright"). On *fama* in Roman politics, see also Laurence 1994, and now Hardie 2012: 226–72 on Livy. Appius Claudius: 10.15.7–8 *cum primo uocatae Q. Fabium consulem dicerent omnes centuriae, Ap. Claudius, consularis candidatus . . . cum suis tum totius nobilitatis uiribus incubuit ut se cum Q. Fabio consulem dicerent* ("When all the centuries, having been summoned, named Q. Fabius consul first, Ap. Claudius, a consular candidate . . . devoted not only his own energies, but also those of the entire nobility to ensure the centuries named him consul along with Q. Fabius").

This passage is quite extraordinary, both for Rullianus' pluck and for Livy's elaborately described skepticism. Characteristically, Livy is simultaneously coy and emphatic: he clearly mistrusts Macer and Tubero and prefers the evidence of Piso, but despite the fact that he takes the Macer–Tubero version as mistaken (*conuenientem errori*), he nevertheless affords it primacy of place, and an equal amount of space as to his debunking of it. More striking, however, is that the Macer–Tubero version assigns Rullianus considerable agency in driving both the result of the election and the historiographical account, which Livy attempts at the end to set straight. The phrase *ipsum auctorem fuisse*, referring to Rullianus, thus puts him on an equal footing with both Livy, the author of the *AUC*, and Piso, whose account makes Livy suspect the Macer–Tubero version, and who is explicitly called *uetustior annalium auctor*, the only named source in this passage to be so called. This ascription of agency implicates Rullianus both as a political actor as well as a historical *auctor*. More ironically, however, Rullianus inverts the standard positioning of the candidate as an active seeker of office, seeking instead a deferral to an unspecified future date. In so doing, he makes use not just of the requisite popularity for election, but also the necessary authority for negotiating, on his own terms, the type of office he would have in any given year. Livy's source criticism turns the passage into a comment on the historiographical role of the magistrate: Rullianus' *auctoritas* has the power to affect the *fasti* themselves, even in years when he seeks not to have his name inscribed in them. This very curiosity in turn ensures his place in the historical narratives.

Rullianus' strong intervention results, as Livy already suggests, in several different kinds of doubling. Livy introduces this idea by repeating *error* twice in 10.9.13 above (*errorem* ~ *errori*), a confusion he claims stems from a doubled *cognomen*, presumably *Maximus*, which he does not repeat. Rullianus eventually holds this deferred consulship in 298 BC, thereby doubling the original election in 10.9, and in that case too Rullianus repeats his negotiations, demanding a consular colleague with whom he had already served. As with the mirrored alternatives in the first episode, doubling dominates the language of this second request as well, presenting Decius as a doublet for Rullianus. The personal pronouns *mihi* and *mecum* bracket the petition itself, and the description of Decius likewise echoes itself, both in the doubling of *dignum* and of the prefix *con/l-* in the noun-phrase *concordi collegio*: 10.13.13 *P. Decium, expertum* <u>*mihi*</u> *<u>co</u>ncordi <u>co</u>llegio uirum,* <u>*dignum*</u> *uobis,* <u>*dignum*</u> *parente suo, quaeso* <u>*mecum*</u> *consulem faciatis.*[60]

[60] On doubling as marked language, see the extensive survey of Wills 1996. On doubling figures in Livy: Kraus 1998. Rullianus' speeches here also make ample use of verbal polyptoton, another

This movement into narrative doublets is stopped, however, once doubles turn into triples. In the third Rullianus episode, Rullianus refuses outright to play any further, and the excuses he offers repeat those he had given the previous year (10.15.9 *Fabius primo de se eadem fere quae priore anno dicendo abnuere*, "Fabius at first refused in much the same words as he had used in the previous year"). Since the phrase *eadem fere* is the standard annalistic way to signal the artistic composition of a speech, this gesture too is self-reflexive, as Livy adverts to his own artistic recomposition of his own prior speechifying. Further, since the discussion revolves around the election of two patricians for the consulship the doubling figure is once again available for negation, as Rullianus agrees to double the patrician candidacies, so long as he himself is not one of them: 10.15.10 *facturum enim se fuisse dixit ut duorum patriciorum nomina reciperet, si alium quam se consulem fieri uideret* ("he said that he would agree to receive the names of two patricians, so long as he saw someone other than him became consul"). What eventually squares this particular circle is that Rullianus refuses this time not because of inconvenience, but because he refuses to become a bad – in fact, the worst – sort of *exemplum* (10.15.11 *pessimo exemplo*) in acting against the laws (*contra leges*). Here too, Livy's exemplary patterning is evident, since Rullianus' refusal to allow his name to be put forward ensures that any doubling will now be a genuine change: two new consuls replacing two old consuls, rather than collapsing ones and twos through the iteration of one (or both) of the consular colleagues.

I shall return to the connection between exemplarity and the laws in a moment, but first I want to draw attention to Rullianus' opposite numbers, the various agents who attempt to cajole him into magistracy. The first of the three instances, Rullianus' election to the consulship and then his switch to the aedileship, sketches out a complex nexus of textual and political agency, where the natural agents, Livy as the author of the text and the people as the dispenser of the electoral *beneficium*, are displaced in favor of competing authorial presences (Macer, Tubero, and especially Piso), and the candidate's own *auctoritas*, which allows him to negotiate his way out from one magistracy and into the other. This already highlights one of the ways in which the Rullianus cycle inverts the narrative paradigms we have seen instantiated elsewhere, in the cases of Flaccus, Africanus, and Flamininus. Unlike the other candidates, Rullianus is warding off not obstruction, but overly enthusiastic support. In the third and last episode Livy even describes the whole nobility flocking to Rullianus' consular chair

rhetorical figure which marks out similiarity in difference: *regi* ~ *regere* (10.13.10), *ferri* ~ *tulissent* (10.13.10, and emphasized by the alliteration of *ferri . . . tulissent fraus fieret*), 10.13.12 *agitis acturique* (for which Oakley 2005b: 182). On the harmony between Fabius and Decius: Lipovsky 1981: 81 n. 1.

(10.15.9 *circumstare sellam omnis nobilitas*), beseeching (*orare*) him to remain in office, in language which shades into the religious. Most emphatically, the tribunes, the normal sources of obstruction and objection, though they appear only in the middle episode, intervene not to obstruct but rather to release Rullianus from any obstruction he himself may come up with:

> acuebat hac moderatione tam iusta studia; quae uerecundia legum restinguenda ratus, legem recitari iussit, qua intra decem annos eundem consulem refici non liceret. uix prae strepitu audita lex est tribunique plebis nihil id impedimenti futurum aiebant: se ad populum laturos uti legibus solueretur. et ille quidem in recusando perstabat: quid ergo attineret leges ferri, quibus per eosdem qui tulissent fraus fieret? iam regi leges, non regere. populus nihilo minus suffragia inibat et, ut quaeque intro uocata erat centuria, consulem haud dubie Fabium dicebat. (Livy 10.13.8–11)
>
> With this moderation, he sharpened such justified enthusiasm; and because he thought that these sentiments might be dampened by reverence for the laws, he ordered the law to be read out, according to which it was not allowed for anyone to be re-elected consul twice within ten years. The law was barely heard over the noise, and the tribunes of the plebs avowed that it would be no obstacle, and that they would bring it to the people that he should be released from the laws. But he, in fact, persisted in refusing: for what was the point, he said, of passing laws, on which the very people who had passed them perpetrated fraud? Now the laws were ruled, not ruling. The people nevertheless began to vote, and as each century was summoned, it elected Fabius as consul, without any doubt.

The law to which Rullianus refers is another of the Genucian plebiscites of 342 BC, reported in Livy as belonging to the same legislative package we have already seen invoked in the campaign of Fulvius Flaccus earlier in this chapter. Unlike Flaccus' case, however, here the citation and recitation of the law achieves precisely the opposite effect, as the tribunes, rather than invoke the law to stop the candidacy, instead volunteer to dismiss it as irrelevant. The change is visible also at the level of the actual citation. I have noted that the tribunes and Flaccus have slightly different interpretations of the relevant Genucian plebiscite, and this interpretative gap paves the way to a vivid political altercation. Here, on the other hand, harmony is apparent. Livy's own description of the plebiscite above, *qua intra decem annos eundem consulem refici non liceret* ("according to which it was not allowed for anyone to be re-elected consul twice within ten years"), is manifestly a paraphrase rather than the language of the law, but it conveys much the same idea as Livy's account of the plebiscite in 7.42.2 *ne quis eundem magistratum intra decem annos caperet* ("that no one should hold the same magistracy again within ten years"). If anything, Livy is both more emphatic and more precise in the Rullianus rendition: the generalizing *ne quis* and *eundum magistratum* are replaced by the more specific *eundem consulem*. The verb change from *caperet* to *refici*, meanwhile, is far more topical – Rullianus is not speaking of any magistracy, but rather a potential reiteration of the consulship, and it is in that technical usage that Livy here employs the verb (*OLD* s.v. *reficio* 4 "to reappoint [to office]").[61] This tension between specificity and generalization recalls, and in dramatic time anticipates, the Flaccus campaign, since there too, as I have argued, Flaccus is the more precise reader of the plebiscite, while the tribunes tend more to generalities and misapprehensions. Here too the tribunes miss the point altogether. Where Rullianus wants the law to release him from the burden of office, they enthusiastically step in to waive it.

The recitation of the law itself is an unusual rhetorical gambit, at least in Livy's electoral paradigms as we have so far seen them. While laws are regularly invoked and their meaning and application debated, it is only here that we learn explicitly that a law was read out.[62] In its formal features, however, the recitation of the law functions in very similar ways to the more informal invocations we have seen earlier, setting up the constitutional premise around which the debate revolves. Further, as in the previous instances, the reading audience remains at some remove from the language of the law. The references presumably go back to a genuine piece of legislation, but they also reach back towards the same set of Genucian plebiscites that will recur allusively in Flaccus' canvass.[63] The law thus becomes something of an echo chamber, wherein Livy replicates his own language both as paraphrase of the law itself as well as part of an intratextual node. This textual layering is part and parcel of the cycle's larger power dynamic, where Rullianus emerges as wielding considerable authority, derived, in this context, entirely from his refusal of candidacy (notwithstanding, of course, the military prestige that made him a desirable candidate to begin with). With the language of the law reducible to paraphrase and repetition, his own interpretation emerges as the one definitive voice. Even when tribunes and

[61] On *reficere* in the sense "to reappoint to office": Oakley 1997: 673. The passive voice of the verb emphasizes the agency of the people over the magistrate and suggests that the prohibition applied to the electorate (which was not allowed to elect) just as it did to the candidate.

[62] For recitations of laws: cf. Oakley 2005a: 426 *ad* 9.33.5 (*recitaret*), who cites our passage (Livy 10.13.8), and App. *Pun.* 112.531.

[63] On the plebiscite, see n. 34 above, and Oakley 2005b: 180. Compare Cic. *Leg.* 3.9 *eundem magistratum, ni interfuerint decem anni, ne quis capito; aeuitatem annali lege seruanto*. Cicero's preoccupation is here with iteration rather than simultaneous holding of two magistracies, though it is possible to argue that the latter is a fortiori prohibited by the former. See Dyck 2004a: 459–60 ad loc. On the vexed problem of iteration, see the succinct summary at Brennan 2000: 647–52.

people largely ignore his refusal, Rullianus continues to assert his authority, demanding and receiving P. Decius as his colleague.

Rullianus here makes this power dynamic both more explicit and more central to his narrative. His recitation of the law turns him into the champion of legality, while the tribunes become perpetrators of fraud rather than guardians of the constitution against the demagoguery of ambitious politicians: *quid ergo attineret leges ferri, quibus per eosdem qui tulissent fraus fieret* (10.13.10 "for what was the point, he said, of passing laws, on which the very people who had passed them perpetrated fraud?"). Rullianus' presentation of his argument casts the laws in quite anthropomorphizing terms, and the switch from the singular *lex* to the plural *leges* likewise elevates Rullianus' point from particular to universal. The laws can be the object of *fraus*;[64] they participate in a reciprocal model of politics, where one governs and is governed in turn;[65] and they can induce the social emotion *uerecundia*, a context-based deference which showed one knew one's place relative to others.[66] All of these phrases are peculiar and distinctive. As Stephen Oakley points out, the sense of *uerecundia legum* is clear enough ("deference for the laws"), but the phrase is rare, appearing only once more in a textually corrupt passage at the end of Livy's fourth book.[67] Likewise, the idea that the laws can be ruled seems to be a Livian *hapax* rather than a stock phrase of political thought, although it fits perfectly within the power dynamics of the episode. Both phrases, however, implicate the laws in a broader social construct and in the political process as actual, almost anthropomorphized participants, rather than as mere instruments. Within this metaphoric participation, further, the laws assume a position of some authority: this is the rhetorical premise from which Rullianus proceeds, whose moral high ground he arrogates for himself, and which he articulates explicitly with the *rego* cognates. Rullianus' hope to arouse the *uerecundia* of his listeners,

64 On legal *fraus*: Oakley 1998: 185, which takes *fraus* in the sense "breach of the law," as in *OLD* s.v. 6. *Fraus*, however, also has an ethical dimension, which involves violating the spirit, rather than the letter of the law. Rullianus' concern here is clearly for both.

65 As Oakley 2005b: 181 points out, the idea of the laws being ruled is without precise parallel. However, the paired active and passive infinitives (10.13.11 *iam regi leges non regere*) evoke the Greek democratic principle as articulated, e.g. in Arist. *Pol.* 1277b12–13: ὡς οὐκ ἔστιν εὖ ἄρξαι μὴ ἀρχθέντα. For the reciprocity of imperium, see, e.g., Cic. *Leg.* 3.5, although the etymological figures here are less precise: *imperandi . . . obtemperandi* and *imperat, paruerit . . . paret . . . imperet.*

66 On *uerecundia* as a social emotion, Kaster 2005: 13–27, and Chapter 1: 38–45.

67 Oakley 2005b: 180. The phrase appears as the culmination of a tribunician refusal of a senatorial request for intervention: *interim patricii soluti legum magistratuumque uiuerent uerecundia, per se quoque tribuni agerent* (Livy 4.56.13 "in the meantime the patricians will live free of the laws and reverence for the magistracies, and they may as well be tribunes themselves"). On the textual problem: Ogilvie 1965: 619–20.

their sense of having stepped too far out of line, also assumes that the law has power to soothe and calm the sentiments Rullianus himself has paradoxically heightened with his moderation (10.13.8 *acuebat hac moderatione iam iusta studia*). But Rullianus' recitation of the law ultimately fails; the *studia* he has sought to extinguish remain unchanged (10.13.11 *nihilo minus*).

Rullianus accepts the nomination, defeated, as it were, by the united will of the commonwealth (10. 13.12 *consensu ciuitatis uictus*), whose opposition to the rule of law is smoothed over by the consistent designation of their electoral expression as *iusta* (10.13.8 *iusta studia*; 13 *iusta suffragatio*). Morality and authority are here aligned, and this union results in the transfer of concrete authority – namely the consulship – into Rullianus' hands. The reluctant candidacy, therefore, is spectacularly successful, as time and again Rullianus is elected to office, with the full complicity of the voters and of the tribunes in his transgression of the law. This is not to assign Rullianus a malicious intent, of course, or to suggest "contional ventriloquism"[68] at work – but the tactic, by which refusal breeds success and power, adverts strongly to the political theatrics of the late republic and early empire.[69] Whatever historical relevance this set of episodes may have, the dynamic at work, wherein the candidate drives the action, is the same as we have seen in Cicero as well as Livy, even if the framework is considerably different. Further, here too we find the familiar tension between the people's wishes and political convention, although unlike previous episodes, the candidate himself generates the opposition rather than submitting to popular demand.

Rullianus finally holds fast in the last of the three episodes, which plays out as a microcosm of previous iterations, where everything is reduced in scope but intensified in specificity. *Consensus ciuitatis* becomes *omnis nobilitatis; fraus legi* becomes *contra legem*; *uerecundia* and its attendant social habitus give way to *pessimo exemplo*. The superlative form, as well as the phrase *eadem fere quae priore* a few lines earlier, invite us to read this episode explicitly as part of the larger set. Read in that way, the episodes dramatize the workings of Roman shame culture, as a fear of becoming a

68 The phrase is from Morstein-Marx 2004: 136–43 and refers to the rhetorical fashioning of speeches to generate applause at specific moments, in order to manipulate the impression of public approval or disapproval. See also p. 142 above, on Flaccus' flirtation with the practice.

69 On the phenomenon under the republic: Oakley 2005b: 181. Tiberius, too, will go on to employ such tactics to good effect: Tac. *Ann.* 1.7 (*ambiguus imperandi*), 11–12 (on which "false refusal" see Flaig 2007, discussing as well the precedents of Pompey, Caesar, and Augustus). On the *recusatio* as a poetic topos influenced by the political atmosphere: Freudenburg 2014.

negative *exemplum* succeeds in making Rullianus stand by his principles where even reverence to the law has not. Rullianus avoids being the worst sort of *exemplum* by stepping down, but his superlative betrays a concern that bad exemplarity was already at play in the earlier episodes, when *uerecundia legum* failed so spectacularly to move the crowds. Livy leaves Rullianus' exemplary value undecided. He is, on the one hand, a hero of the state, as Rullianus himself says in one of his recusal speeches, whose standards of glory set an example for others to follow.[70] On the other, he is a self-confessed negative *exemplum*, or at least potentially one, in his actions *contra legem*, and in his submission to the consensus of citizens. This is a new interpretation of the familiar *uoluntas populi–leges* binary we have seen so far, and it brings in a moral coloring that has been largely absent. The distinctive contribution of the reluctant magistrate, however, is perhaps the explicit articulation of the ease with which this people–laws binary can collapse: the same people pass and manipulate the law, and the same people are both a positive and negative sort of *exemplum*.

Elections, and their problems and querying, are therefore an important site for thinking about how magisterial authority is constructed and how it operates – not just as the result of some kind of electoral magic, but as subject to all kinds of negotiations, from subsequent trials, to legal parsing, to rhetorical manipulation. What electoral narratives do best, however, is to act as a mechanism for producing and testing definitions of magistracy, as each candidate and each narrative fashions and promotes a different set of competing criteria. Elections further highlight the importance of context in understanding magistracy as a narrative rather than legal institution: the legal strictures which apply in some cases need not always apply, and as Cicero's example shows, even the law was subject to expert storytelling. Magistrates conformed to fluid and highly particularized conditions, but they also did so within largely stable horizons of expectations. Narrative, with its attention to causes, explanations, and a panoramic view of actors,

[70] Although the word *exemplum* itself is missing, the theme is clear. 10.13.7 *et se gloriae seniorum succreuisse et ad suam gloriam consurgentes alios laetum adspicere; nec honores magnos fortissimis uiris Romae nec honoribus deesse fortes uiros* ("he had risen to the glory of his ancestors, and he was happy to see others rising to his own glory; Rome lacked neither great offices for the bravest of men, nor brave men to fill them"). For exemplary self-fashioning, another Augustan characteristic, compare *Res Gestae* 8 *legibus nouis me auctore latis multa exempla maiorum exolescentia iam ex nostro saeculo reduxi et ipse multarum rerum exempla imitanda posteris tradidi* ("Having passed new laws under my authorship, I brought back many examples of our ancestors forgotten in our time, and I myself passed down examples of many things to be imitated by posterity").

decisions, and behaviors, captures the tension between repetition and originality, a tension which was anyway at the heart of exemplary thinking and Roman self-fashioning, but which influenced also the criteria Romans applied to the choice of their elected officials.[71]

[71] On the exemplary tension between uniqueness and imitability: Roller 2009a.

Epilogue: staging authority

One of the threads in this book's argument has been the distinctive image of magistracy as a textual and literary phenomenon, which is to say, a phenomenon expressed in literary terms and through literary forms, rather than an entirely fictive creation of something that never existed. Conflicts and tensions, albeit often of the low-grade kind, are at the center of the book, and each of the episodes discussed deals with the processes of resolving them. The idea of a conflict of interests, and especially its dense literary representation, is a commonplace of dramatic art. This structure of thought goes back to Greek tragedy, with its stylized tensions between abstractions – "the state" versus "the family," to take only the most hackneyed of examples, in Sophocles' *Antigone*. These macro-tensions interact in turn with more topical tensions enacted in the play: Antigone, a heroine so isolated on stage that she does not once use the plural form "we" or "us," is at best a problematic representation of idealized resistance to state authority.[1] The human cost of the tragedy, meanwhile, as Creon finds out, threatens to nullify the value of successful enforcement of the law, both for the characters on stage and for the watching audience. These tensions cannot be resolved, of course, and there is some interpretative value to acknowledging their resistance to simple solutions. They are also, as various critics have shown, profoundly political tensions, revealing many of the anxieties of fifth-century Athens, and continuing to speak to political anxieties in the present day.

[1] E.g. Hammond 2009: 95–6 and Goldhill 2012: 31–2, 231–48. The agonistic mindset is characteristic of Athenian democratic thinking and represented across the genres, from tragedy to epic to historiography: Barker 2009. The democratic nature of the Roman republic has been an issue of some contention following a series of provocative articles by Fergus Millar (1984, 1986, 1989, all reprinted in Cotton and Rogers 2002, as well as Millar 1998 and 2002: 135–82), and it is here worth noting that the written texts of the Roman republic and early empire have a different relationship to their audience than did the state-mandated performances of Greek tragedy.

There is now little doubt that historiography and drama were genres in dialogue, as were Roman politics "on the ground" and Rome's theatrical world, even if the precise nature of that interaction is not yet perfectly clear.[2] For my purposes, however, drama provides a clear instantiation of the generative power of conflicts of interest, not least because the genre enjoys a robust critical tradition which has seen conflict and tension as the central tenet of the artistic form.[3] Moreover, this capacity of drama, together with its value as a heuristic for readers of historiography, extends beyond the confines of classical antiquity. Take, for example, the following extract from Shakespeare's *Richard II*:[4]

> Things sweet to taste prove in digestion sour.
> You urged me as a judge; but I had rather
> You would have bid me argue like a father.
> O, had it been a stranger, not my child,
> To smooth his fault I should have been more mild:
> A partial slander sought I to avoid,
> And in the sentence my own life destroy'd.
>
> (*Richard II*, 1.3)

John of Gaunt's dilemma – "but I had rather . . . " – captures a whole host of conflicting roles in a few verses, in line with the play's interest in the tension between natural and political identities. In this early scene Gaunt's son Bolingbroke, the future Henry IV, has been exiled, partly because his father has so counseled the king. Faced with the stark reality of his son's exile, Gaunt finds that he cannot advocate as both father and impartial

2 It is worth noting too that drama was a way to speak about and criticize politics and politicians at Rome: for the republic see, e.g., Boyle 2006: 109–42. On drama as a source for history: Wiseman 1998. Feldherr 1998: 165–212 connects historiography's concern for *enargeia* with the visual spectacle of the theater, while also keeping to the fore Livy's insistence on the generic differences between historiography and drama. Walter 2001: 249–52 discusses drama as an alternative medium of communication. On the spectacle-culture of the republic and early empire, see the general remarks in Flower 2004. Hölkeskamp 2011 discusses the consuls as primary actors in Rome's "theater of power" (161). Sumi 2005 discusses the performativity of politics in the early empire; on rituals of power, see also Hopkins 1991, Gargola 1995.

3 Goldhill 2012 discusses in depth the critical history of Greek tragedy and argues for a reception-centered view of how that critical history shapes the philological procedures and questions we employ today.

4 I follow the text printed in the 2011 Oxford Shakespeare edition (Dawson and Yachnin, eds.). The play as a whole is one deeply concerned with the multiple identities that inhere in political roles, especially that of the king. This polysemy found political and theological expression in the doctrine of the King's two bodies, which separated the King's natural body from his institutional role as the Crown. It thereby codified and resolved some tensions Roman magistrates would have been familiar with. On the King's two bodies and *Richard II*: Kantorowicz 1957: 24–41; Dawson and Yachnin 2011: 16–19.

judge, and that the authority of the king ("you urged me . . . you would have bid me") has determined and defined his role for him. The scene therefore stages, however microscopically, not only the absolute authority of the King of England, but also the emotive conflicts that authority generates, together with the rigors of serving the king in any official capacity. The judge places burdens on the father, which Gaunt is unable to reconcile. In this regard, the scene is no different from Livy's depiction of Brutus' execution of his sons, with which this book's first chapter concluded. Both scenes stage a live tension between personal obligation and public duty, which evokes feelings of pity and empathy, and encourages a reassessment of institutional public roles. Historiography brings with it a different set of resources, but the final result, as this book has argued, is of much the same stripe as its more exalted poetic brethren: a vivid depiction of conflict and resolution, action and reaction, causes and motivations, emotional choices, and a didactic framework to leverage the aesthetic into the morally useful. Drama, with its archetypes, offers also an exemplary framework, since its protagonists, like those of epic, must be simultaneously the everyman and the uniquely heroic. The didactic role of poetry is likewise obvious: *Richard II* teaches kingship, just as the *Aeneid* teaches *pietas*, or the *Iliad* heroic excellence. Textual performance thus relies on exemplarity – the connection between the singularly unique and the reader's everyday experience – for its impact and its ethical didacticism. Fraught moments like John of Gaunt's sobering realization of his own miscalculation teach not only their own substantive lessons – say what you mean and mean what you say – but also invite reflection on their embedding framework: what use is a counselor who repents immediately, or a king who forces his counselors to advise against their better instincts? Exemplarity thus frames political performances as both substantive and self-reflexive, signifying both itself and the values of the state for which public officialdom stand.

By way of drawing some of these threads together, let me turn to one final example, which shows the impact of encountering magistracy experientially as well as legally. The episode is Livy's *précis* on Cn. Flavius the aedile, a talented man from humble stock (his father, like seemingly many Augustan worthies, was a freedman), who, despite his trade as a scribe, was elected aedile, though the sources differ on how early he had put away his tools.[5]

[5] Among the majority of the sources (see the conspectus in Oakley 2005a: 600–3, though many of these refer to his later career), Macer (*ap.* Livy 9.46.3) is unique in giving Flavius a longer career between his resignation as a scribe and his aedilician election (cf. Oakley 2005a: 619). An alternative tradition, focusing more on sumptuary legislation, is preserved in Pliny, *HN* 33.17–9 and derives

He became known as a scourge of the nobility and made his career out of thumbing his nose at their prejudices. As the sources present it, at least, he began as he meant to continue, and this anecdote, in which he discomfits a posse of snobbish young aristocrats, comes from early in his career:

> ad collegam aegrum uisendi causa Flauius cum uenisset consensuque nobilium adulescentium, qui ibi adsidebant, adsurrectum ei non esset, curulem adferri sellam eo iussit ac sede honoris sui anxios inuidia inimicos spectauit. (Livy 9.46.9)
>
> When Flavius went to visit his sick colleague, and no one rose in his honor among the throng of young nobles seated there, he ordered his curule chair brought to him, and watched his enemies rattled by envy of the seat of his office.

At the most basic level, this episode describes a magistrate asserting – or more accurately, having to assert – his *auctoritas* against a perceived, and reasonably petty, breach of decorum. In this it has much in common with Fabius meeting his father at the crossroads, which I discuss in Chapter 1, or the more complex case of Cicero and Murena, faced with a charge of bribery, in Chapter 4. The problem is one of according due honor and deference – the noble youths refuse to honor Flavius by rising, and their defiance is embodied in their physical posture. The situation is resolved, at least to some degree, through a reliance on the trappings of office: Flavius flaunts his curule chair, a visible emblem of his office, to which the young nobles have no adequate response other than seething jealousy.

The episode is as much about class and snobbery as it is about magistracy, if not more so. The youths refuse to rise in the aedile's honor because they feel his low social position invalidates the show of respect typically owed to the office. The aedile, for his part, asserts his own authority over his rivals' class-based claims, and the episode ends with his implicit victory. The accouterments of office allow Flavius to affirm for himself the dignity that the company of youths would not accord him, and they are rattled because his self-sufficiency demonstrates that his office trumps their birth. As such, this episode is also very much about a Roman culture of authority, that is to say, it is about the interaction of two societal structures, both of which were determinative of political success or failure, and both of which occasionally ran up uncomfortably against each other. Focalization, too, plays a role here. The reason why these two structures – magistracy and nobility – require such reconciliation is that, from the point of view of

probably from Fenestella; see the discussion in Forsythe 1994: 339–41. For Livy's account: Oakley 2005a: 600–45.

the young nobles, magistracy and nobility should be mutually implicated: people of Flavius' social status should not be made aediles, because the privileges of magistracy and honor belong strictly to those already born to it. Indeed, they disdain Flavius because he represents (to their minds) an unnatural intrusion into the proper order of things, and they feel free to shun him because of their social superiority.

Flavius does not refute that assertion, at least within the confines of this particular interaction, but his political authority allows him to turn the tables on his rivals, turning them and their emotional response (*inuidia*) into a spectacle (*spectauit*) for his own benefit. This aspect of the episode represents, in fact, a muted version of one of Livy's annalistic sources, the historian Lucius Piso Frugi, who gives a more elaborate punch line to the event: (Gell. *NA* 7.9.6 = Piso fr. 27 P = F 37 Forsythe [1994] = Beck and Walter 30 = *FRHist* F 29) *Cn. Flavius Anni filius aedilis id arrisit, sellam curulem iussit sibi afferi, eam in limine apposuit, ne quis illorum exire posset utique hi omnes inuiti uiderent sese in sella curuli sedentem* ("Cn. Flavius, son of Annius, aedile, laughed at this, and ordered that his curule chair be brought. He put it right within the door frame facing them, so that none of them would be able to leave and so that all of them, though unwilling, would see him seated in his curule chair"). Piso's version stresses the magistrate's activity even more, turning him from the albeit superior audience he is in Livy into both dramaturge and star of this little scene. He calls for props in commanding language (*iussit*), arranges them in the landscape (*in limine apposuit*), and has a clear intention not only to trap his audience (*ne exire posset, inuiti*), but also to establish himself as the focus of attention.[6] In stark contrast to Livy, Piso's Flavius seems to have little interest in watching the young men *per se*, but rather in making them watch him, presumably as he watches them. The scene thus becomes a potential *mise-en-abyme*, a device with rich metapoetic overtones, though we possess too little of Piso's text to know how, if at all, he deployed it.

For Livy, further, the episode as a whole was exemplary: 9.46.8 *haud memorabilem rem per se, nisi documentum sit aduersus superbiam nobilium plebeiae libertatis, referam* ("I shall relate something, hardly worth mentioning in its own right, except that it is proof of plebeian freedom against the haughtiness of the nobility"). The singular instance becomes typical of all plebeians, or at least the ones who showed *libertas* in the face of *superbia*, and Flavius' later career certainly illustrates not only how

[6] Rabun Taylor points out to me that Flavius' positioning overturns the usual spatial dispositions, according to which the person in authority would sit axially to the door.

such an attitude manifests itself, but also its deep and long-lasting effects.[7] Flavius becomes typical also of a more broadly Roman mentality, which valorized *libertas* as against the *superbia* of kings and tyrants and saw magistracy as a bulwark of that freedom against tyranny and oppression. The framing of the anecdote as exemplary explains also Livy's attention to the emotional spectacle; a *documentum* was, as Livy outlined in his preface, something to look at, and to learn from. The lesson of the episode, however, is multi-layered, and while Flavius sets out to teach the noble youths a lesson, that moral is never spelled out; instead, the whole vignette becomes exemplary. The *sella curulis*, already freighted with symbolism, becomes a token of greater social currents at work, of the various responses to those currents, and of the various abilities and obligations of the various participants.[8] Magistracy, although not the explicit topic of the *exemplum*, thus becomes its enabling mechanism: plebeian *libertas* comes about through public office. The episode stresses, therefore, that the magistrate has the power to enforce his will on a situation, to coerce a response, and to shape events to his liking. In both variants the episode suggests also that such behavior came at a cost, in this case the making of political enemies, and in consequence also exposed the enabling fictions and even more so the productive tensions that drove Roman political life.

As the case of Flavius illustrates, exemplarity underpins the textual reconstruction of the magisterial *persona*, and the textual exploration of the values, behaviors, and models which went into creating that *persona*. Several other themes have emerged as well: the primacy of elections as *loci* for generating images, exemplary and otherwise, of the magistrate; the overlapping spheres of competence and their competing demands; the impositions made by political office on other relationships; and the situatedness of all of the above within the broader antitheses which shaped Roman politics in its literary representation, as well as its manifestation in the formal features and rhetorical structures of the text. The image of the textualized magistrate is distinctive, in some ways, for its amorphous qualities: it does not produce a definitive set of qualities or skills which a magistrate must

7 Livy 9.46.4 *ceterum, id quod haud discrepat, contumacia aduersus contemnentes humilitatem suam nobiles certauit* ("what is certain, though, is that he stubbornly strove against the nobility who spurned his humble origins"). *Contumacia* is an interesting choice here, because in its negative connotation it suggests precisely the arrogance the nobility directed towards Flavius and emphasizes that the feeling must have been mutual. His main achievements (Livy 9.46.4–8) included the publication of legal formulas, the calendar, and the formulas for dedication of the temple of Concord.

8 For the heightened effect of props in drama see, e.g., Goldhill 2012: 50 (the urn in Sophocles' *Electra* as metapoetic emblem, following Segal 1981: 287; Ringer 1998; and Batchelder 1995), and Gill 1980 (Philoctetes' bow). From a very different perspective, see Alföldi 1959 on the *hasta* as a token of sovereignty in Rome, and Schäfer 1989 on the *sella curulis*.

possess, but rather a fluid sequence of overlapping images, highlighting some aspects of the job over others to suit the occasion. This composite image illustrates the myriad ways of negotiating a relationship between a set of political qualities and historical contexts and a timeless abstraction of "magistracy" as an institution, an exemplary bricolage relying as much on the failed experiments and political compromises as on any single heroized instance. Any given magistrate might attain more or less of the ideal, but they all had in common its authority, and they were all ultimately judged on how well, how often, and how much they manifested that intangible quality. More problematically, being a magistrate enmeshed one in a set of discourses and obligations, many of which demanded an active choice between roles, or an uncomfortable acknowledgment that some values must be somehow reconciled, or two contradictory ideas held together in some productive tension. These choices themselves both fueled the exemplary tradition and actively reflected the values, ideologies, and political commitments of the Roman state, or, as the republic receded into memory, perceptions and recollections, as well as transhistoricist lessons in leadership. But this book argues above all that magistracy offered a unique opportunity to think both in exemplary terms and about exemplarity as a fluid discourse, that it was both an individual and institutional *exemplum*, and that it provided, for a variety of reasons, a mechanism for meta-exemplary reflection.

The vibrancy of politics and the authority vested in those who practice it has not faded since the heyday of Rome. The story of politics and of political progress and development has been told frequently, by historians both ancient and modern, whose narratives have been mined for information on the political institutions they depict. But what has frequently been left by the wayside, especially for the ancient world, is a sense of the vividness of political activity – the emotion it arouses, the aggressiveness it entails, its sheer performativity and the constant friction it generates with the myriad other activities and values which govern human societies. The preceding pages have argued that this rich drama around the political acts, and especially the political and exemplary discourses on which they rely, themselves constitute an important part of how literary texts articulate what political authority was and meant. This understanding in turn helps to shape and define how readers made sense of their experience of political authority. Attention to that drama therefore produces a more holistic and three-dimensional image of how that authority was perceived. From that vantage point, this project has explored the cultural concept of political authority in republican Rome, as well as the ways in which authors of prose narrative and rhetoric, chiefly Livy and Cicero, imagined, understood, and described that authority. In other words, this book has focused on the intersection of politics and literature, and it has argued that magistracy offered a political phenomenon, and exemplarity a textual mannerism, with which to think about the Roman state as well as the discourses that shaped its political self-awareness.

Bibliography

Adamietz, J. 1986. "Ciceros Verfahren in den Ambitus-Prozessen gegen Murena und Plancius." *Gymnasium* 93: 102–17.

Adler, E. 2003. *Vergil's Empire: Political Thought in the Aeneid.* Lanham, MD.

Alföldi, A. 1959. "*Hasta–Summa imperii*: The Spear As Embodiment of Sovereignty in Rome." *AJA* 63: 1–27.

Arena, V. 2012. *Libertas and the Practice of Politics in the Late Roman Republic.* Cambridge.

Asmis, E. 2005. "A New Kind of Model: Cicero's Roman Constitution in *De Republica*." *AJP* 126.3: 377–416.

Astin, A. E. 1958. *The Lex Annalis before Sulla.* Brussels.

1967. *Scipio Aemilianus.* Oxford.

1978. *Cato the Censor.* Oxford.

1982. "The Censorship of the Roman Republic: Frequency and Regularity." *Historia* 31.2: 174–87.

Austin, R. G. 1971. *P. Vergili Maronis Aeneidos: liber sextus.* Oxford.

Badian, E. 1971. "The Family and Early Career of T. Quinctius Flamininus." *JRS* 61: 102–11.

1990. "The Consuls, 179–40 BC." *Chiron* 20: 371–413.

1996. "*Tribuni plebis* and *res publica*." In: Linderski, J. (ed.), *Imperium sine fine: T. Robert Broughton and the Roman Republic.* Stuttgart: 187–213.

Balsdon, J. P. V. D. 1963. "The *commentariolum petitionis*." *CQ* 13.2: 242–50.

Baraz, Y. 2009. "From Vice to Virtue: The Denigration and Rehabilitation of *superbia* in Ancient Rome." In Sluiter, I. and R. Rosen (eds.), *Kakos: Badness and Anti-Value in Classical Antiquity.* Leiden: 365–98.

Barker, E. T. E. 2009. *Entering the Agon: Dissent and Authority in Homer, Historiography and Tragedy.* Oxford.

Batchelder, A. G. 1995. *The Seal of Orestes: Self-Reference and Authority in Sophocles' Electra.* Lanham, MD.

Batstone, W. 1988. "The Antithesis of Virtue: Sallust's 'Synkrisis' and the Crisis of the Late Republic." *ClAnt* 7.1: 1–29.

Batstone, W. and C. Damon 2006. *Caesar's Civil War.* Oxford.

Bauman, R. 1967. *The crimen maiestatis in the Roman Republic and Augustan Principate.* Johannesburg.

1969. *The duumviri in the Roman Criminal Law and in the Horatius Legend.* Wiesbaden.
Beck, H. 2005. *Karriere und Hierarchie: Die römische Aristokratie und die Anfänge des cursus honorum in der mittleren Republik.* Berlin.
2011. "Consular Power and the Roman Constitution: The Case of *imperium* Reconsidered." In Beck, Duplá, Jehne, and Pina Polo 2011: 77–96.
Beck, H., A. Duplá, M. Jehne, and F. Pina Polo 2011. *Consuls and res publica: Holding High Office in the Roman Republic.* Cambridge.
Beck, H. and U. Walter 2001. *Die frühen römischen Historiker.* 2 vols. Darmstadt.
Berger, A. 1953. *Encyclopedic Dictionary of Roman Law.* Philadelphia.
Berlin, I. 1958. *Two Concepts of Liberty.* Oxford.
Bleicken, J. 1955. *Volkstribunat der klassischen Republik; Studien zu seiner Entwicklung zwischen 287 und 133 v. Chr.* Munich.
Bloomer, W. M. 1992. *Valerius Maximus and the Rhetoric of the New Nobility.* Chapel Hill, NC and London.
Botteri, P. 1983. "Figli pubblici e padri privati: 'tribunicia potestas' e 'patria potestas.'" In Pellizer, E. and N. Zorzetti (eds.), *La paura dei padri nella società antica e medievale.* Rome: 56–9.
Boyle, A. J. 2006. *Roman Tragedy.* London and New York.
Braet, A. 1987. "The Classical Doctrine of 'Status' and the Rhetorical Theory of Argumentation." *Philosophy and Rhetoric* 20.2: 79–93.
Brennan, T. C. 2000. *The Praetorship in the Roman Republic.* 2 vols. Oxford.
2004. "Power and Process under the Republican 'Constitution.'" In Flower, H. (ed.), *The Cambridge Companion to the Roman Republic.* Cambridge: 31–65.
Briscoe, J. 1973. *Commentary on Livy, Books XXXI–XXXIII.* Oxford.
2008. *Commentary on Livy, Books XXXVIII–XXXX.* Oxford.
2012. *Commentary on Livy, Books XXXXI–XXXXV.* Oxford.
Bruckmann, H. 1936. *Die römischen Niederlagen im Geschichtswerk des T. Livius* Diss. Münster.
Bruno, L. 1966. "'Crimen regni' e 'superbia' in Tito Livio." *GIF* 19: 236–59.
Brunt, P. A. 1988. *The Fall of the Roman Republic and Related Essays.* Oxford.
Bücher, F. 2006. *Verargumentierte Geschichte. Exempla Romana im politischen Diskurs der späten römischen Republik.* Stuttgart.
Burton, P. 2000. "The Last Republican Historian: A New Date for the Composition of Livy's First Pentad." *Historia* 49.4: 429–46.
Cantarella, E. 2003. "Fathers and Sons in Rome." *CW* 96.3: 281–98.
Carawan, E. M. 1988. "*Graecia liberata* and the Role of Flamininus in Livy's Fourth Decade." *TAPA* 118: 209–52.
Carney, T. F. 1960. "Cicero's Picture of Marius." *WS* 73: 83–122.
Castro, L. C. P. 2005. "Naturaleza y composición del *sermo castrensis* latino." *Emerita* 73.1: 73–96.
Champion, C. 2004. *Cultural Politics in Polybius's Histories.* Berkeley.
Chaplin, J. 2000. *Livy's Exemplary History.* Oxford.
2010. "Scipio the Matchmaker." In Kraus, Marincola, and Pelling 2010: 60–72.

2013. "Alluding to Reality: Towards a Typology of Historiographical Intertextuality." Paper given in Historiography, Poetry, and the Intertext seminar, American Philological Association Annual Meeting 2013, Seattle, WA.

Chaplin, J. and C. S. Kraus (eds.) 2009. *Oxford Readings in Classical Studies. Livy.* Oxford.

Christenson, D. 2002. "*Superbia* in Vergil's *Aeneid*: Who's Haughty and Who's Not?" *Scholia* 11: 44–54.

Clarke, M. L. 1968. *Rhetoric at Rome: A Historical Survey.* London.

Connolly, J. 2007. *The State of Speech.* Princeton.

2009. "Virtue and Violence: The Historians on Politics." In Feldherr 2009: 181–94.

Corbeill, A. 2005. "Gesture in Early Roman Law: Empty Forms or Essential Formalities?" In Cairns, D. (ed.), *Body Language in the Greek and Roman Worlds.* Swansea: 157–74.

Cotton, H. and G. Rogers (eds.) 2002. *Rome, the Greek World, and the East.* Vol. 1: *The Roman Republic and the Augustan Revolution.* Chapel Hill.

Coudry, M. and T. Späth (eds.) 2001. *L'invention des grands hommes de la Rome antique. Die Konstruktion der grossen Männer Altroms. Actes du Colloque du Collegium Beatus Rhenanus, Augst. 16–18 Septembre 1999.* Paris.

Courtney, E. 1999. *Archaic Latin Prose.* Atlanta.

Craig, C. P. 1985. "Dilemma in Cicero's *Divinatio in Caecilium.*" *AJP* 106.4: 442–6.

Crawford, M. H. 1973. "*Foedus* and *sponsio.*" *PBSR* 41: 1–7.

Crook, J. 1967. "*Patria potestas.*" *CQ* 17.1: 113–22.

Damon, C. 1999. "The Trial of Cn. Piso in Tacitus' *Annals* and the 'Senatus Consultum de Cn. Pisone Patre': New Light on Narrative Technique." *AJP* 120.1. Special Issue: *The "Senatus Consultum de Cn. Pisone Patre": Text, Translation, Discussion*: 143–62.

2010. "Déjà vu or déjà lu? History as intertext." *Papers of the Langford Latin Seminar* 14: 375–88.

Daube, D. 1951. "The Peregrine Praetor." *JRS* 41: 66–70.

Dawson, A. and P. Yachnin (eds.) 2011. *The Oxford Shakespeare: Richard II.* Oxford.

Degrassi, A. 1954. *Fasti Capitolini.* Paravia.

De Martino, F. 1958–72. *Storia della costituzione Romana.* 6 vols. Naples.

Deniaux, E. 1987. "De l'*ambitio* à l'*ambitus*: les lieux de la propagande et de la corruption électorale à la fin de la République.' In *L'Urbs: espace urbain et histoire.* Rome: 279–304.

Develin, R. 1976. "C. Flamininus in 232 BC." *AC* 45: 638–43.

1979. *Patterns in Office-Holding 366–49 BC.* Brussels.

1985. *The Practice of Politics at Rome, 366–167 BC.* Brussels.

Dixon, S. 1997. "Continuity and Change in Roman Social History: Retrieving 'Family Feeling(s)' from Roman Law and Literature." In Golden, M. and P. Toohey (eds.), *Inventing Ancient Culture: Historicism, Periodization, and the Ancient World.* London and New York: 79–90.

Dugan, J. 2012. "*Scriptum* and *voluntas* in Cicero's *Brutus.*" In M. Citroni (ed.), *Letteratura e civitas: transizioni dalla Repubblica all'Impero. In ricordo di Emanuele Narducci.* Pisa: 119–28.

Dutoit, E. 1948. "Silences, dans l'oeuvre de Tite-Live." In *Mélanges de philology, de literature et d'histoire anciennes offerts à J. Marouzeau*. Paris: 141–51.
Dyck, A. 1996. *A Commentary on Cicero's De Officiis*. Ann Arbor.
2004a. *A Commentary on Cicero's De Legibus*. Ann Arbor.
2004b. "Cicero's 'Devotio': The Rôles of Dux and Scape-Goat in His 'Post Reditam' Rhetoric." *HSPh* 102: 299–314.
Earl, D. C. 1961. *The Political Thought of Sallust*. Cambridge.
Easterling, P. E. 1999. "Plain Words in Sophocles." In Griffin J. (ed.), *Sophocles Revisited: Essays Presented to Sir Hugh Lloyd-Jones*. Oxford: 95–108.
Eckstein, A. 1987. *Senate and General: Individual Decision-Making and Roman Foreign Relations, 264–194 BC*. Berkeley.
Edwards, C. 1993. *The Politics of Immorality in Ancient Rome*. Cambridge.
Ehrenberg, V. 1953. "*Imperium maius* in the Roman Republic." *AJP* 74.4: 113–36.
Elliot, J. 2009a. "Ennius' 'Cunctator' and the History of a Gerund in the Roman Historiographical Tradition." *CQ* 59.2: 532–42.
2009b. "Livy's Papirius Cursor and the Manipulation of the Ennian Past." *CQ* 59.2: 650–3.
2013. *Ennius and the Architecture of the Annales*. Cambridge.
Elster, M. 2003. *Die Gesetze der mittleren römischen Republik: Text und Kommentar*. Munich.
Fantham, E. 2013. *Cicero's Pro L. Murena Oratio*. Oxford.
Farrell, J. 1997. "The Phenomenology of Memory in Roman Culture." *CJ* 92.4: 373–83.
2001. *Latin Language and Latin Culture: From Ancient to Modern Times*. Cambridge.
Feeney, D. C. 1984. "The Reconciliations of Juno." *CQ* 34.1: 179–94.
1998. *Literature and Religion at Rome: Cultures, Contexts, and Belief*. Cambridge.
2010. "Fathers and Sons: the Manlii Torquati and Family Continuity in Catullus and Horace." In Kraus, Marincola, and Pelling 2010: 205–23.
Feig Vishnia, R. 1996a. *State, Society and Popular Leaders in Mid-Republican Rome 241–167 BC*. London and New York.
1996b. "Cicero *De Senectute* 11, and the Date of C. Flaminius' Tribunate." *Phoenix* 50.2: 138–45.
2012. *Roman Elections in the Age of Cicero: Society Government and Voting*. Florency, KY.
Feldherr, A. 1997. "Livy's Revolution: Civic Identity and the Creation of the *res publica*." In Habinek, T. and A. Schiesaro (eds.), *The Roman Cultural Revolution*. Cambridge: 136–57.
1998. *Spectacle and Society in Livy's History*. Berkeley.
(ed.) 2009. *The Cambridge Companion to the Roman Historians*. Cambridge.
Fezzi, L. 2007. "Il *commentariolum petitionis*: sguardi dalle democrazie contemporanee." *Historia* 56.1: 14–26.
Flaig, E. 2007. "Falsche Bescheidenheit: Die *cunctatio* des Tiberius – ein misslungener Rite de passage." In Reinhard, W. (ed.), *Krumme Touren. Anthropologie kommunikativer Umwege*. Cologne: 77–106.
Flobert, P. 1985. *La Langue latine: Livre 6*. Paris.

Flower, H. I. 1996. *Ancestor Masks and Aristocratic Power in Roman Culture.* Oxford.

2000. "The Tradition of the *spolia opima*: M. Claudius Marcellus and Augustus." *ClAnt* 19.1: 34–64.

2003. "Memories of Marcellus." In Eigler, U. (ed.), *Formen römischer Geschichtsschreibung von den Anfängen bis Livius: Gattungen, Autoren, Kontexte.* Darmstadt: 39–52.

2004. "Spectacle and Political Culture in the Republic." In Flower, H. I. (ed.), *The Cambridge Companion to the Roman Republic.* Cambridge: 322–43.

2006. *The Art of Forgetting: Disgrace and Oblivion in Roman Political Culture.* Chapel Hill, NC.

Forsythe, G. 1994. *The Historian, L. Calpurnius Piso Frugi, and the Roman Annalistic Tradition.* Lanham, MD.

1999. *Livy and Early Rome: A Study in Historical Method and Judgment.* Stuttgart.

Freudenburg, K. 2014. "*Recusatio* as Political Theater: Horace's Letter to Augustus." *JRS* 104: 1–28.

Frier, B. W., and T. A. J. McGinn 2004. *A Casebook on Roman Family Law.* Oxford.

Fries, J. 1985. *Der Zweikampf: historische und literarische Aspekte seiner Darstellung bei T. Livius.* Meisenheim.

Fronda, M. 2011. "*Privata hospitia, beneficia publica?* Consul(ar)s, Local Elite, and Roman Rule in Italy." In Beck, Duplá, Jehne, and Pina Polo 2011: 232–56.

Galinsky, G. K. (ed.) 2014. *Memoria Romana: Memory in Rome and Rome in Memory.* Ann Arbor.

Gallagher, C. and S. Greenblatt 2001. *Practicing New Historicism.* Chicago.

Gallia, A. 2012. *Remembering the Roman Republic: Culture, Politics, and History under the Principate.* Cambridge.

Gardner, J. 1993. *Being a Roman Citizen.* London and New York.

Gargola, D. J. 1995. *Lands, Laws, and Gods: Magistrates and Ceremony in the Regulation of Public Lands in Republican Rome.* Chapel Hill, NC.

Gaughan, J. 2010. *Murder Was Not a Crime: Homicide and Power in the Roman Republic.* Austin, TX.

Geertz, C. 1973. *The Interpretation of Cultures: Selected Essays.* New York.

Gildenhard, I. 2010. *Creative Eloquence: The Construction of Reality in Cicero's Speeches.* Oxford.

Gill, C. 1980. "Bow, Oracle, and Epiphany in Sophocles' *Philoctetes.*" *G&R* 27.2: 137–46.

Gilmartin, K. 1975. "A Rhetorical Figure in Latin Historical Style: The Imaginary Second Person Singular." *TAPA* 105: 99–121.

Gladhill, C. 2008. "*Foedera*: A Study in Roman Politics and Society." Diss. Standford.

Goldhill, S. 1994. "The Failure of Exemplarity." In De Jong, I. J. F. and J. P. Sullivan (eds.), *Modern Critical Theory and Classical Literature.* Leiden: 51–73.

2012. *Sophocles and the Language of Tragedy.* Oxford.

Goldsworthy, A. 1998. "'Instinctive Genius': the Depiction of Caesar the General." In Welch, K. and A. Powell (eds.), *Julius Caesar as Artful Reporter: The War Commentaries as Political Instruments*. Swansea: 193–219.

Gowing, A. 2005. *Empire and Memory: The Representation of the Roman Republic in Imperial Culture*. Cambridge.

Greenblatt, S. 1985. "Invisible Bullets: Renaissance Authority and Its Subversion, Henry IV and Henry V." In Dollimore, J. and A. Sinfield (eds.), *Political Shakespeare: New Essays in Cultural Materialism*. Manchester: 18–47.

1997. "The Touch of the Real." *Representations* No. 59, Special Issue: *The Fate of "Culture": Geertz and Beyond*: 14–29.

Grethlein, J. 2006. "*Nam quid ea memorem*: The Dialectical Relation of *res gestae* and *memoria rerum gestarum* in Sallust's *Bellum Jugurthinum*." *CQ* 56.1: 135–48.

Grillo, L. 2012. *The Art of Caesar's Bellum Civile: Literature, Ideology, and Community*. Cambridge.

Gruen, E. S. 1991. "The Exercise of Power in the Roman Republic." In Molho, A., K. Raaflaub, and J. Emlen (eds.), *City States in Classical Antiquity and Medieval Italy*. Stuttgart: 251–68.

1992. *Culture and National Identity in Republican Rome*. Ithaca.

Gunderson, E. 2003. *Declamation, Paternity, and Roman Identity. Authority and the Rhetorical Self.* Cambridge.

Hahm, D. 1995. "Polybius' Applied Political Theory." In Laks, A. and M. Schofield (eds.), *Justice and Generosity. Studies in Hellenistic Social and Political Philosophy*. Cambridge: 7–47.

Haimson Lushkov, A. 2010. "Intertextuality and Source Criticism in the Scipionic Trials." In Polleichtner, W. (ed.), *Livy and Intertextuality*. Bochum: 93–133.

2014. "Narrative and Notice in Livy's Fourth Decade: The Case of Scipio Africanus." *ClAnt* 33.1: 102–29.

Hall, J. 1998. "The Deference-Greeting in Roman Society.' *Maia* 50: 413–42.

Hammer, D. C. 2008. *Roman Political Thought and the Modern Theoretical Imagination*. Norman.

Hammond, P. 2009. *The Strangeness of Tragedy*. Oxford.

Hampton, T. 1990. *Writing from History: The Rhetoric of Exemplarity in Renaissance Literature*. Ithaca.

Hansen, M. H. 1993. "The Battle Exhortation in Ancient Historiography. Fact or Fiction?" *Historia* 42.2: 161–80.

1998. "The Little Grey Horse: Henry V's Speech at Agincourt and the Battlefield Exhortation in Ancient Historiography." *Histos* 2: 1–11.

Hardie, P. 1998. *Virgil.* Greece & Rome: New Surveys in the Classics 28. Oxford.

2012. *Rumour and Renown: Representations of Fama in Western Literature.* Cambridge.

Harris, W. V. 1976. "The Development of the Quaestorship, 267–81 BC." *CQ* 26.1: 92–106.

1986. "The Roman Father's Power of Life and Death." In Bagnall, R. and W. V. Harris (eds.), *Studies in Roman Law in Memory of A. Arthur Schiller*. Leiden: 81–95.

1990. "On Defining the Political Culture of the Roman Republic: Some Comments on Rosenstein, Williamson, and North." *CP* 85.4: 288–94.

Harrison, S. 1988. "Vergil on Kingship: The First Simile of the *Aeneid*." *CCJ* 34: 55–9.

Hellegouarc'h, J. 1972. *Le Vocabulaire latin des relations et des partis politiques sous la République*. Paris.

Henderson, M. I. 1957. "Potestas Regia." *JRS* 47: 82–7.

Hölkeskamp, K.-J. 1996. "*Exempla* und *mos maiorum*: Überlegungen zum kollektiven Gedächtnis der Nobilität." In Gehrke, H.-J. and A. Möller (eds.), *Vergangenheit und Lebenswelt: Soziale Kommunikation, Traditionsbildung und historisches Bewusstsein*. Tübingen: 301–38.

2003. "Ikonen der *virtus*. Exemplarische Helden(-taten) im monumentalen Gedächtnis der römischen Republik." In Barzanò, A. (ed.), *Modelli eroici dall'antichità alla cultura europea*. Rome: 213–37.

2004. *Senatus Populusque Romanus. Die politische Kultur der Republik – Dimensionen und Deutungen*. Tübingen.

2010. *Reconstructing the Roman Republic: An Ancient Political Culture and Modern Research*. Princeton and Oxford.

2011. "The Roman Republic as Theater of Power: The Consuls as Leading Actors." In Beck, Duplá, Jehne, and Pina Polo 2011: 161–81.

Hopkins, K. 1991. "From Violence to Blessing: Symbols and Rituals in Ancient Rome." In Molho, A., K. Raaflaub, and J. Emlen (eds.), *City-States in Classical Antiquity and Medieval Italy*. Stuttgart: 479–81.

Hopkins, K. and G. Burton 1983. "Political Succession in the Late Republic (249–50 BC)." In Hopkins, K., *Death and Renewal*. Cambridge: 31–119.

Hornblower, S. 2004. "'This Was Decided' *edoxe tauta*: The Army as Polis in Xenophon's *Anabasis* – and Elsewhere." In Lane Fox, R. (ed.), *The Long March: Xenophon and the Ten Thousand*. New Haven: 243–63.

Horsfall, N. 1982. "The Caudine Forks: Topography and Illusion." *PBSR* 50: 45–52.

1985. "Illusion and Reality in Latin Topographical Writing." *G&R* 32.2: 197–208.

2004. *The Culture of the Roman Plebs*. London.

Hurlet, F. 2011. "Consulship and Consuls under Augustus." In Beck, Duplá, Jehne, and Pina Polo 2011: 319–35.

Jaeger, M. 1997. *Livy's Written Rome*. Ann Arbor.

2006. "Livy, Hannibal's Monument, and the Temple of Juno at Croton." *TAPA* 136.2: 389–414.

Jehne, M. 2011. "The Rise of the Consular as a Social Type in the Third and Second Centuries BC." In Beck, Duplá, Jehne, and Pina Polo 2011: 211–31.

Kantorowicz, E. H. 1957. *The King's Two Bodies: A Study in Mediaeval Political Theology*. Princeton.

Kapust, D. 2011. *Republicanism, Rhetoric, and Roman Political Thought: Sallust, Livy, and Tacitus*. Cambridge.

Kaster, R. 2005. *Emotion, Restraint and Community in Ancient Rome*. Oxford.
2007. Review of McDonnell 2006. *Bryn Mawr Classical Review* 2007.02.08.
Kennedy, G. 1994. *A New History of Classical Rhetoric*. Princeton.
Konstan, D. 2001. *Pity Transformed*. London.
Kraus, C. S. 1991. "'Initium turbandi omnia a femina ortum est': Fabia Minor and the Elections of 367 BC." *Phoenix* 45.4: 314–25.
1994a. *Livy: Ab Urbe Condita Book VI*. Cambridge.
1994b. "'No Second Troy': Topoi and Refoundation in Livy, Book V." *TAPA* 124: 267–89.
1998. "Repetition and Empire in the *Ab Vrbe Condita*." In Foss, C. and P. Knox (eds.), *Style and Tradition: Studies in Honor of Wendell Clausen*. Stuttgart: 264–83.
2005. "From *exempla* to Exemplar? Writing History around the Emperor in Imperial Rome." In Edmonsen, J., S. Mason, and J. Rives (eds.), *Flavius Josephus and Flavian Rome*. Oxford: 181–200.
Kraus, C. S., J. Marincola, and C. Pelling 2010. *Ancient Historiography and Its Contexts. Studies in Honor of A. J. Woodman*. Oxford.
Kraus, C. S. and A. J. Woodman 1997. *The Latin Historians*. Oxford.
Krostenko, B. A. 2001. *Cicero, Catullus, and the Language of Social Performance*. Chicago.
Kunkel, W. and R. Wittman 1995. *Staatsordnung und Staatspraxis der römischen Republik*. Munich.
Lacey, W. K. 1986. "Patria potestas." in Rawson, B. (ed.), *The Family in Ancient Rome: New Perspectives*. Ithaca: 121–44.
Langlands, R. 2006. *Sexual Morality in Ancient Rome*. Cambridge.
2008. "'Reading for the Moral' in Valerius Maximus: The Case of *severitas*." *Cambridge Classical Journal* 54: 160–87.
2011. "Roman *exempla* and Situation Ethics: Valerius Maximus and Cicero *de Officiis*." *JRS* 101: 1–23.
Last, H. 1947. "*Imperivm maivs*: A Note." *JRS* 37: 157–64.
Laurence, R. 1994. "Rumour and Communication in Roman Politics." *G&R* 41.1: 62–74.
Lavery, G. 1971. "Cicero's 'Philarchia' and Marius." *G&R* 18: 133–42.
Lendon, J. E. 2005. *Soldiers and Ghosts: A History of Battle in Classical Antiquity*. New Haven.
2009. "Historians without History: Against Roman Historiography." In Feldherr, A. (ed.), *Cambridge Companion to the Roman Historians*. Cambridge: 41–61.
Levene, D. S. 1993. *Religion in Livy*. Leiden.
1997. "Pity, Fear and the Historical Audience. Tacitus on the Fall of Vitellius." In Morton Braund, S. and C. Gill (eds.), *The Passions in Roman Thought and Literature*. Cambridge: 128–49.
2006. "History, Metahistory, and Audience Response in Livy 45." *ClAnt* 25.1: 73–108.
Levene, D. S. 2010. *Livy and the Hannibalic War*. Oxford.

Levick, B. 1981. "Professio." *Athenaeum* 59: 378–88.

Levithan, J. 2013. *Combat Motivation and Siege Warfare in the Roman Army*. Ann Arbor.

Libero, L. de 1992. *Obstruktion: Politische Praktiken im Senat und in der Volksversammlung der ausgehenden römischen Republik (70–49 v. Chr.)*. Stuttgart.

Linderski, J. 1985. "Buying the Vote. Electoral Corruption in the Late Republic." *AncW* 11: 87–94.

Lintott, A. 1990. "Electoral Bribery in the Roman Republic." *JRS* 80: 1–16.

1999. *The Constitution of the Roman Republic*. Oxford.

Lipovsky, J. 1981. *A Historiographical Study of Livy: Books VI–X*. Salem, NH.

Lippold, A. 1963. *Consules: Untersuchungen zur Geschichte des römischen Konsulates von 264 bis 201 v. Chr*. Bonn.

Litchfield, H. 1914. "National *exempla virtutis* in Roman Literature." *HSPh* 25: 1–71.

Lowrie, M. 2009. *Writing, Performance, and Authority in Augustan Rome*. Oxford.

Luce, T. J. 1965. "The Dating of Livy's First Pentad." *TAPA* 96: 209–40.

1990. "Livy, Augustus, and the Forum Augustum." In Raaflaub, K. and M. Toher (eds.), *Between Republic and Empire: Interpretations of Augustus and His Principate*. Berkeley: 123–38.

Lundgreen, C. 2011. *Regelkonflikte in der römischen Republik: Geltung und Gewichtung von Normen in politischen Entscheidungsprozessen*. Stuttgart.

Mackie, N. 1992. "'Popularis' Ideology and Popular Politics at Rome in the First Century BC." *RhM* 135: 49–73.

Marincola, J. 2008. *A Companion to Greek and Roman Historiography*. Malden, MA and Oxford.

Marshall, B. A. 1985. *A Historical Commentary on Asconius*. Columbia.

Martin, R. H. and A. J. Woodman 1989. *Tacitus, Annals, Book Four*. Cambridge.

Masi Doria, C. 2000. *Spretum Imperium*. Naples.

Matthes, M. 2000. *The Rape of Lucretia and the Founding of Republics. Readings in Livy, Machiavelli, and Rousseau*. University Park, PA.

May, J. 1988. *Trials of Character. The Eloquence of Ciceronian Ethos*. Chapel Hill, NC.

McDonnell, M. 2006. *Roman Manliness: Virtus and the Roman Republic*. Cambridge.

Merola, F. R. 2001. *Iudicium de iure legum: senato e legge nella tarda Repubblica*. Naples.

Miles, G. 1995. *Livy: Reconstructing Early Rome*. Ithaca.

Millar, F. 1984. "The Political Character of the Classical Roman Republic, 200–151 BC." *JRS* 74: 1–19.

1986. "Politics, Persuasion and the People before the Social War (150–90 BC)." *JRS* 76: 1–11.

1989. "Political Power in Mid-Republican Rome: *curia* or *comitium*?" *JRS* 79: 138–50.

1998. *The Crowd in Rome in the Late Republic*. Ann Arbor.

2002. *The Roman Republic in Political Thought*. Hanover.

Moles, J. 1994. "Livy's Preface." *PCPhS* 39: 141–68.
Mommsen, T. 1887. *Römisches Staatsrecht*. Leipzig.
Morello, M-R. 1996. "*Ars imperatoria*: Three Studies of Leadership in Livy's Second Pentad." Diss. Cornell.
2002. "Livy's Alexander Digression (9.17–19): Counterfactuals and Apologetics." *JRS* 92: 62–85.
2003. "Place and Road: Neglected Aspects of Livy 9.1–19." In *Studies in Latin Literature and Roman History XI. Collection Latomus* 272: 290–306.
Morgan, T. 2007. *Popular Morality in the Early Roman Empire*. Cambridge.
Morstein-Marx, R. 1998. "Publicity, Popularity and Patronage in the 'commentariolum petitionis.'" *ClAnt* 17.2: 259–88.
2004. *Mass Oratory and Political Power in Late Republican Rome*. Cambridge.
Mouritsen, H. 2001. *Plebs and Politics in the Late Roman Republic*. Cambridge.
Niccolini, G. 1934. *I fasti dei tribuni della plebe*. Milan.
Nicolet, C. 1989. *The World of the Citizen in Republican Rome*. Berkeley.
2000. *Censeurs et publicains. Économie et fiscalité dans la Rome antique*. Paris.
Nisbet, R. G. M. 1961. "The *commentariolum petitionis*: Some Arguments against Authenticity." *JRS* 51: 84–7.
Nisbet, R. G. M. and M. Hubbard 1970. *A Commentary on Horace: Odes 1*. Oxford.
Noreña, C. 2011. *Imperial Ideas in the Roman West*. Cambridge.
North, J. 1990a. "Democratic Politics in Republican Rome." *PP* 126: 3–21.
1990b. "Politics and Aristocracy in the Roman Republic." *CP* 85.4: 277–87.
2006. "The Constitution of the Roman Republic." In Rosenstein, N. and R. Morstein-Marx (eds.), *A Companion to the Roman Republic*. Oxford: 256–77.
Nousek, D. 2010. "Echoes of Cicero in Livy's Bacchanalian Narrative (39.8–19)." *CQ* 60.1: 156–66.
Oakley, S. P. 1985. "Single Combat in the Roman Republic." *CQ* 35.2: 392–410.
1987. Review of Fries 1985. *CR* 37: 34–6.
1997. *A Commentary on Livy: Books VI–X*. Vol. I: *Book VI*. Oxford.
1998. *A Commentary on Livy: Books VI–X*. Vol. II: *Books VII–VIII*. Oxford.
2005a. *A Commentary on Livy: Books VI–X*. Vol. III: *Book IX*. Oxford.
2005b. *A Commentary on Livy: Books VI–X*. Vol. IV: *Book X*. Oxford.
2010. "Dionysius of Halicarnassus and Livy on the Horatii and the Curiatii." In Kraus, Marincola, and Pelling 2010: 118–38.
Oesterreicher, W. 1997. "Types of Orality in Text." In Bakker, E. and K. Ahuvia (eds.), *Written Voices, Spoken Signs*. Cambridge, MA: 190–214.
Ogilvie, R. M. 1965. *A Commentary on Livy: Books 1–5*. Oxford.
O'Gorman, E. 2009. "Intertextuality and Historiography." In Feldherr 2009: 231–42.
Ostwald, M. 1986. *From Popular Sovereignty to the Sovereignty of Law: Law, Society, and Politics in Fifth-Century Athens*. Berkeley.
O'Sullivan, T. 2009. "Death *ante ora parentum* in Vergil's *Aeneid*." *TAPA* 139.2: 447–86.
Otis, B. 1964. *Virgil: A Study in Civilized Poetry*. Norman.
Pascal, C. B. 1990. "The Dubious Devotion of Turnus." *TAPA* 120: 251–68.

Patterson, M. L. 1942. "Rome's Choice of Magistrates during the Hannibalic War." *TAPA* 73: 319–40.

Paul, G. A. 1984. *A Historical Commentary on Sallust's Bellum Jugurthinum*. Liverpool.

Pelling, C. 1980. "Plutarch's Adaptation of His Source Material." *JHS* 100: 127–40.

Pfeilschifter, R. 2005. *Titus Quinctus Flamininus: Untersuchungen zur römischen Griechenlandpolitik*. Hypomenmata 162. Hamburg.

Pina Polo, F. 1996. *Contra arma verbis: Der Redner vor dem Volk in der späten römischen Republik*. Stuttgart.

2011. *The Consul at Rome: The Civil Functions of the Consuls in the Roman Republic*. Cambridge.

Pinsent, J. 1964. "Cincius, Fabius, and the Otacilii." *Phoenix* 18.1: 18–29.

Pitcher, L. 2010. *Writing Ancient History: An Introduction to Classical Historiography*. London.

Pittenger, M. R. P. 2008. *Contested Triumphs: Politics, Pageantry, and Performance in Livy's Republican Rome*. Berkeley.

Popov-Reynolds, N. 2010. "The Heroic Soldier as *exemplum* in Cato and Livy." in W. Polleichtner (ed.), *Livy and Intertextuality*. Trier: 169–202.

Pöschl, V. 1962. *The Art of Vergil: Image and Symbol in the Aeneid*. Ann Arbor, MI.

Powell, J. G. F. and J. A. North (eds.) 2001. *Cicero's Republic*. London.

Quint, D. 1993. *Epic and Empire: Politics and Generic Form from Virgil to Milton*. Princeton.

Rich, J. 2009. "Structuring Roman History: The Consular Year and the Roman Historical Tradition." In Chaplin and Kraus 2009: 118–47.

Richardson, J. 1971. "The 'Commentariolum Petitionis.'" *Historia* 20.4: 436–42.

2008. *The Language of Empire. Rome and the Idea of Empire from the Third Century BC to the Second Century AD*. Cambridge.

Riggsby, A. 1991. "Elision and Hiatus in Latin Prose." *ClAnt* 10.2: 328–43.

1999. *Crime and Community in Ciceronian Rome*. Austin, TX.

2006. *Caesar in Gaul and Rome: War in Words*. Austin, TX.

Rilinger, R. 1976. *Der Einfluss des Wahlleiters bei den römischen Konsulwahlen von 366 bis 50 v. Chr*. Munich.

Ringer, M. 1998. *Electra and the Empty Urn: Metatheater and Role Playing in Sophocles*. Chapel Hill, NC.

Robb, M. A. 2010. *Beyond Populares and Optimates: Political Language in the Late Republic*. Wiesbaden.

Roller, M. 2001. *Constructing Autocracy: Aristocrats and Emperor in Julio-Claudian Rome*. Princeton.

2004. "Exemplarity in Roman Culture: The Cases of Horatius Cocles and Cloelia." *CP* 99.1: 1–56.

2009a. "The Exemplary Past in Roman Historiography and Culture." In Feldherr 2009: 214–30.

2009b. "The Politics of Aristocratic Competition: Innovation in Livy and Augustan Rome." In Dominik, W., J. Garthwaite, and P. A. Roche (eds.), *Writing Politics in Imperial Rome*. Leiden: 153–72.

2010. "Demolished Houses, Monumentality, and Memory in Roman Culture." *ClAnt* 29.1: 117–80.

2011. "The Consul(ar) as *exemplum*: Fabius *Cunctator*'s Paradoxical Glory." In Beck, Duplá, Jehne, and Pina Polo 2011: 182–210.

Rosenstein, N. 1986. "*Imperatores Victi*: The Case of C. Hostilius Mancinus." *ClAnt* 5.2: 230–52.

1990. *Imperatores Victi: Military Defeat and Aristocratic Competition in the Middle and Late Republic*. Berkeley.

Rosillo López, C. 2010. *La Corruption à la fin de République romaine (IIe–Ier s. av. J.-C.). Aspects politiques et financiers*. Historia Einzelschriften 200. Stuttgart.

Rotondi, G. 1912. *Leges publicae populi Romani*. Hildesheim.

Rüpke, J. 1990. *Domi militiae: Die religiöse Konstruktion des Krieges in Rom*. Stuttgart.

Russell, A. 2013. "Speech, Competition, and Collaboration: Tribunician Politics and the Development of Popular Ideology." In Steel, C. and H. van der Blom (eds.), *Community and Communication: Oratory and Politics in Republican Rome*. Oxford: 101–16.

Sailor, D. 2006. "Dirty Linen, Fabrication, and the Authorities of Livy and Augustus." *TAPA* 136.2: 329–88.

Sailor, D. 2011. *Writing and Empire in Tacitus*. Cambridge.

Saller, R. 1980. "Anecdotes as Historical Evidence for the Principate." *G&R* 27.1: 69–83.

1994. *Patriarchy, Property and Death in the Roman Family*. Cambridge.

Salmon, E. T. 1929. "The *Pax Caudina*." *JRS* 19: 12–18.

Sandberg, K. 2001. *Magistrates and Assemblies. A Study of Legislative Practices in Republican Rome*. Rome.

Santoro L'Hoir, F. 1990. "Heroic Epithets and Recurrent Themes in *Ab Urbe Condita*." *TAPA* 120: 221–41.

Scafuro, A. 1987. "Pattern, Theme and Historicity in Livy Books 35 and 36." *ClAnt* 6.2: 249–85.

1989. "Livy's Comic Narrative of the Bacchanalia." *Helios* 16.2: 119–42.

Schäfer, T. 1989. *Imperii insignia, sella curulis und fasces: Zur Repräsentation römischer Magistrate*. Mainz.

Scheidel, W. 2009. "When Did Livy Write Books 1, 3, 28 and 59?" *CQ* 59.2: 653–8.

Schmähling, E. 1938. *Die Sittenaufsicht der Censoren. Ein Beitrag zur Sittengeschichte der römischen Republik*. Stuttgart.

Searle, J. 1995. *The Construction of Social Reality*. New York.

Segal, C. P. 1981. *Tragedy and Civilization: A New Interpretation of Sophocles*. Cambridge.

Shackleton-Bailey, D. R. 1996. "On Valerius Maximus." *RFIC* 124.2: 175–84.

Shaw, B. 2001. "Raising and Killing Children: Two Roman Myths." *Mnemosyne* 54.1: 31–77.

Shenhav, S. 2006. "Political Narratives and Political Reality." *International Political Science Review / Revue internationale de science politique* 27.3: 245–62.

Sivonen, P. 2006. *Being a Roman Magistrate. Office Holding and Roman Identity in Late Antique Gaul.* Helsinki.

Skinner, Q. 1979. "The Idea of a Cultural Lexicon." *Essays in Criticism* 29: 205–24. Revised and reprinted in Q. Skinner, *Visions of Politics.* Vol. 1: *Regarding Method.* Cambridge: 158–74.

Smith, C. J. 2006. *The Roman Clan: The Gens from Ancient Ideology to Modern Anthropology.* Cambridge.

2010. "Rhetorical History: The Struggle of the Orders in Livy." In Berry, D. H. and A. Erskine (eds.), *Form and Function in Roman Oratory.* Cambridge: 264–80.

Smith, R. E. 1944. "The Sources of Plutarch's *Life of Titus Flamininus.*" *CQ* 38.3/4: 89–95.

Solodow, J. 1979. "Livy and the Story of Horatius, 1.24–26." *TAPA* 109: 251–68.

Staveley, E. S. 1956. "The Constitution of the Roman Republic (1940–1954)." *Historia* 5.1: 74–122.

1963. "The *fasces* and *imperium maius.*" *Historia* 12.4: 458–84.

1972. *Greek and Roman Voting and Elections.* Ithaca.

Steel, C. 2010. "Tribunician Sacroscantity and Oratorical Performance in the Late Republic." In Berry, D. H. and A. Erskine (eds.), *Form and Function in Roman Oratory.* Cambridge: 37–50.

Steel, C. and H. van der Blom (eds.) 2013. *Community and Communication: Oratory and Politics in Republican Rome.* Oxford.

Stemmler, M. 2000. "*Auctoritas exempli*: Zur Wechselwirkung von kanonisierten Vergangenheitsbildern und gesellschaftlicher Gegenwart in der spätrepublikanischen Rhetorik." In Linke, B. and M. Stemmler (eds.), *Mos maiorum: Untersuchungen zu den Formen der Identitätsstiftung und Stabilisierung in der römischen Republik.* Stuttgart: 141–205.

Stewart, R. 1998. *Public Office in Early Rome: Ritual Procedure and Political Practice.* Ann Arbor.

Stroup, S. 2010. *Catullus, Cicero, and a Society of Patrons: The Generation of the Text.* Cambridge.

Sumi, G. 2005. *Ceremony and Power: Performing Politics in Rome between Republic and Empire.* Ann Arbor, MI.

Suolahti, J. 1963. *The Roman Censors.* Helsinki.

Syme, R. 1959. "Livy and Augustus." *HSPh* 64: 27–87.

Tatum, W. J. 2007. "*Alterum est tamen boni viri, alterum boni petitonis*: The Good Man Canvasses." *Phoenix* 6.1/2: 109–35.

2013. "Campaign Rhetoric." In Steel, C. and H. van der Blom (eds.), *Community and Communication: Oratory and Politics in the Roman Republic.* Oxford: 133–50.

Taylor, L. R. 1939. "Cicero's Aedileship." *AJP* 60.2: 194–202.

1960. *The Voting Districts of the Roman Republic.* Rome.

1966. *Roman Voting Assemblies from the Hannibalic War to the Dictatorship of Caesar.* Ann Arbor.

Tempest, K. 2007. "Saints and Sinners: Some Thoughts on the Presentation of Character in Attic oratory and Cicero's Verrines." In Prag, J. R. W. (ed.), *Sicilia nutrix plebis Romanae: Rhetoric, Law, and Taxation in Cicero's Verrines*. London: 19–36.

Thiele, G. 1893. *Hermagoras: Ein Beitrag zur Geschichte der Rhetorik*. Strassburg.

Timpe, D. 1996. "*Memoria* und Geschichtsschreibung bei den Römern." In Gehrke, H.-J. and A. Möller (eds.), *Vergangenheit und Lebenswelt: Soziale Kommunikation, Traditionsbildung und historisches Bewusstsein*. Tübingen: 277–300. Translated by M. Beck and reprinted in 2011. "*Memoria* and Historiography at Rome." In Marincola, J. (ed.), *Oxford Readings in Classical Studies: Greek and Roman Historiography*. Oxford: 150–74.

Thompson, L. A. 1962. "The Relationship between Provincial Quaestors and Their Commanders-in-chief." *Historia* 11.3: 339–55.

Ungern-Sternberg, J. 1986. "The Formation of the 'Annalistic Tradition': The Example of the Decemvirate." In Raaflaub, K. (ed.), *Social Struggles in Archaic Rome: New Perspectives on the Struggle of the Orders*. Malden, MA and Oxford: 75–97.

Valditara, G. 1989. *Studi sul magister populi: dagli ausiliari militari del rex ai primi magistrati repubblicani*. Milan.

van der Blom, H. 2010. *Cicero's Role Models: The Political Strategy of a Newcomer*. Oxford.

2011. "Historical *exempla* as Tools of Praise and Blame in Ciceronian Oratory." In Smith, C. J. and Covino, R. (eds.), *Praise and Blame in Roman Oratory*. Swansea: 49–68.

Vanggaard, J. H. 1988. *The Flamen: A Study in the History and Sociology of Roman Religion*. Copenhagen.

Vasaly, A. 1987. "Personality and Power: Livy's Depiction of the Appii Claudii in the First Pentad." *TAPA* 117: 203–26.

1993. *Representations. Images of the World in Ciceronian Rhetoric*. Berkeley.

Viparelli Santangelo, V. 1978. "Ironia e ideologia nell'excursus del 9 libro delle Storie di Livio." *BStudLat* 8: 43–55.

Vlassopoulos, K. 2009. *Politics: Antiquity & Its Legacy*. Oxford.

Walbank, F. 1957–79. *A Historical Commentary on Polybius*. 3 vols. Oxford.

1964. "Polybius and the Roman State." *GRBS* 5: 239–60.

1998. "A Greek Looks at Rome." *SCI* 17: 45–59.

Walbank, F. and C. Brink 1954. "The Construction of the Sixth Book of Polybius." *CQ* 48(n.s. 4).3–4: 97–122.

Walsh, P. G. 1961. *Livy: His Historical Aims and Methods*. Cambridge.

(ed.) 1994. *Livy Book XXXIX*. Warminster.

1996. "Making a Drama out of a Crisis: Livy on the Bacchanalia." *G&R* 43.2: 188–203.

[1954] 2009. "The Literary Techniques of Livy." In Chaplin and Kraus 2009: 201–21.

Walter, U. 2001. "Die Botschaft des Mediums. Überlegungen zum Sinnpotential von Historiographie im Kontext der römischen Geschichtskultur zur Zeit der Republik." In Melville, G. (ed.), *Institutionalität und Symbolisierung. Verstetigungen kultureller Ordnungsmuster in Vergangenheit und Gegenwart.* Cologne: 241–79.

2004. *Memoria und res publica. Zur Geschichtskultur im republikanischen Rom. Studien zur Alten Geschichte.* Vol. 1. Frankfurt am Main.

Watson, A. 1979. "The Death of Horatia." *CQ* 29.2: 436–47.

Welch, K. 1998. "Caesar and His Officers in the Gallic War Commentaries." In Welch, K. and A. Powell (eds.), *Julius Caesar as Artful Reporter.* Swansea: 85–110.

Wiedemann, T. 2005. "Reflections of Roman Political Thought in Latin Historical Writing." In Rowe, C. and M. Schofield (eds.), *The Cambridge History of Greek and Roman Political Thought.* Cambridge: 517–31.

Wikander, O. 1976. "Caius Hostilius Mancinus and the *Foedus Numantinum.*" *ORom* 11: 85–104.

Wilcox, A. 2005. "Paternal Grief and the Public Eye: Cicero 'Ad Familiares' 4.6." *Phoenix* 59.3/4: 267–87.

Williams, B. 1981. "Conflict of Values." In Williams, B., *Moral Luck.* Cambridge: 71–82.

Wills, J. 1996. *Repetition in Latin Poetry: Figures of Allusion.* Oxford.

Wirszubski, C. 1968. *Libertas as a Political Idea at Rome during the Late Republic and Early Principate.* Cambridge.

Wiseman, T. P. 1974. "Legendary Genealogies in Late-Republican Rome." *G&R* 21.2: 153–64.

1994. *Historiography and Imagination: Eight Essays on Roman Culture.* Exeter.

1998. *Roman Drama and Roman History.* Exeter.

Woodman, A. J. 1988. *Rhetoric in Classical Historiography: Four Studies.* London.

Yakobson, A. 1992. "*Petitio et largitio*: Popular Participation in the Centuriate Assembly of the Late Republic." *JRS* 82: 32–52.

1999. *Elections and Electioneering in Rome: A Study in the Political System of the Late Republic.* Historia Einzelschriften 128. Stuttgart.

Yardley, J. C. 2006. *Livy. Hannibal's War. Books 21–30.* Oxford.

Zetzel, J. 1995. *Cicero: De Republica.* Cambridge.

Index locorum

General index